C000175830

WITH 6TH AIRBORNE DIVISION IN PALESTINE 1945–1948

GENERAL SIR ALAN CUNNINGHAM, K.C.B., D.S.O., M.C., HIGH
COMMISSIONER OF PALESTINE, WITH MAJOR-GENERAL H. C.
STOCKWELL, C.B., C.B.E., D.S.O., COMMANDER 6TH AIRBORNE
DIVISION, APRIL, 1948.

Frontispiece

WITH 6TH AIRBORNE DIVISION IN PALESTINE 1945–1948

Major General R. Dare Wilson
CBE MC

Pen & Sword
MILITARY

First published in Great Britain in 1949 by Gale and Polden Ltd
Reprinted in the United States of America in 1984 by The Battery Press, Inc.
Republished in this format in 2008 by
PEN AND SWORD MILITARY
an imprint of
Pen & Sword Books Ltd
47 Church Street
Barnsley
South Yorkshire
S70 2AS

Copyright © R. Dare Wilson, 1949, 1984, 2008

ISBN 978 1 84415 7 716

The right of R. Dare Wilson to be identified as author
of this work has been asserted by him in accordance with the
Copyright, Designs and Patents Act 1988.

A CIP catalogue record for this book is
available from the British Library

All rights reserved. No part of this book may be reproduced or
transmitted in any form or by any means, electronic or mechanical
including photocopying, recording or by any information storage and
retrieval system, without permission from the Publisher in writing.

Printed and bound in Great Britain
By CPI UK

Pen & Sword Books Ltd incorporates the Imprints of
Pen & Sword Aviation, Pen & Sword Family History,
Pen & Sword Maritime, Pen & Sword Military, Wharncliffe Local History,
Pen & Sword Select, Pen & Sword Military Classics, Leo Cooper,
Remember When, Seaforth Publishing and Frontline Publishing

For a complete list of Pen & Sword titles please contact
PEN & SWORD BOOKS LIMITED
47 Church Street, Barnsley, South Yorkshire, S70 2AS, England
E-mail: enquiries@pen-and-sword.co.uk
Website: www.pen-and-sword.co.uk

A TRIBUTE
TO THOSE OFFICERS AND OTHER RANKS
WHO GAVE THEIR LIVES
IN THE SERVICE OF THEIR COUNTRY
AND
WHOSE DEEDS ARE RECORDED
IN THE PAGES WHICH FOLLOW

FOREWORD

BY MAJOR-GENERAL SIR HUGH STOCKWELL, K.B.E., C.B., D.S.O.

THROUGHOUT its history, the British Army has from time to time been called upon to carry out tasks in peace time which are often akin to war. They are often difficult and sometimes distasteful; they require tact, forbearance, cheerfulness, determination and courage, and the British soldier has shown himself to be supreme under such conditions.

The last two years of the British Mandate in Palestine was one such task, when the British soldier stood for the maintenance of law and order in a country where Jew and Arab vied with each other for the control of the country, and were bent upon each other's destruction.

This story of 6th Airborne Division in Palestine, so ably and accurately told by Major Dare Wilson, serves to record their task in Palestine and follows their history after the completion of their task in the Second World War. This has already been told by Lieutenant-General Gale, in his book, "With the 6th Airborne Division in Normandy."

Major Wilson served on the Headquarters Staff of the Division where he was in close contact with all the activities and happenings that took place between 1945 and 1948, and this book will prove of real interest to all who served with the Division throughout this period and to those who served either under command of the Division or alongside it during these difficult years. It will, too, be of great interest to any student of the intricate problem that Palestine presents.

I am sure that I am voicing the opinions of everyone in the Division when I say that the task was made so much easier by the tremendous support it was given by the Higher Command in Palestine and the Middle East; by the British Government in

Palestine, and by the close co-operation it always had from the Royal Navy, the Royal Air Force and the Palestine Police.

It was but part of a team which held together and won through successfully in completing the final evacuation from Palestine in June, 1948, without let or hindrance.

H. Stockwell.

THE ROYAL MILITARY ACADEMY SANDHURST

January, 1949

CONTENTS

APPENDICES

ACKNOWLEDGEMENTS

The thanks of the author are due to many who have assisted in one way or another in the writing of the book. Foremost among those who played a major part in its production was the late commander of 6th Airborne Division, Major General Sir Hugh Stockwell, KBE, CB, DSO.

Major General E L Bols, CB, DSO and Major General A J H Cassels CBE, DSO, former commanders of the Division, were both kind enough to read and improve those parts of the book dealing with the periods in which they were in command. Major General G W Lathbury, DSO, MBE, late Commander 3rd Parachute Brigade, Brigadier F D Rome, CBE, DSO, late Commander 1st and 3rd Parachute Brigades, and Brigadier C H Colquhoun, OBE, late Commander Royal Artillery, 6th Airborne Division, also read through those parts concerning their late formations, and made many suggestions which have been incorporated. Mr K G Boswell, TD, BA, head of the Faculty of Modern Subjects at the Royal Military Academy Sandhurst, gave much useful advice. Lieutenant Colonel H H van Straubenzee, DSO, OBE, late GSO (Operations) of the Division, helped in a variety of ways, and Captain D E C Russell and Captain E M Rolley between them prepared most of the appendices. Lance Corporal R Stockwell of The Parachute Regiment, made a most valuable contribution by producing all the maps and plans. Many of the photographs have been kindly provided by The Associated Press Ltd, Keystone Press Ltd, The Imperial War Museum and various members of the Division. Finally, the author's thanks are due to those who played minor, but none the less vital parts in the production of the book, but who are so numerous that it would be difficult to mention them all individually. They are asked to accept this collective acknowledgement of their assistance.

In addition to the above, the author wishes to thank Richard Gardner of The Battery Press Inc who republished *Cordon and Search* in the USA in 1984 and Henry Wilson of Pen and Sword Books Limited, who suggested this edition under the title *With 6th Airborne Division in Palestine 1945 – 1948*.

PREFACE

The purpose of this book is to place on record the main tasks and achievements of 6th Airborne Division between September 1945 and April 1948 in Palestine where, in an atmosphere of hatred and violence, the Division was faced with a responsibility in many respects more unpleasant and difficult to carry out than any it had to fulfil in war. It is a story of which those who served with the Division at that time may feel justly proud; not because of any mastery achieved over the civil population, but because of the efficient, humane and tolerant manner in which a distasteful duty was discharged. Such was the provocation that few forces in the world other than the British Army would have had either the discipline or patience to restrain themselves from counter-violence. The only reward was the satisfaction of a difficult job well done, and yet this in itself inspired the maintenance of an extremely high morale among all ranks of the Division.

In telling the story the aim has been to give the reader an accurate idea of the problems confronting the Division and how they were tackled. It is, however, important to remember that the events described are part and parcel of one of the most controversial problems of modern times. No one is yet in a position to pass judgment on the action of any government or individual, whether soldier or statesman. Opinions, where they are expressed, are the product of moral conviction, but are necessarily those of the soldier and will inevitably give rise to controversy.

If the narrative shows in an unfavourable light some of those with whom the Division had dealings, that is because of the prevailing conditions, and it is hoped that the reader will understand why it is so. The intention has been to record events and their effects on the troops at the time, and not conveniently to pass over the more difficult or unpleasant facts; to omit or soften them would present a false picture, and the production of the book would be pointless. But nothing has been included in this account with the object of exacting retribution against a people who, it is believed, were misguided enough to regard the British Army as their oppressor.

It is now nearly 60 years since the three paragraphs above appeared as part of the Preface to an account written by a young officer, at the suggestion of the last Divisional Commander, Major General Hugh

Stockwell, recording 6th Airborne Division's three years in Palestine. The previous year had seen the end of the British Mandate for Palestine, which came into being in September 1923 under the League of Nations, its basis being the Balfour Declaration of 1917. This opened a new phase in the history of a small country so closely associated in many minds with Biblical times. British involvement with Palestine, aside from the Crusades between the 11th and 13th centuries, was minimal until 1917 when General Allenby, in the course of a brilliant campaign, defeated the Turkish Army and wrested the country from the Ottoman Empire. Thence, for some 30 years, Britain was responsible for its government, administration and defence.

It was mainly owing to Palestine's geographic location at the eastern end of the Mediterranean, forming a bridge between Africa and Asia, coupled with its ancient history as the Holy Land to Christians, Jews and Moslems alike, that contributed to its sense of international importance. The era that followed the Second World War saw new problems arising from conflicts of national interest, none more so than the sudden increase in Jewish immigration from Europe. It was characterised by the lawlessness and terrorism of dissident organisations that necessitated the presence of considerable British security forces, which soon increased to a field force of three divisions supported by base garrisons and lines of communication forces.

6th Airborne Division, which had been dropped in Normandy on D-Day and later across the Rhine, was heavily involved in the final defeat of the formidable enemy forces in North West Europe. The end of hostilities found it next to the Russians close to the Baltic, but soon it returned to England for a pause to refit and absorb reinforcements, with further active service in prospect in the Far East. However, the dropping of the atomic bombs on Hiroshima and Nagasaki removed that commitment and, by September 1945, it was on the move to Palestine. Having been sent initially for a period of training, by the time it had arrived internal security had become threatened by lawlessness and the Division remained in the country for nearly three years of further active service.

It was in some ways an unpleasant time and certainly costly in lives, but once again the men of this great Division rose to the occasion, maintaining law and order against terrorists who enjoyed the protection and support of a community, soon to gain nationhood, which chose to overlook all that Britain had done at such cost on its behalf throughout the six preceding years. Nevertheless, the years 1945–1948 in Palestine remain for Britain a chapter of history to which those former members of her Armed Forces who served there contributed with honour.

PART ONE

SOUTHERN PALESTINE
SEPTEMBER, 1945—JANUARY, 1947

CHAPTER I

PRELUDE TO PALESTINE

THE end of the war in Germany in May, 1945, found the Division at Wismar on the Baltic. Here for about two weeks it rested after its rapid advance from the Rhine, until orders were received for it to return immediately to England.

In the Pacific the war against Japan was gathering momentum, but there was yet no sign of the enemy capitulating in that theatre. Plans had been drawn up for the operations in South-East Asia which were to make possible the final overthrow of the Japanese, and in these plans an important part was to be played by 6th Airborne Division.

As soon as it became known that the Division had been selected for service in the Far East, preparations went ahead on the vast number of administrative and training problems involved. Early in July a Divisional Tactical Headquarters flew out to Bombay with Headquarters 5th Parachute Brigade. This Brigade was at that time part of the Division, and was to be given an independent role in an operation in Burma which necessitated its arrival in advance of the Division. At the conclusion of this operation it would return to the Division in time for a major airborne operation which was planned to take place later.

At Headquarters S.A.C.S.E.A. (Supreme Allied Commander South East Asia) the Divisional Commander learned of the task which had been assigned to the Division, and together with his small staff set about the planning of what was to be the Division's third airborne operation. As soon as the preliminary planning was completed the Divisional Commander returned to England, where much remained to be done and time was desperately short. In the meantime, 1st Airborne Division, which had been engaged in the liberation of Norway, had been earmarked as part of the Imperial Strategic Reserve in the Middle East.

Early in August atomic warfare was opened on Japan, which

gave the *coup de grâce* to a regime already beginning to totter. Capitulation soon followed, and that led to an immediate modification in the plans of the operations in which 6th Airborne Division was to have taken part. Now that the Division was no longer required, even in an occupational role, in the Far East, the employment of the two British Airborne Divisions was replanned. One had to be disbanded; 6th Airborne Division was the younger Division, but after relative strengths and age-group composition had been taken into account, it was decided that 1st Airborne Division would be disbanded and 6th Airborne Division retained. Thus the Division stepped into the role of part of the Imperial Strategic Reserve, and plans were made for its dispatch as soon as possible to the Middle East. In order to make the Division up to strength, the place of 5th Parachute Brigade was taken by 2nd Parachute Brigade, recently returned from Greece.

On 24th September the Divisional Commander with his Tactical Headquarters flew out in advance of the Division in order to make the preliminary reconnaissances and to discuss plans with G.H.Q. Middle East Forces. Here it must be emphasized that the choice of Palestine was by no means primarily concerned with the political situation in that country. The Division was assigned to Palestine (as opposed to Egypt, Cyrenaica or any of the other possible stations) primarily on account of the better air training facilities (including several suitable airfields) which Southern Palestine afforded. This is not to say that a requirement for more troops in Palestine at that stage was not foreseen, but nevertheless the emphasis inside and outside the Division until several weeks after its arrival was on the concentrated air training which was to be carried out. Every effort was to be made to prevent the Division becoming involved in internal security duties. How these hopes miscarried is told in the following chapters.

ARRIVAL OF THE DIVISION IN PALESTINE

The move of the Division from England to Palestine took place over the period 15th September—6th November, 1945. The period immediately preceding the move was occupied, among other things, with alterations to the order of battle, most of which were the result of wider changes in the Army as a whole. 2nd Parachute Brigade which, as already stated, took the place of 5th Parachute Brigade, came under command of the Division on 3rd September, 1945. The place of the 12th Battalion The Devonshire Regiment in 6th Airlanding Brigade was taken by 1st Battalion The Argyll and Sutherland Highlanders.

Among the first troops of the Division to set foot in Palestine was 286 Airborne Park Squadron, Royal Engineers (later redesignated 249 and finally 147), which arrived on 16th September. The 3rd The King's Own Hussars were already in Syria and moved south into Palestine on 4th October. Though at that time not part of the Division, the regiment soon came under command. Later it was included in the order of battle as the Divisional Reconnaissance Regiment in place of 6th Airborne Armoured Reconnaissance Regiment, which was disbanded.

Main Divisional Headquarters was established initially in Palestine at Nuseirat Hospital Camp, near Gaza. It was here that the main body, which had just arrived by sea, was joined by Tactical Headquarters on 27th September, having flown out from England via Egypt. The Division was still under the command of Major-General E. L. Bols, C.B., D.S.O., who had commanded it in the Ardennes and Rhine-crossing operations in the North-West Europe campaign.

The first of the brigades to arrive was 3rd Parachute Brigade, under the command of Brigadier G. W. Lathbury, D.S.O., M.B.E., which disembarked at Haifa on 3rd October. This was followed by 6th Airlanding Brigade, under the command of Brigadier R. H. Bellamy, D.S.O., which disembarked on 10th October. 2nd Parachute Brigade, under the command of Brigadier C. H. V. Pritchard, D.S.O., followed on 22nd October. All formations and units arrived by sea at Haifa and from there were moved by rail to the Gaza district.

The Division concentrated on arrival in a group of camps which lay about six miles south of the large Arab town of Gaza. Here all the brigades, arms and services lay almost within sight of each other. Conditions were bad, but that was to be expected, and in any case this was only a concentration area. The weather was still hot and the Division needed to acclimatize itself to this barren and sandy region which verged on the Sinai Desert. After the ten-days voyage emphasis was laid on getting all ranks properly fit again, in which bathing and marching played a big part. Bathing was one of the blessings of Palestine. It was rarely altogether safe, and, in spite of life-saving precautions, as a result of the treacherous currents, a small number of troops were drowned each year. Nevertheless, bathing ranked very high among the few forms of recreation available.

The camps themselves were almost primitive, and the Divisional Engineers worked unceasingly to improve them. The main reason for this state of affairs was that whenever a camp was left vacant (and these were taken over in that condition), the Arabs would descend on it by day and night and carry off every movable fitting. To prevent this was quite beyond the ghaffirs (Arab watchmen), and to have stopped it altogether would have taken a small army of guards. In these circumstances lucky was the unit which marched into a camp with even the most essential structures untouched.*

One of the first lessons to be learned was the safeguarding of property. This was almost a science in itself and the battle of wits on either side went on unceasingly. The custody of arms was the main problem. After that came all other articles which could be removed by any number of Arabs working quite noiselessly during the hours of darkness. At this stage the problem was confined to pilferage by Arabs only. The Arab worked by stealth, and very rarely attacked sentries. He was a specialist at penetrating the best defences undetected, and after visiting one or more tents occupied by sleeping soldiers, left silently with his loot. The risk of his being shot in so doing was small deterrent.†

---

* From time to time, and particularly as the end of the Mandate approached, camps would be closed down. Within a few days, not only any fittings which remained, but the very structures of the huts, cookhouses and ablutions themselves would vanish into the desert, laden on the backs of the Bedouin and his ass. The only signs left which suggested that there had ever been a camp were a few tent hard-standings.

† Instances at first were not rare in which individuals (in one case a Commanding Officer) would wake in the morning to find their bed and the blankets over them were the only articles left in the tent or hut. Pistols could disappear from under pillows, and even tents themselves if unoccupied would vanish without trace on a dark night. These operations would take place while sentries prowled around the camp, and were only curtailed by the installation of perimeter lighting and searchlights.

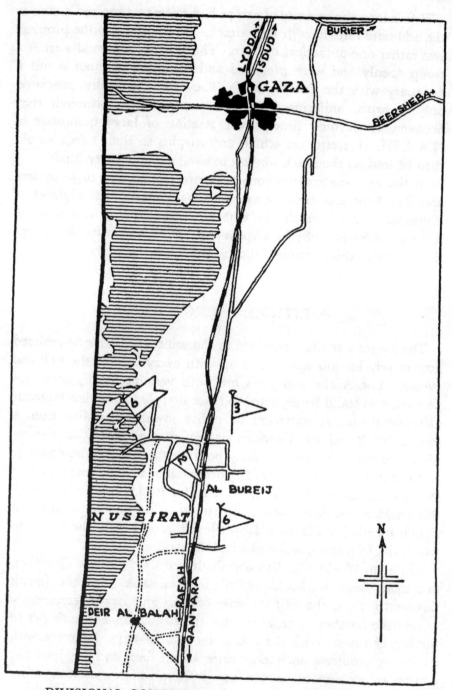

DIVISIONAL CONCENTRATION AREA, OCTOBER, 1945.

Before long the security of camps had to be reorganized owing to the additional threat of Jewish attack. To counter this the problem was rather one of tactical defence. The Jews would usually enter a camp openly and were prepared and equipped to shoot it out if necessary with the camp guard. They were normally interested only in arms, uniforms and military equipment, although they occasionally devoted time to the stealing of large quantities of N.A.A.F.I. cigarettes, of which any surplus to their needs would then be sold on the Black Market to swell gang or party funds.

At the week-ends recreational trips were organized to Jerusalem and Tel Aviv and educational visits were made to the places of historical interest which lay within reach. After a few months, leave was allowed to Syria, Cyprus and Egypt, and, with the exception of Syria, this continued during the following years.

POLITICAL BACKGROUND

The longer a soldier remained in Palestine, the better he realized how closely his job was bound up with every turn of the political events. The Arabs and Jews are both very politically-conscious peoples, and could be expected to react sharply to any development affecting them. A statement on policy towards Palestine from a responsible British or American statesman might easily alter overnight the entire internal security position throughout the country, and to this reason as much as any other might be attributed the fact that life for the soldier was never dull for long. Practically everything which the Army was called upon to do had some political significance behind it, so it is worth outlining briefly the situation which the Division found on arrival in 1945.

The 1939 World War had overshadowed the Palestine Question, and apart from the Mufti and his irreconcilables, and the Jewish dissident groups, the vast majority of Jews and Arabs temporarily buried the hatchet in order to turn their thoughts and energies to the bigger issue. With the end of the war in 1945, Palestine with its thorny problems once more came to the fore, and the Jews lost no time in pressing the issue of immigration, which was all the more acute as a result of the vast numbers of displaced Jews in Europe, many of whom, with no home left to them, turned their eyes towards the Holy Land. The Arabs kept relatively quiet, but watched each move of the Jews keenly and as time went on, apprehensively.

To understand this problem more clearly it is necessary to go back to the British Government's White Paper of May, 1939, which limited Jewish immigration to a maximum of 75,000 for the next five years, after which no further immigration would be permitted without Arab consent. In 1944 His Majesty's Government decided to extend the time limit owing to the delay incurred by the war, but no increase was made in the total of 75,000. By the end of 1945 that quota was practically exhausted and the problem was more acute than ever before.

Gradually, as tension rose on this issue, it became obvious that the British Government would have to reconsider its Palestine policy as laid down in the White Paper in the light of the events and effects of the war years. What soon became known as the "Expected Statement" gained more and more prominence, until the whole of the Jewish community hung on its advent.

In Palestine itself it appeared that neither the British nor the Jews could understand the attitude of the other. On the one hand, the Jews were openly accusing the British of a policy towards them which was designed to perpetuate Nazi anti-Semitism. To them, the most vital problem of the world was the opening of the gates of Palestine to the remnants of Europe's displaced Jewry. To them, the imposition at this stage of an immigration quota was unnecessary and inhuman; furthermore, if immigrants could not be admitted legally, no opportunity would be missed for bringing them in illegally. On the other hand, the British were still bound by the terms of their White Paper; they had also to consider the Arabs. The latter, in the meantime, remained solid and (on this issue) as uncompromising as ever. It was not through lack of patience or effort on Britain's part that the problem remained a bone of contention until the end of the Mandate.

As so much of the Army's attention was taken up in Palestine with the actions and reactions of the various sections of the Jewish community, it is necessary to examine briefly at this stage the characteristics and functions of those bodies and organizations, both legal and illegal, which will feature from time to time throughout this book. In so doing it will also be necessary to outline their relations with the Government of the country.

Palestine was administered by Great Britain under a Mandate of the League of Nations which came into force officially in 1923. One of the terms of the Mandate provided for the formation of a Jewish body for the purpose of advising the Government of Palestine on questions affecting the Jewish National Home and the interests of the Yishuv (Jewish community in Palestine). Until 1929 the duties of this Agency were performed by the Zionist Organization, but in that year its basis was broadened, an equal number of non-Zionists were admitted, and the Jewish Agency emerged in its later form as a world-wide organization. Although it was not entitled to share in the government of the country, it exercised a great degree of control over the community by virtue of its functions.

The system of Jewish social government provided for the existence of an Elected Assembly, which corresponded in some ways to a Parliament, and which from time to time elected the Vaad Leumi, an inner council, whose function was to administer the lay affairs of the community in accordance with the resolutions of the Elected Assembly. There was, in addition, a very wide range of political parties varying from extreme right to extreme left. To probe deeper than this point into the complexities of Jewish politics would be unwise as well as unnecessary.

Closely allied to other problems affecting the Jewish way of life in Palestine was the vital matter of defence. A succession of pogroms and anti-Jewish riots throughout the ages, which have maintained their frequency in the present century, have made the Jews particularly conscious of the need for some form of defence organization for the protection of their settlements and land in Palestine. Armed watchmen were authorized by the Turks for this purpose, and Jewish Settlement Police were later raised under the authority of the British. However, in spite of these measures, and various other undertakings by the British Government, the Jews remained ever convinced that a Defence Organization of their own was a necessity. Thus the Hagana was born following the anti-Jewish riots of 1920 and 1921. Throughout the succeeding years this organization grew steadily and underwent several changes in character. Not being recognized by the British, it had perforce to remain underground and maintain a high standard of secrecy regarding its strength, organization, and capabilities. The Jews never denied its existence, but rather took every opportunity of justifying it, and though originally raised for defence and maintained primarily for that purpose, they were not slow at hinting at its offensive potentiality when the time came for a "final settlement" in Palestine.

The Hagana eventually became virtually a Jewish National Army in which the majority of able-bodied males and a large number of females were obliged to enlist and give part-time service. Following the Second World War, it benefited from the number of trained recruits which became available, and also from the amount of arms, ammunition, and military equipment which it was possible to acquire from the jetsam of the various campaigns. It was ultimately organized on modern lines and very adequately equipped with small arms, machine guns and mortars.

Within the main organization of the Hagana came the Palmach (abbreviation for Plugot Machatz, Spearhead Groups) which, as the name suggests, was the élite of the army. The Palmach was a regular armed force whose members gave full-time service and were subject to continuous military discipline. It was highly trained in offensive warfare and led by experienced commanders. Many of its members served in the British-raised Palestine Regiment, while others had been trained in foreign armies. This was the force which was committed by the Jewish authorities on specific tasks of sabotage directed against the Government and usually in connection with illegal immigration.

The Hagana was essentially a moderate organization when compared to the so-called "terrorist" groups. When employed on tasks of sabotage which involved the use of force, the instructions were always to avoid loss of life to British personnel if possible, and their plans were framed with this object in view. If some task was decided upon which could not fulfil this requirement, or if the British Government was to be given a special demonstration of the degree of force which the Jews were able to apply, there were other less scrupulous organizations who were only too willing to participate. It may be recalled here that in July, 1946, the British Government, in a White Paper, furnished proof of the complicity of certain prominent politicians and the Hagana Command with the campaign of murder and sabotage carried out by the terrorist groups.

In 1937 a small body of Revisionists and other political extremists in the Hagana, who were at variance with the political views of that organization, broke away under the leadership of one Jabotinski and formed their own group which they called Irgun Zvai Leumi (National Military Organization), usually abbreviated to I.Z.L. or N.M.O. One of the main reasons for a break with the parent body was a disagreement over the question of armed reprisals against Arab aggression. In later years its allegiance and its outlook, together with its attitude towards the Government, underwent several changes. During the war it was quiescent until February, 1944, when it embarked on a general campaign of violence and sabotage against the Government, and from that time it remained in open opposition to Britain, planning and executing a wide range of murderous attacks. The I.Z.L. followed an extreme political policy and for some years claimed that the Jews are the rightful heirs not only to the whole of Palestine but also Transjordan. Their badge depicted a map of these two countries superimposed with an arm holding a rifle and the words "Only thus." Their strength fluctuated and was never actually known, but possibly towards the end of the Mandate it reached several thousands.

After the outbreak of war in 1939 the relations between the Revisionists and the Government improved considerably, and the Irgun co-operated under the leadership of one David Raziel. A party of some fifty members, however, under the leadership of Abraham Stern, strongly opposed this policy and, denouncing Raziel as a British agent, they started to follow their own line. Stern worked actively, first for the Italians and then for the Germans, and all the time was engaged in an underground war against the British with his gang of desperadoes. They specialized in assassinations, and most of these were of British members of the Palestine Police. In 1942 Stern was cornered and shot dead in a gun fight with the police, and command of the gang passed to a Pole named Nathan Freedman Yellin. For a time Yellin was detained in Latrun, but, after escaping by means of a tunnel together with nineteen others, he continued to direct the gang until after the end of the Mandate. In 1943 the gang adopted the name of Lochmei Heruth Israel (Fighters for the Freedom of Israel).

The members of these two dissident organizations were universally termed "terrorists" until the word was banned by the Army in Palestine early in 1947. The word implies that those who were engaged with them had cause to be terrified by them. This, of course, could not have been farther from the truth—the perpetual regret of all ranks was that there were so few opportunities of getting to grips with them. The term was an unfortunate journalistic choice which, despite the efforts of the Army, persisted until the end in general use by the Press and B.B.C. The Stern Gang also raised its voice on this issue of nomenclature when it circulated a copy of the following letter to newspaper representatives in Palestine in April, 1947:—

"Dear Sir,

"May we direct your attention upon the fact that the English name of our underground is Fighters for the Freedom of Israel, not ' Stern Gang ' or ' Stern Group.' The Hebrew press, *Eretz-Israel*, quite familiar with the nature of our organization, uses, when referring to us, the original name of Lechamey Heruth Israel (the Hebrew Fighters for the Freedom of Israel) or just the abbreviation L.H.I.

" ' Stern Gang ' has been the name sponsored by the alien Government of oppression in this country. The enemy quite naturally seek to misrepresent our legal and legitimate fight for freedom as gangster activities, exactly as the Germans did with regard to the French maquis or the Balkan partisans.

"This nickname is the more misleading as our underground is not merely a combat organization, but a fighting movement, based upon deeply rooted ideological principles and pursuing a clear home, as well as foreign, policy.

"We should consequently be very obliged if, for the sake of equity and historic truth, you used in your despatches our proper name or the abbreviation F.F.I.

"Yours sincerely,

"FIGHTERS FOR THE FREEDOM OF ISRAEL."

At this point, having completed an outline of the illegal armed organizations of the Jews and an even briefer reference to their political bodies, it would be logical to cover in a similar manner the Arab political picture. But to dwell on this subject is unnecessary for two reasons. Firstly, from the end of the war until the closing stages of the Mandate, when both Arabs and Jews started to clear their decks for action, the Arabs by their exemplary behaviour caused neither the Government nor the security forces the slightest embarrassment. This being the case, there was neither the necessity nor the inclination for the soldier to become interested in their politics. Secondly, if there had been that necessity, it is doubtful whether the soldier would ever have succeeded in penetrating the fringe of such a confused and incomprehensible muddle, for the Palestinian Arabs, though united in their desire for independence and the cessation of the Mandate, were so absorbed in the evils of tribal faction that the demands of national unity were relegated to a status of minor importance. The dominant personality was Haj Amin al Husseini, the exiled Mufti of Jerusalem. He commanded a greater following than any other, but, not being allowed into the country, he was at a considerable disadvantage, although he had a number of loyal lieutenants on whom he could count to carry out his policy.

In 1936 a committee, known as the Arab Higher Executive Committee, composed of the heads of the various political parties, was formed under the presidency of the Mufti with the object of co-ordinating the disturbances of 1936. This was actually declared illegal by the Government, and during the war years nothing took its place. In November, 1945, the Arab Higher Committee was re-formed on an all-party basis, but dissension between its members soon brought about its downfall. On instructions of the Arab League,* a new body, the Arab Higher Executive was formed under the leadership of Jamal Husseini, cousin of the Mufti. It remained in existence with the object of producing national unity from the various political factions until the end of the Mandate.

---

* The Arab League, which was formed in 1945, was of importance to Palestinian Arab Nationalist politics by virtue of its wide interest in the political, economic and cultural affairs of all Arab countries. Its influence was also possibly accentuated in that country because of the conspicuous lack of Arab political organization there. The policy of the League was formulated by its council, which consisted of representatives of all the Arab States.

This short diversion should indicate something of the instability of Arab politics in Palestine. But to what extent did the intricacies, or even the fundamentals of Jewish or Arab politics, affect the soldier when 6th Airborne Division first set foot in Palestine? It affected him not at all for some time, but other impressions were not slow in making themselves felt. He was intensely mystified by the attitude of the Jews towards his country and towards him as a soldier. If he had expected to find an atmosphere of friendliness and hospitality, he was disappointed. Indeed, such was his reception that soon he was asking himself what he had been fighting for during the past five years.

It was in an uneasy and strained atmosphere, therefore, that the Division found itself on arrival from England. Few soldiers serving with it had ever been in Palestine before, and of the few who had, their experience only dated back to the Arab Rebellion of 1936, in which the Army acted in defence of, and in co-operation with, the Jews.

On the troopships coming out from home it was noticeable how open-minded—ignorant might be more truthful—were the troops on the Palestine Question. They were quite prepared to take things as they found them. As far as their sympathies went at the time, these probably lay in favour of the Jews, as a result of what these troops had seen in North-West Europe earlier that year. It might not be considered altogether surprising that this attitude was put severely to the test during the following two and a half years, and in the majority of cases failed to stand up to the strain.

THE MILITARY SITUATION

The arrival of the Division in Palestine was only one of several significant changes in the order of battle and military organization within the Command during the autumn of 1945. There was in the country at that time the 1st British Infantry Division together with one or two British cavalry and infantry units, and certain ancillary troops, most of whom were colonial, engaged on guard duties. Among them were units of West Africans, Cypriots, Indians, Transjordan Frontier Force and Arab Legion. One British infantry brigade was also due to arrive from Egypt in the middle of October.

It has already been mentioned that Palestine had been comparatively quiet internally during the war; the command organization, therefore, which existed during this period was designed to function in a role which was largely administrative. The country was divided into three military sectors: 15 Area in the north with Headquarters at Haifa, 21 Area in the south with Headquarters at Sarafand, and 156 Sub-Area in the east with Headquarters at Jerusalem.

During the war, Palestine had been used for the training, equipping, and resting of a series of divisions which had passed through it. It would have been inconvenient at that time for them to have been saddled with internal security duties, so these were handled where necessary by the Area Headquarters under the overall direction of the General Officer Commanding British Troops in Palestine. But such problems of this nature that had arisen had been more or less within the control of the Palestine Police. With the end of the war, however, and the threat of trouble in Palestine itself, it was necessary to revise the system under which control was exercised by the Army when acting in aid of the Civil Power, and it was decided to vest in the field formations in that country the necessary powers for the maintenance of law and order should that become necessary. The Area Headquarters would continue in being as their landlords and for the purpose of controlling the various static units and installations. Simultaneously, the deployment of the field formations was to be undertaken in such a way as to maintain the maximum measure of control in the event of civil disturbances.

On the arrival of the Division in Palestine, then, it became apparent that the internal security role was likely to become a matter of growing importance. Furthermore, living and training in the Gaza area was likely to be disturbed every time there was a call for troops to maintain or restore order farther north. The Division was not concentrated before anticipatory orders were received for a regrouping of forces in Palestine in the likely event of trouble, in which case the whole of the southern sector* would become the responsibility of the Division. However, such a course was not considered likely for at least three weeks. In the meantime,

---

* The Southern Sector consisted of the civil districts of Lydda, Gaza, and Samaria, less the sub-district of Jenin.

as units and formations of the Division arrived, they were given their future tasks and they set about their reconnaissances from the Gaza area without delay.

Law and order in Palestine were maintained under a dual system consisting of the Civil Administration (the High Commissioner and the Government of Palestine) and the Military Power (G.O.C. British Troops in Palestine and Transjordan). All the normal powers of government in Palestine were placed in the hands of the High Commissioner. The Orders in Council which clothed him with full legislative authority, entitled him to pass on to the military authorities extensive powers. The High Commissioner exercised his authority in this respect by enacting from time to time sets of regulations to meet the changing situations, and it was from the Defence Emergency Regulations of 1945 that the Army derived its power during the period under review. Under these regulations the High Commissioner delegated very comprehensive powers to the General Officer Commanding in Palestine, who in turn was permitted to delegate a great measure of responsibility to his appointed military commanders, i.e., the Divisional Commanders. The Defence Emergency Regulations were extremely powerful, and in fact, the powers of the security forces were equivalent to those which they would have had under Martial Law.

Thus in theory in each military sector there was the authority to meet most situations with firm handling and without the delay which might have been imposed by referring all such matters to higher authority. In practice, however, this was not always the case, and the implications of firm military action, however well justified, were charged with political dynamite. Unfortunately, the possible political repercussions in Palestine were often overshadowed and outweighed by factors farther afield which played an important part behind the scenes. In the words of the leading article of *The Times* of 1st November, 1946: "The Army is the right arm, sometimes almost the whole body, of the Government, but it cannot be the controlling brain or enjoy freedom to do as it might think fit." The consequences of decisions entailing a strong line of action were likely to be such that if they (the decisions) were not actually made at the highest level, at least they had to receive the necessary sanction. The point is stressed, for while there is no denying the fact that technically the Army and its formations were empowered to take any action deemed fit, in practice the demands of political expedience often decreed otherwise. This, it is hoped, will explain in advance why the sequels, or counter-action, to so many vile acts by the opposition were not as they might have been, had the issues been more straightforward. It should also illustrate what was at the time bound to be a cause of the greatest frustration to all ranks. It cannot be left unrecorded that although this feeling continued to have a profound effect throughout the Division, and for that matter, the Army in Palestine as a whole, yet neither its spirit nor its efficiency were at any time affected in the smallest degree.

CHAPTER II

TRAINING FOR INTERNAL SECURITY DUTIES

THE study of Internal Security in a country such as Palestine is far removed from that of modern war. In 1945 the Division had reached a standard of training in offensive warfare of which it was justly proud. But the requirements of Internal Security duties necessitate the application of minimum force; and, when the Division had to adapt its ideas from its previous doctrine of the use of maximum force, an entirely fresh approach was clearly needed.

In this special role, discipline, leadership, fitness, alertness and weapon training are as fundamentally important as in any form of soldiering. The conversion from one role to the other, however, required special study, and the danger of over-simplifying the problem had to be watched.

One of the mental adjustments to be made by every individual was in his attitude towards the people with whom he was dealing. In war it is the enemy. He must be neither underrated nor over-rated, and should be fought by all means within the rules of war. This is such a simple outlook when compared to that required in Imperial Policing. The nature of the problem in Palestine made this adjustment even more difficult by adding its own complications. Here were two communities with practically no characteristic in common and either of whom was liable to cause trouble. Each had to be studied in detail and each would respond to different treatment.

The soldier therefore had always to try and keep one move ahead, and have the answer ready in advance to any situation with which he might be faced. Not only was it necessary to consider the correct counter-action to a move by Arab or Jew against the Mandatory Power, but there were also all the situations that could arise in which the soldier would have to act as mediator between the two, or protect one from the other.

One of the first things to be done, therefore, was to make a close study of the characteristics and habits of the two main communities. Here the Palestine Police were of the utmost assistance and the very closest co-operation was established with them. This liaison was maintained during the years which followed and became a feature of all the operations carried out.

While learning the principles of Internal Security duties, the Division was assisted by a G.H.Q. training team which specialized in the subject. A study was made of how to search Arab villages and Jewish settlements for illegal arms or wanted men; how to throw a cordon round any area before those inside could slip out undetected; how to obviate the use of force unless it was quite unavoidable, and even then to exert only the minimum to achieve the object or safeguard lives and property. The "powers of the military" were straightforward but needed knowing; they included regulations on the imposition of curfews, road restrictions and powers of search and arrest. Much of this information had to be passed down to all ranks. The sentry had to know when he was justified in opening fire and when he was not. A high standard of discipline was necessary in the searching of houses, and in order to avoid unnecessary offence or embarrassment it was necessary to know something of the religions and customs of both communities. There was much to be learned where the Arabs were concerned from the lessons of the Arab Rebellion of 1936. It was anticipated quite naturally that if trouble came from that quarter again similar tactics would be employed.

Finally, it was necessary to know something of the manner in which the country was governed and administered, the system of civil administration by District Commissioners who were responsible to the Chief Secretary, and the boundaries of the six Civil Districts. The police organization also had to be known: the composition of Districts and Divisions, and the duties of the various branches of the force. If due attention were not paid to the structure of the government of the country and its administration, the tendency would be for troops to forget that they were there to aid the Civil Power and not to act in place of it. In some of the situations which arose in later years, it was occasionally difficult to determine just which problems should be dealt with in each of the spheres— military, police or civil administration. However, the correct action usually lay in a tripartite handling, and though the Army usually assumed the executive role, there was much to be gained from the knowledge and experience of the other partners. On the comparatively infrequent occasions when friction or misunderstanding occurred it was due to one or more of those engaged not fully understanding the problems of the others.

DEPLOYMENT

It has been mentioned that no major regrouping of troops in the Command was considered likely to take place for approximately three weeks after the arrival of the Division. That, however, was an optimistic estimate and, in fact, owing to the political situation it took place earlier. The plan which was issued to brigades on 7th October provided for the takeover by the Division of operational command in the southern sector from 21 Area as soon as the situation demanded it, and after at least 3rd Parachute Brigade was ready for action. In the meantime 3rd Parachute Brigade was to be made available in its present semi-mobile condition to Headquarters 21 Area if required. The plan also provided for the restoration of law and order by force on receipt of the code word "Footlights," and the imposition of further preventive measures in the form of curfews and road restrictions on the receipt of the code word "Flourish."

On 14th October this plan was replaced by a similar one to be put into action on receipt of code word "Benzine." It was a more detailed order, and gave the dispositions to be adopted by all field formations and garrison units in an emergency. It also made special reference to the keeping open of the railways and main roads. In the meantime 3rd Parachute Brigade was ordered to provide two mobile columns at six hours' notice on call from Headquarters 21 Area.

During this period there was one of the uneasy lulls which the Division came to know so well during the next few years. Rumours and false alarms were rife and a miniature war of nerves developed. There were a few minor incidents, but everyone was waiting for the expected announcement on the White Paper. The generally accepted theory was that the Jewish Agency had prevailed on the dissidents to hold their hand and so not jeopardize their cause. However, signs were not lacking that a political crisis might develop, and this resulted in the code word "Benzine" being issued on 20th October to come into force at 0800 hours the following day. "Benzine" was looked upon at the time and even for a period after it came into force as a short-term deployment. As far as was known, the Division was only required to move north for a limited period and ultimately when all was peace and quiet again it would reconcentrate either in the Gaza or Julis camps and devote itself once more to air raining. Certainly no one anticipated that it would remain deployed on internal security duties not only for a matter of months but years. Indeed, it was not expected that the Division would remain in the country for more than a year.

On 21st October, 3rd Parachute Brigade moved north to its "battle stations" in the Lydda District, which was likely to be by far the most difficult of the three districts to control, as it contained Tel Aviv together with all its surrounding settlements, and Jaffa. The previous day Tactical Divisional Headquarters had moved to Sarafand alongside Headquarters 21 Area. It stayed there for two days, controlling the deployment, before moving to Bir Salim, two and a half miles away, where it was joined by Main Head-quarters. It was in the same building in which General Allenby had his Headquarters in 1918 during his Palestine Campaign, when his Chief of Staff was Major-General Sir Louis Bols, K.C.B., K.C.M.G., D.S.O., father of the present Divisional Commander. In the meantime, 6th Airlanding Brigade was preparing for its move to the Samaria District. Brigade Headquarters moved to Lydda Airport on 23rd October, and the battalions, with the exception of 1st Battalion The Argyll and Sutherland Highlanders, took up their new stations in that area a few days later. Under command also was 6th Battalion The Gordon Highlanders, stationed at Tulkarm.

On 22nd October, 2nd Parachute Brigade arrived from England, and, being the last brigade out, it was assigned to the Gaza District, which was expected to be the quietest of the three brigade areas. It was intended that the brigade stationed there should devote its time and energy to ground and air training. The long-term policy was to change brigades round at approximately

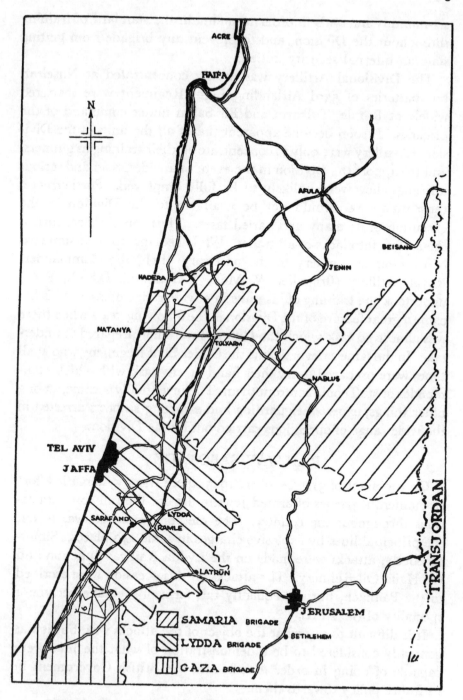

DIVISIONAL LAYOUT IN SOUTHERN PALESTINE, 1945-6.

six-monthly intervals in order to maintain the standard of training throughout the Division, and to prevent any brigade from getting stale on internal security duties.

The Divisional Artillery was mostly concentrated at Nuseirat, but batteries of 53rd Airlanding Light Regiment were scattered widely at Ramle, Tulkarm and Bir Salim under command of the brigades. It soon became apparent that if all the units of the Divisional Artillery were only to concentrate on their training as gunners, and to support the Division in the event of a widespread and serious uprising, they were unlikely to be fully employed. Furthermore, their manpower would not be available to the Division in the execution of its many and varied tasks. Thus the Gunners turned themselves into jacks-of-all-trades. While keeping up their standard of training in gunnery to the necessary pitch, the Commander, Royal Artillery (Brigadier W. McT. T. Faithfull, D.S.O., R.A.) undertook the training of his units in a wide range of tasks. This became a great feature of the Division in the following years when there was almost no task which the Gunners were not prepared to undertake. In the same category came the Glider Pilot Regiment, who at all times were prepared to try their hand at any task with which commander or staff could confront them. They eventually became, among other things, experts at guarding and escorting suspects arrested in the wide range of operations carried out by the Division.

RAILWAY SABOTAGE

On the night of 31st October, 1945, there was a systematic effort by numerous parties of armed Jews to disrupt the rail communications throughout the country. The method employed was to cut the principal lines by explosive charges in some 240 places. Simultaneously, attacks were made on the Lydda Railway Junction and the Haifa Oil Refinery. The attacks on this occasion were ascribed to the Palmach, but subsequently this form of sabotage became a speciality of the I.Z.L.

It is difficult to say what the object of the attacks was, but it was generally considered to be a demonstration of what the Jews were capable of doing in order to influence the British Government in its future policy towards them.

The only known casualties suffered were at Lydda in the

Divisional area, where there were some dozen casualties, including four dead, suffered by the Army, police and railway staff (mostly among the latter). The attack was typical of many to follow; carried out with skill and determination, based on faultless information, and though the object was not to take life, the method had little regard for the loss of it.

Only one casualty was suffered by the saboteurs, but the next day a police party with tracking dogs followed a trail into Ramat Hak Kovesh, an outlying Jewish settlement midway between Tel Aviv and Tulkarm. At the approach of the party the school bells were rung and a large part of the population turned out to bar its entry to the settlement. The trail was soon obliterated, and the police, faced with overwhelming numbers and an ugly situation, were obliged to withdraw.

The widespread attack on the railway, in spite of its thoroughness, only succeeded in putting the main line out of action for two days. This fact seems remarkable, but it is only one illustration of a well-known principle; it requires a powerful and unceasing effort to keep a railway out of action by the sabotage of its permanent way, except when the effort can be applied to some vital point such as a bridge or viaduct which will itself take time to repair.* On the other hand, it is partly offset by the small risk incurred by railway saboteurs. Both these principles were well illustrated in Palestine. In the Divisional sector during the two and a half years under review there were some fifty major incidents of railway sabotage, mostly on the main line from Haifa to Gaza.† None of these incidents closed the line for more than a day or two, and on only three occasions were Jewish saboteurs caught or killed, and then by troops who were not at the time engaged on patrolling the railway. The distance patrolled by troops of the Division employed on railway protection duties is not likely to have been less than 20,000 miles,

---

* In Palestine most railway bridges were guarded by detachments of Railway Police in block-houses.
† The standard-gauge lines in Palestine were as follows: The main north–south line running for most of its length parallel with the coast, which in normal times connected Egypt with Syria (this was the most vital), the Lydda–Jerusalem line, and the Lydda–Tel Aviv line. The narrow-gauge lines ran from Haifa to Trans-jordan via Beisan and Samakh, from Tulkarm to Nablus, and from Afula to Nablus via Jenin. (The lines from Gaza to Beersheba and Beersheba to Artuf built by Allenby in the First World War were no longer in use.)

and the constant attention to the railway was probably some deterrent to the extremists.* Nevertheless, in the course of these patrols no record exists of a single saboteur being shot or arrested.

Again, in 1946, almost the full strength of the security forces was made available during a short and vital period to keep the railway running. Even so, the scale of effort was only enough to afford security by day to the engine drivers, who at that time were refusing to work without a guarantee of safety. The operation will be described more fully in a later chapter and is only mentioned here to illustrate the points already raised.

RIOTS IN TEL AVIV

On 13th November the Foreign Secretary made the British Government's long-awaited statement of policy on the Palestine Problem. His main points were as follows: Firstly, Palestine by itself could not provide the solution to the Jewish problem. Secondly, an Anglo-American Committee would be appointed "to examine the political, economic and social conditions in Europe as they bear on the problem of Jewish immigration and settlement . . . and to examine the position of Jews in Europe where they have been victims of Nazi and Fascist persecution." Lastly, the British Government would in the meantime "consult the Arabs with a view to an arrangement which will ensure that, pending the receipt of the *ad interim* recommendations, there is no interruption of Jewish immigration at the present monthly rate" (1,500).†

To what extent this announcement was the bitter disappointment which the Jews avowed is a debatable point. Many were without doubt, secretly satisfied, though it would have been inexpedient for them to have made this admission. But it did mean that if any reaction involving violence by the Jews should be inspired or condoned by the Jewish Agency, their cause and hopes would

---

* This estimate does not include the mileage covered by the armoured rail cars operated by the 3rd The King's Own Hussars, 12th Royal Lancers and 17th/21st Lancers, which probably exceeded the figure several times.

† Negotiations on this point with the Arabs were opened soon after, but resulted in a complete deadlock. The Arabs were adamant in refusing to give their assent to any further Jewish immigration at this stage. As a result, on 6th January, 1946, the British Government announced that, in spite of the attitude of the Arabs, "for cogent reasons" it had been decided to permit 1,500 Jews a month to enter Palestine as an interim measure.

be seriously impaired in front of the Anglo-American Committee. The Jewish authorities were thereby placed in a dilemma. On the one hand, they could not help voicing their bitter disappointment (which was shared by the whole Jewish community); on the other, they could not jeopardize their cause by adopting or approving a course of violence. However, after the Vaad Leumi (National Council) proclaimed a twelve-hour protest strike for the following day (14th November), the matter was taken out of their hands in Jerusalem and Tel Aviv by the hooligan elements of the community. who harboured no such feeling of restraint.

The rioting which resulted from the British Government's statement of policy was confined to the Jewish communities of Jerusalem, and Tel Aviv (which is an all-Jewish city), but, whereas the disturbances in Jerusalem were soon brought under control by the security forces, the situation in Tel Aviv deteriorated rapidly, and led to the occupation of the town by the whole of 3rd Parachute Brigade for a period of five days.

The first incidents developed from a number of semi-organized processions conducted through the town during the afternoon of 14th November. A wave of feeling among irresponsible elements led to a series of incidents in which British offices and shops were attacked and military vehicles and their occupants stoned in the streets.

The first serious incident was an attack at 1815 hours on the District Offices, which were set on fire by hooligans. The police became heavily involved in several parts of the town and were compelled to make numerous baton charges to try and hold the mob in check. However, they were soon obliged to send for the inlying company of 8th Parachute Battalion at Sarona, which arrived on the scene at 1840 hours.* The company took up positions in Colony

---

* At this time the Division had no troops permanently stationed in Tel Aviv, the nearest battalion being 8th Parachute Battalion on the outskirts. The Battalion maintained a company at short notice to move into the town in support of the police, but the maintenance of law and order was wholly in the hands of the police. If the situation should demand it, the company could be called upon to act under police instructions. If further troops were required, the operation would become a military one with the police in support. This is an orthodox principle which later had to be adjusted in Palestine when a proportion of each army formation was permanently on Internal Security Duties. It then became a matter of defining clearly the responsibilities of the Army and Police alike, and all operations involving the use of more than a company of troops were normally controlled by a senior Army officer. Through the wholehearted co-operation and good spirit shown by all concerned, the arrangement worked admirably.

Square and drew the attentions of a large crowd which subjected the troops to heavy stoning. Fresh from their recent training in the principles of internal security, and having been briefed repeatedly on the importance of avoiding the use of firearms if humanly possible, these soldiers displayed a most remarkable restraint. The same high standard of conduct was later displayed in this operation by the remainder of the Brigade. The mobs which gathered on the first evening, and until order was finally restored, were several thousand strong and consisted largely of the hooligan elements of the town. The heavy stoning tactics which they adopted inflicted some serious and many minor injuries on both police and troops. Eventually, after repeated warnings, fire was opened by the troops, a small number of rounds being fired by a specified number of men under the direct supervision of an officer. The fire had the desired effect of making the mob withdraw, but it soon turned its attention to other parts of the town. At 1935 hours the Post Office was attacked, and later the Income Tax Offices and other government offices were raided and set on fire.

At 2040 hours the remainder of 8th Parachute Battalion, under command of Lieutenant-Colonel G. Hewetson, D.S.O., arrived and was soon heavily involved. After an hour the situation was under control and at 2330 hours a curfew was imposed on the town.

Early the following day (15th November) the curfew was broken by large crowds who again, after due warnings, had to be dispersed with fire. More buildings were destroyed by fire and there was much looting. In view of this recrudescence, the Brigade Commander, after discussing the situation with the Divisional Commander, ordered the remainder of 3rd Parachute Brigade into Tel Aviv. The troops started to arrive at midday, and Operation "Bellicose," for the restoration of law and order and the imposition of a curfew began.

The balance of the Brigade consisted of 3rd Parachute Battalion, under command of Lieutenant-Colonel W. P. B. Bradish, and 9th Parachute Battalion under command of Lieutenant-Colonel N. Crookenden, D.S.O. Under command was "A" Squadron 3rd The King's Own Hussars.

With the aid of the additional troops the situation was soon restored, and the curfew was imposed and maintained without further incident. The night was a quiet one, and plans were made to raise the curfew the following morning at 0700 hours (16th November). In order to avoid the risk of further damage or bloodshed, and to enable the curfew to be reimposed at 1600 hours, additional troops were placed under command of 3rd Parachute Brigade. These consisted of the balance of 3rd The King's Own Hussars, 6th Airborne Armoured Reconnaissance Regiment, and 1st Battalion The Royal Ulster Rifles. With the increased number of troops available, there were no further incidents, and the curfew was reimposed according to plan.

The operation was continued on 17th, 18th and 19th November, and the curfew was finally revoked at 0520 hours on 20th November, when all troops who had not already left returned to their stations.

The casualties inflicted on the Jews were estimated from reports at 6 killed and 60 wounded. British casualties amounted to 12 wounded and 30 treated for superficial injuries.

As this was the first operation carried out by the Division in Palestine, all the more credit was due to those who took part. There were many extremely difficult situations to handle, and if criticism can be made in the light of subsequent experience, it is possible that the troops were called upon to hold their fire long after it was merited.

The brunt of the operation (apart from the police) was borne by 8th Parachute Battalion. Lieutenant-Colonel G. Hewetson, D.S.O., was particularly prominent in his handling of many dangerous situations and was subsequently awarded the O.B.E. for his part in this, and one or two later operations. As a result of the firm handling which the troops applied during these six days, there was never any subsequent trouble on a comparable scale involving mass disorders in Tel Aviv.

CHAPTER III

THE FIRST SETTLEMENT SEARCHES

ON the night of 22nd/23rd November, a naval patrol vessel boarded a Greek schooner, S.S. *Demetrius*, which was in the process of landing illegal Jewish immigrants on the coast about twelve miles north of Tel Aviv. The vessel was escorted into Haifa, where the crew were arrested and 20 Jews on board were sent to Athlit Detention Camp. It was estimated that possibly 200 Jews had landed and made good their escape to the nearby settlements before the *Demetrius* was arrested.

As a result of this incident, and in view of the manner in which the Jews reacted on issues connected with the prevention of immigration into Palestine, it was anticipated that some form of reprisal would be undertaken by them. Moreover, the Intelligence Branch of Headquarters Palestine accurately forecast that an attack of some kind would take place in the same region.

On the night of the 24th/25th, two strong assault parties of Jews (almost certainly Palmach) attacked the coastguard stations at Givat Olga and Sidna Ali, respectively fifteen miles north and three miles south of the spot at which the *Demetrius* had been boarded. Both attacks were well planned and executed, and were covered by heavy fire from automatic weapons. After the wire defences had been penetrated both buildings were blown up with gelignite. Fourteen police were wounded in the attacks. The Jews withdrew, taking their casualties with them, and mining the roads round Givat Olga to delay any pursuit.

The ensuing action by the Security Forces was primarily a police operation with the Army in support and was designed to find and arrest those who had taken part in the attacks on the coastguard stations. Owing to the distance between the two localities, the subsequent searches were organized as two separate operations. Givat Olga was in 1st Infantry Division's sector, but the settlements concerned in the attack were in 6th Airborne Division's area. The operation, as far as it affected the Army, therefore, became a joint one, with 1st Infantry Division being prominent in the initial stages and 6th Airlanding Brigade moving north to assist in the searches which were to be made.*

Although the two operations which followed took place fifteen miles apart, the resistance, in each case, to the police and Army, followed an almost identical pattern and it is possible to consider them together. With the aid of tracking dogs, the police traced the attackers of Givat Olga to the two Jewish settlements of Givat Haiyam and Hogla, which are close together about four miles south-east of Hadera. The attackers of Sidna Ali were similarly traced to the two settlements of Rishpon and Shefayim, respectively one and two miles distant from the coastguard station.

Early on the 25th, troops were called for in each locality to support the police. 2nd Infantry Brigade provided two battalions for the north, and 3rd Parachute Brigade sent 8th Parachute Battalion to Sidna Ali. The police entered the settlements and explained what they had come for, and how they proposed to screen all male members of the population. Their progress was opposed at each stage by the inhabitants of the settlements who resorted to stoning and the use of clubs in trying to evict them. In the meantime, large numbers of reinforcements from neighbouring settlements poured into these areas to assist the Jews. The troops which were deployed in cordoning the settlements prevented the majority of reinforcements from entering them, although many had done so before the cordons were established. These eventually tried to break out, and clashes with the troops ensued. Inside the settlements the police were bitterly opposed and were forced to make several baton charges. During the afternoon, after no progress had been made in the searches, the police were forced to withdraw, and the cordons were strengthened by further troops, and left in position overnight. By this stage, the troops deployed in the north consisted of 1st Battalion The Loyal Regiment, 2nd Battalion The North Staffordshire Regiment (both 2nd Infantry Brigade), 1st Battalion

---

* These operations received more than the usual share of publicity, particularly in the Jewish Press, and became known as the "Sharon Searches." That their purpose was misrepresented goes almost without saying, and there was little or no mention of the fact that they were the direct outcome of two particularly ruthless attacks.

The Argyll and Sutherland Highlanders, ist Battalion The Royal Ulster Rifles (both 6th Airlanding Brigade), 2nd/7th Battalion The Middlesex Regiment, ist Reconnaissance Regiment, 6th Battalion The Gordon Highlanders, and one company ist Battalion The Hertfordshire Regiment. In the south, 8th Parachute Battalion had been reinforced by 3rd Parachute Battalion, and and Battalion The Oxfordshire and Buckinghamshire Light Infantry (placed under command of 3rd Parachute Brigade from 6th Airlanding Brigade). One squadron 3rd The King's Own Hussars was placed under command of each brigade of the Division taking part, and 195 Airlanding Field Ambulance and 224 Parachute Field Ambulance each supported their respective brigades. The operations were under command of Brigadier R. H. Bower, C.B.E., Commanding 6th Airlanding Brigade (having just taken over command from Brigadier' R. H. Bellamy, D.S.O.), and Brigadier G. W. Lathbury, D.S.O., M.B.E., Commanding 3rd Parachute Brigade.

The following day (26th November) in the north the police made a further attempt to carry out a search without the assistance of troops, but were again heavily involved inside the settlements in hand-to-hand fighting with the Jews, who were armed with bricks and clubs and who resisted violently. At 1120 hours troops were ordered into the settlements and all resistance soon became passive. Shortly after, further efforts were made by mobs of Jewish reinforcements from neighbouring settlements to break through the cordon by weight of numbers. After due warnings had been given, the troops were obliged to open fire and a number of casualties was inflicted.

At Rishpon and Shefayim to the south, the Brigade Commander's plan, agreed by the police, was for 8th Parachute Battalion to enter Shefayim at 0700 hours with the police. Their entry was opposed and resort had again to be made to baton charges, and for the first time to the use of tear gas, before any form of order was established. Following this, difficulties were encountered with the inhabitants, who refused to go into their houses as instructed; 900 were eventually arrested and placed under guard. In the meantime the cordon round Rishpon became hard pressed by a crowd, estimated at 1,500, which tried to break into the settlement. Several rounds were fired, and casualties were inflicted on the Jews. Later, a large crowd, estimated at 3,000, approached a platoon on the outer cordon. The ringleader, who was on horseback exhorting the mob, was picked off, and the situation was restored.

At 1200 hours the search of Shefayim was completed, and soon after Rishpon was entered. Here there were no major incidents, though 175 pounds of ammonal and some other explosives were found. Eleven inhabitants, including the Mukhtar,* were arrested.

The searches of the four settlements were completed by 1700 hours and police and troops withdrew after sending 160 Jews for further interrogation to Athlit. Casualties to the Jews amounted to 6 killed and (estimated) 42 wounded. A number of minor injuries were sustained by the Security Forces.

Several points of interest were noted as a result of these operations.† Firstly, it was quite obvious that a highly developed local organization had been into action. There were numerous examples of this, such as the movement of Jewish reinforcements in answer to summons by alarm gongs, sirens, and signalling from settlement watch-towers. There was also an efficient medical organization which treated all Jewish casualties.

Secondly, it demonstrated that a comparatively minor situation could develop rapidly into one involving many thousands of Jews, armed with clubs and stones and all inspired by the will to forestall the Security Forces in the execution of their duty. It also showed, however, that the Jews considered it not worth while to offer full armed resistance.‡

Thirdly, on the tactical side, one new lesson was learned and an old one relearned. In future searches of this type, it was resolved to intercept Jewish reinforcements farther afield, and thus prevent interference with the troops concerned in the search. And finally, it also confirmed the fact that this type of operation should be carried out by the largest available force, a proportion of which should be held in immediate reserve. In these operations the Army produced the equivalent of eleven infantry battalions, and this

---

* Headman of a village or settlement.
† The search of Rishpon and Shefayim was afterwards named Operation "Guy Fawkes."
‡ There was in fact one instance in which fire was opened by Jews in this operation, but this was probably an act of irresponsibility on the part of an individual.

force, which at first might have appeared unnecessarily strong, was finally only sufficient to deal with the situation without resorting to extreme measures. On occasions such as these, the more troops that could be made available, the less force had to be employed.

TEL AVIV AGAIN

Following the operations in the Plain of Sharon, Palestine was comparatively quiet for a month. That means to say that there were no attacks on troops or military installations by the dissidents, and no searches were carried out by the Security Forces. But even during the lulls there was an undercurrent of activity. The I.Z.L. and Stern Gang were, for example, unable to let any great interval pass without staging the robbery of a bank or organizing some other means of contributing towards their funds. This, of course, though necessary for them in order to meet their expenses, was only a sideline. Such time as was not actively spent in prosecuting the "war" against their "enemy" was used in development of the "war effort"—the manufacturing of arms and explosives, the endless gathering of information, the reconnaissances and the preparation of plans. Nor in the camp of the Law was there any relaxation. The police had the task of keeping in touch with the underworld, and, by exerting a continual pressure on the opposition, they strove hard to retain the initiative. Their efforts were not always successful, but undoubtedly they had the effect of directing much of the energies of the dissident groups towards their own security, when the latter would rather have been on the offensive against our forces. Meanwhile the Army was no less occupied, and the daily round of guards, patrols, and occasionally some training, went on unceasingly.

During this lull, which almost lasted to the end of the year, the dissidents presumably had to make a decision. In view of the forthcoming visit of the Anglo-American Committee, should they curtail their campaign of lawlessness and show how well they could behave ? Or should they take the stronger line, and demonstrate how their patience was exhausted, what their capabilities were, and how they would stick at nothing in the pursuit of their ideals ? If the decision had rested with the community, the former course would no doubt have been chosen, but it lay with an unbalanced, fanatical and ruthless element, which decided in favour of a renewal of bloodshed.

On the night of 26th/27th December, operations were resumed. Attacks were carried out against Police Headquarters in Jerusalem and Jaffa, a R.E.M.E. armoury in Tel Aviv, and railway installations at Lydda. The methods and traces savoured strongly of the I.Z.L., who showed less regard than ever for taking lives.

As a result of this renewal of activity, the Security Forces went into action in strength. 3rd Parachute Brigade was again launched into Tel Aviv, where a curfew was imposed, this time with no opposition. The extremists had suffered a certain number of casualties in these attacks and information was followed up in each case. It appeared that those who had carried out the attacks in Jaffa and Tel Aviv had probably gone into hiding at Ramat Gan, a large settlement on the outskirts of Tel Aviv. Here 3rd Parachute Brigade, with 4th Parachute Battalion under command, carried out Operation "Pintail" on 29th December. This was a detailed search, in conjunction with the Police, for the thugs who had taken part in the recent attacks; 1,500 persons were subjected to a detailed investigation, and of these, 59 were taken into custody. Thirty curfew breakers were also arrested. Following "Pintail" came Operation "Heron" on 8th January, 1946—again conducted by 3rd Parachute Brigade—in which Rishon-le-Zion was searched by the police, with the Army enforcing the curfew and providing the cordon troops; 55 suspects were detained. After this came a period of routine minor operations in support of the police, and a rather larger one (Operation "Pigeon") on 30th January, again in Tel Aviv, where 3rd Parachute Brigade assisted the police in searching the Shapiro Quarter.

So for many months to come, one search was followed by another. Before long a standard drill had been perfected, and most operations followed the same basic design. The hardest part was by no means the search itself; that was a matter of straightforward routine. Broadly speaking, the troops had to produce all possible suspects in front of the police screening teams, who were trained in interrogation and identification. This was probably the simplest part of the whole; the hardest was to get the cordon into position before the alarm was raised. The difficulties started at the very beginning,

D

and the best way of illustrating them is to describe briefly the development of a search operation from its inception onwards.

A SEARCH IS PLANNED

Searches were undertaken for varying reasons. The most common was to trace certain members of an extremist group who were known to have carried out an attack, and who were believed to be hiding in a particular area. Then there was a search, again for suspects, based on intelligence, which was carried out in order to forestall an attack. Thirdly, there was the arms search; this was a more thorough and detailed type of operation and invariably took longer to complete. Finally, there was the punitive search which was at one time contemplated but never actually executed. It might be for arms or suspects, but was designed principally as a punishment for a community which had obstructed the law in one way or another.

Whatever the reason for a search, the idea was conceived as a result of information from the Police or Intelligence, and it was undertaken following either an order from higher authority or a request from the Police. The plan was formulated between the Divisional Commander, the Brigade Commander and the District Superintendent of Police. All proposed searches of any magnitude were Top Secret operations. Each level of commander and staff officer was introduced to the plan according to a carefully calculated schedule, just as in any operation of war, which was known as the Briefing Timetable. The security of information regarding future operations and intentions lay on a place of importance above all other problems connected with them. One slip in security and the operation was doomed to failure ; and the slips were far more easily made in this respect than in war. It was as though the enemy permanently had a vast and highly trained intelligence service with admittance to all indiscreet conversations and access to all written orders and correspondence not under guard or lock and key. It would be impossible to detail all the methods by which information on forthcoming operations could go astray, but most were variations on one of several fundamental causes. Where our own troops were concerned, any leakage would not be the outcome of malicious intent, but lack of thought, so the danger was obviated by leaving it as late as possible before the briefing for a search was carried out. One of the greatest dangers was careless references to forthcoming operations by unthinking officers. Civilian employees, whether Arab or Jew, were all totally untrustworthy in this respect. That planning and preparations had to go on before their eyes in some form which they would not recognize was one of the complications which made the use of cover-plans essential. At a certain time immediately prior to each operation, the camps of all troops taking part had to be sealed in order that the briefing of troops could be carried out. One of the factors which set the time for this was the normal routine of the civilian employees. It was desirable to seal the camps after they had left, but on occasions it was necessary for them to be sealed inside and placed under temporary guard. Reconnaissance was nearly always out of the question. Detailed plans for the approach of the cordon troops (which were the first to arrive) had to be made from air photos and large-scale maps. Fortunately, these were plentiful and normally accurate, but the greatest asset of all was in knowing the area from a study of the ground carried out during previous months.

Neither wireless nor telephone could be used for either open or guarded reference to a future operation. Plans had to be discussed and agreed in offices where overhearing was impossible, and any alterations to plans had to be notified by personal contact.

Written orders were kept to an absolute minimum, and on occasions were dispensed with altogether. No previously made arrangements could suddenly be cancelled when a unit or formation was warned for an operation. That meant that chaos had to be accepted in all other less vital matters, which led to some unusual and amusing situations. For example, a Commanding Officer might have to let the organization for an athletic meeting go ahead, well knowing that it would not be able to take place on the day arranged. His task was then to cut the losses without the motive being sensed.

Even when planning and briefing were completed, and troops were moving off in their transport, it was often worth while moving away in the reverse direction to that in which the objective lay. By this means it was hoped to mislead the "agents" who watched the camps in order to get early warning of operations. In the case of one of the biggest operations which involved so many troops that it was impossible to cover it up, the movement of columns was carried out in such a way as to give the impression that the operation was taking place many miles from the chosen spot.

No doubt should remain in the reader's mind by now as to the magnitude of the problem of the security of information. But even when this was successfully overcome, the planning for the actual conduct of the search was little less complex.

Some 23 parties from at least 16 different units might play a part in a brigade search. Each party had to fit into the general plan, and if it should fail to turn up at the right time and place, correctly equipped and prepared for its task a breakdown might result. A frequent problem on occasions was when and how to assemble the transport when this was provided by the R.A.S.C. Its arrival might so easily be interpreted as a sign of future operations if seen by civilian employees. The best time for most searches to begin was dawn, as this enabled troops taking part to assemble under cover of darkness, and also, at that time any wanted persons were more likely to be found in their houses. Concentration of forces in the dark demanded a high standard of training and a thorough knowledge of the country.

The brunt of the operation was borne by the infantry (or parachute troops), who had to establish the outer and inner cordons, impose the curfew and conduct the search. In addition to the obvious commitments, it was necessary for them to provide baton parties in case of resistance, guides to the place of screening, guards for the suspect cages, escorts to the detention camp, and reserves in case of emergency. In any of these duties they were frequently assisted by the Gunners and the Glider Pilots acting in an infantry role.

The Arms and Services all played their part. A *coup de main* party from the Divisional Signals Regiment might have to precede the main columns in order to take over a civilian telephone exchange on the way and cut communications; the Divisional Engineers had to be present and equipped to make, or break, anything; and the R.A.M.C. had to be prepared to undertake midwifery as well as deal with the casualties of both sides. All these units had to be given time to plan and prepare, and yet the longer they were given the greater the risk of leakage of information. It followed, therefore, that the operations which were mounted at the shortest notice normally had the best chance of success. Eventually, when the standard of training reached its peak, a brigade search could be organized in just under six hours.

The foregoing description relates principally to military searches in which the Palestine Police were normally in support. Many other operations which were within the means of the police were planned and carried out by them with possibly a military detachment in reserve and under their command. The command of all operations was a matter of vital importance—there could be no dual control; it was clearly either a police or military responsibility. At the same time, operations were frequently initiated by the police, and, at some intermediate stage, control was passed to the Army if the situation warranted it. In this respect certain factors made it difficult for both forces to adhere strictly to the normal rules of "Duties in Aid of the Civil Power." In fairness to the police, it should be pointed out that they were faced by several crippling handicaps. Following the war they found themselves terribly depleted in British personnel, and those who remained were often overworked and in need of rest. The Arab and Jewish elements in the force were rarely altogether reliable, particularly in situations where there were opposing calls on their loyalty. In such circumstances they were largely partisan and this fact had to be accepted. As far as the Army was concerned, it meant that when referring to forthcoming operations with the police, even more care than usual was necessary in order to maintain security, and it soon became the rule for formations and units to deal only with the Superintendents of Police Districts in these matters, and anything in writing was passed to them personally by hand. Such a state of affairs in turn gave rise to the inevitable calls for small detachments ("penny packets" as they were known), of troops to guard various vital installations. These were often difficult to resist, for if such V.Ps. were liable to sabotage, the only hope for their security might lie with the provision of a British guard. At a time when British police could not be spared owing to their shortage of numbers, many commitments had to be reluctantly accepted by the Army. These calls for dispersion clashed with the necessity for concentration and mobility of all available forces, and confronted the Higher Command with a dilemma which had far-reaching effects and was never satisfactorily solved.

ARMS RAID AT SARAFAND

On the night of 25th February, 1946, the I.Z.L. carried out raids against the R.A.F. airfields at Lydda, Petah Tiqva and Qastina with the object of destroying as many aircraft as possible. Aircraft dispersed round an airfield are not easy to defend against this form of attack, and the raids were very costly, the damage being estimated at some £750,000. One of the attacking force was killed but otherwise there was nothing to show for the losses sustained. The immediate effect of the raids as far as the Division was concerned, was the departure of its aircraft to Egypt in order to avoid further loss or damage. For some time plans were discussed for sending troops from the Division to the Delta for air training but for a variety of reasons this course was not adopted. In the end, the aircraft returned to their former bases and on the Division devolved the responsibility for their protection, which increased further the already heavy guard commitments by night.

On 6th March, which incidentally was the date on which the Anglo-American Committee arrived in Palestine, the I.Z.L. carried out a bold and ambitious raid on the ammunition store of 3rd The King's Own Hussars, who were stationed in the cantonment at Sarafand. The raid achieved very little, cost them two casualties, and was probably classed as a failure by the I.Z.L.

The party, which was estimated to be about nine strong, arrived at the Rishon Gate dressed as Airborne soldiers complete with red berets and camouflage smocks, in a stolen military vehicle and a private car. At the check post they held up the Jewish gate guard, one of whom they later shot in cold blood. Leaving a small covering party at the gate, the remainder of the gang moved into the camp and drew up alongside the ammunition tent of the 3rd Hussars. Here they held up the ammunition sentries and an unsuspecting officer who happened to be there, and started loading ammunition onto their truck. They were careful to choose lunch-time in which to carry out the raid, so there were not many troops about.

It was not long before the alarm was raised and the party of

Jews was compelled to depart hurriedly, followed by a fusillade
of shots from the Regiment. Before leaving the camp, they placed
a time bomb in the ammunition tent, which destroyed the tent but
failed to cause any casualties.

In the meantime, Captain G. E. Barrow, at that time the Signals
Officer of the 3rd Hussars, had run to the Rishon Gate in order to
close it, but found it held by the I.Z.L. covering party. He
grappled with, and overpowered one of the thugs, but, as fire
was directed at him from point-blank range, he was eventually
forced to take cover and was unable to prevent their getaway.
For his gallantry he was later awarded the M.B.E.

The pursuit was taken up by armoured cars, but contact was
lost at Rishon-le-Zion. However, two of the thugs, both seriously
wounded, were captured later, as were the two vehicles, one of
which had been badly damaged by the small-arms fire of the 3rd
Hussars. Of the very small amount of ammunition which they had
succeeded in loading on to their truck practically all was recovered.
The only British casualty caused by the indiscriminate fire of the
gangsters during the raid, was a particularly tragic one—Mrs.
Marjoribanks, one of the Division's voluntary canteen workers,
was hit and seriously wounded. Fortunately she made a wonderful
recovery.

No account of the Division in Palestine would be complete without a reference to Mrs. Marjorie Fildes and her team of Y.M.C.A.
helpers, or "cygnets" as they were known by all. They consisted
of Mrs. Jean Marjoribanks, Miss Pat Kindersley and later Miss
Felicity Archdale. Between them they ran a canteen service,
particularly during parachute dropping, in the same way as they
had done in England. In a country where normal social life was at
a standstill, their presence and work were very greatly appreciated,
and they were the true friends of all ranks.

Following the raid at Sarafand, a thorough investigation was
made into the ways in which camp defences might be further
strengthened. As a result of various recommendations which were
adopted, there were no further incidents of this kind in the Division,
and in fact, as far as was known, the opposition made no further
attempt to gain entry into any Divisional unit camp. It was not
so easy to prevent such incidents in the case of outlying detachments,
as will be seen later.

CHAPTER IV

CHANGES IN ORDER OF BATTLE

ON 5th March the Division underwent a change of command— Major-General A. J. H. Cassels, C.B.E., D.S.O., who had lately commanded the 51st Highland Division in Germany, arrived to take over from General Bols, who went to the Imperial Defence College.

The following month there was a major change in the Divisional Order of Battle—the replacement of 6th Airlanding Brigade by 1st Parachute Brigade. This Brigade consisted of the 1st, 2nd and 17th Parachute Battalions. The 1st and 2nd Battalions had seen a great deal of war service in 1st Parachute Brigade, while the 17th Battalion had been raised in 1945. The arrival of the Brigade meant that the whole of the infantry of the Division was now parachute-trained, and no longer included a glider-borne element.

The Brigade, under the command of Brigadier R. H. Bellamy, D.S.O., arrived at Port Said, in H.M.T. *Orontes*, on 1st April, 1946, and reached Camp 21 near Nathanya, in Central Palestine, in the course of the following week. In the meantime, 6th Airlanding Brigade had moved, less one battalion, to Jerusalem on 29th and 30th March in order to take over the East Sector (Jerusalem) from 7th Infantry Brigade, which meant that the normal method of relief had to be dispensed with for the Nathanya Brigade. Control of the area was assumed temporarily by 1st Battalion The Royal Ulster Rifles, with 3rd The King's Own Hussars and 6th Battalion The Gordon Highlanders under command. Headquarters 1st Parachute Brigade arrived on 3rd April, and by 7th April the Brigade was complete in Camp 21. It was in full operational control of the Samaria Civil District (less the Jenin Sub-District) by 8th April.

This was a sad period for 6th Airlanding Brigade. Two of its battalions had been in the Division since its formation, and had distinguished themselves with the Division in action. The time had

MAJOR-GENERAL E. L. BOLS, C.B., D.S.O.

MAJOR-GENERAL A. J. H. CASSELS, C.B.E., D.S.O.

Facing page 42

now come for them to lose their coveted Airborne affiliation, and on 15th April, the Brigade became 31st Independent Infantry Brigade. On 26th April the Divisional Commander attended a farewell parade in Jerusalem at which red berets and Pegasus signs were worn for the last time. The Brigade remained in Palestine until its disbandment in November, 1946. 2nd Battalion The Oxfordshire and Buckinghamshire Light Infantry ultimately joined 3rd Infantry Brigade, 1st Battalion The Argyll and Sutherland Highlanders went to the 8th Infantry Brigade, and 1st Battalion The Royal Ulster Rifles left for Austria.

Also in March, 1946, there took place the disbandment of 6th Airborne Armoured Reconnaissance Regiment which was commanded in Palestine by Lieutenant-Colonel C. P. D. Legard. The Regiment became unoperational on 1st February and some of the officers and the majority of the men were transferred to 3rd The King's Own Hussars, which regiment had assumed its role in the Division.

On 5th August, 5th Parachute Brigade less 13th Parachute Battalion arrived in Camp 22, Nathanya, from South-East Asia Command. Since leaving the Division in England in July, 1945, the Brigade had served in Malaya and Java. On arrival, 7th Parachute Battalion amalgamated with 17th Parachute Battalion in 1st Parachute Brigade. Though the amalgamated unit was founded on 17th Battalion, the designation of the senior battalion was retained. 12th Parachute Battalion was disbanded and its members were transferred to battalions throughout the Division.

On 13th September, 21st Independent Parachute Company was disbanded. Its pathfinder role in war was to be assumed by the Divisional Reconnaissance Regiment, so many of its members were transferred to 3rd The King's Own Hussars. The remainder was absorbed into the Parachute Battalions.*

SUCCESSFUL ACTION AGAINST I.Z.L.

On the night of 2nd/3rd April the I.Z.L. carried out two widely separated attacks on the railway. One took place north of

---

* Various other changes in the designation of units also took place from time to time, and when not mentioned in the text they will be apparent in the annual Orders of Battle included in the appendices.

Haifa, where a party of some twenty saboteurs first overpowered a police guard, and then seriously damaged a railway bridge at Na'amin. The other attack was of greater proportions but was less successful, and took place in the Isdud-Yibna area between Lydda and Gaza. Here, five railway bridges were slightly damaged, and the roads in the area were mined. One railway engine was also destroyed near Isdud and the line was cut in several places. Several railway police posts in the area were engaged during the night and some spirited fighting took place.

The attack in the south was executed by a party estimated at 30-40 in strength, working to a plan which, as usual, had been carefully thought out. There was, however, a weakness in the timings of the withdrawal. The first phase of the attack was directed at the Yibna railway station and a railway police blockhouse just outside it. The Arab police, however, put up a stout resistance, which, together with the poor quality of the Jewish fuses attached to the explosive charges, resulted in the operation only having a limited success.

While the attack was still in progress, a patrol from 9th Parachute Battalion travelling in transport arrived in the Yibna area. As the patrol was crossing a bridge over a wadi just outside the village, the leading jeep exploded a mine. The 3-ton truck following did likewise, and as part of the patrol dismounted they exploded a third. Three soldiers were wounded as a result of these explosions, though had the mines been of the usual type the casualties would have been greater.

The patrol then went off in search of the attackers, who, however, withdrew before them, and the patrol was fiercely engaged by the Arab railway police who failed to recognize them in the dark. For over an hour efforts were made to convince the police that the patrol was British. These were at last successful, and in the meantime fortunately no further casualties had been sustained. While minor confusion reigned here, another patrol, from 5th Parachute Battalion, arrived, and deployed in the opposite direction to contact the next police post. It appeared that all the posts in the area had been attacked and the Arabs manning them were in a very excited frame of mind.

After midnight a company of 6th Parachute Battalion joined in the operation farther to the south, where they also found the police triumphant because they had driven off the attackers with only one minor casualty to themselves. Nothing remained to be done until daybreak as it was obvious by this time that all the attackers, less one killed in Yibna station, had withdrawn.

In the morning the chase was taken up at first light. Three trails were followed: the first based on a report from an Arab that 30 armed Jews were moving north across the Rishon ranges, the second on a trail followed by dogs to the settlements of Kefar Marmorek and Ezra Bitsaron (respectively near Rehovoth and Rishon-le-Zion), and the third on a trail followed by dogs from Isdud.

Nothing sensational resulted from the last two trails, although both the settlements mentioned were searched and several suspects were detained. The first trail, however, led up the coast through open country, and a weary and unfit party of gangsters found the going much harder than they had anticipated. Here, still some distance from their base, they were spotted by an observation plane sent up for the purpose, and troops of 8th Parachute Battalion soon closed in. The final action was fought between 24 Jews and one section only of the Battalion. In spite of their superiority in numbers and lavish scale of automatic weapons, the Jews after losing 2 seriously, and 12 slightly wounded, soon lost heart in the fight and surrendered. No casualties were suffered by the British section. This was one of the few occasions on which British troops fought an action with the dissidents in the open. Whenever such engagements took place the outcome was never in doubt.

TEL AVIV CAR PARK ATTACK

On 25th April, 1946, the Stern Gang carried out an attack which for cold-blooded brutality could hardly have been surpassed. In the preface to this book reference is made to the absence of bitterness which was shown towards the Jews by those who served with the Division in Palestine. This remark cannot, however, apply to these extremists. No man, whatever his rank, who was serving in the Division on this day will easily forget the feeling of revulsion and frustration which he experienced as a result of this despicable act.

The Division had taken over in Tel Aviv some time previously a car park which was bounded by houses on three sides, and faced the sea on the fourth. The car park was used largely by recreational transport from all formations and units which came into the town on certain afternoons and most evenings. In it, living in tents, was a guard provided by the Lydda Brigade, and which on the night in question came from 5th Parachute Battalion. The object of the guard was primarily to prevent the vehicles, or anything in them, from being stolen, and in order to make their task easier, the park was well surrounded with wire. The strength of the guard on this night was 8 men including 2 N.C.Os.

At 2030 hours (after dark), three vehicles stopped at a house opposite to the entrance to the car park, and between 25 and 30 men, dressed in civilian clothes, entered the house. Here they immediately held up the occupants, and unseen from the car park, established fire positions overlooking the guard tents. Fifteen minutes later a bomb was thrown at the front of the guard tents as a signal for the attack to start. Automatic fire was then directed at the sentries on duty and any soldiers in sight. Those who were not killed had to take cover from the fire which was at very short range. Under the covering fire some twenty or more of the gangsters crossed the road and entered the car park. They entered the first tent in which there were two soldiers off duty, and the sergeant of the guard who was unlocking the rifle rack. While shining torches on the two soldiers who were taking cover on the floor of the tent from the fire outside, they shot them with tommy-guns at point-blank range. A burst was also fired at the sergeant who, unable to reply and having by chance been missed, fell to the ground, feigning death. While he lay at their feet the arms rack was emptied and all the weapons were stolen. Arms, however, were only a secondary consideration; the object of the raid was mass murder, as rapid and complete as possible. It is not known what happened in the next tent, as both the occupants were killed, but they also were unarmed.

Finally, two further soldiers of the Division, who came up to the car park during the attack presumably to assist the guard, were also shot. The casualties to our own troops totalled 7, all killed. After laying mines to cover their escape, the attackers withdrew into the Yemenite section of the Karton quarter, leaving behind them a trail of blood which suggested that at least one had been hit.

It might be explained here that up to this point the stage had not yet been reached when deliberate attacks on British Army personnel were expected. Thus the defence for this guard in the shape of protective sandbag walls round the tents, gunpits for sentries, and a well-defended gate at the entrance had not been generally adopted. These came later, together with many other additional security measures, as a result of this attack and others which followed. It is too easy to be wise after the event, but by that time the situation had not deteriorated sufficiently to suggest that the defences were in any way inadequate. At least, however, this bitter lesson had never to be relearned.

The following day the Karton quarter was searched and 79 suspects were detained, though no proof of complicity could be found. The same morning the Divisional Commander addressed the Mayor of Tel Aviv. To him he expressed in the strongest terms his belief, which was fully shared by the civil and police authorities, that there existed at least some citizens who, if they chose, could come forward with information. He expected more, he said, than messages of sympathy. No such assistance was forthcoming, however, nor was any visible effort made by the Jewish authorities to encourage it.*

This was one of the many occasions when serious thought was given to devise some method of punishing the Jewish community

* Statement by Major-General A. J. H. Cassels, C.B.E., D.S.O., G.O.C. 6th Airborne Division, to the Mayor of Tel Aviv on 26th April, 1946: "I have received your message of regret, but I have sent for you today to say how horrified and disgusted I am at the outrage committed by Jews on the night of 25th April, when seven British soldiers were wilfully and brutally murdered by members of your community. As a result I have decided to impose certain restrictions on the Jewish community as a whole. My decision to restrict the whole community has been made both in order to maintain public security and because I hold the community to blame. There is no doubt whatsoever in my mind that many members either knew of this project or could have given some warning before it happened. Further, I am quite certain that if you, as representative of the community of Tel Aviv, chose to do so you could produce sufficient information to lead to the arrest of the criminals.

"I have therefore decided, with effect from tomorrow and until further orders, to reimpose the road curfew from 6 p.m. to 6 a.m. and also to close all cafes, restaurants and places of public entertainment in Tel Aviv from 8 p.m. to 5 a.m. The necessary orders to enforce this are now being prepared and will be announced shortly."

48

for turning a blind eye to such acts of horror, and making no effort to help the authorities. Many methods were suggested but apart from curfews and road restrictions, which incidentally put a great strain on the troops themselves, no methods were allowed to be enforced. It was difficult to make the soldiers understand such apparent lack of decision, and naturally they and their commanders suffered at times from a very considerable sense of frustration. There was a strong body of opinion in the Army in Palestine which felt that had the community been held to blame more frequently for these outrages, and treated accordingly, the perpetrators would not have received the same measure of support from the Jew-in-the-street.

Much has been written and said about the measure of restraint shown by British troops in Palestine towards a community which condoned and frequently supported the murderous conduct of its extremists. This was attributed to the bonds of discipline and various qualities in the British character which enable forbearance to overcome the instinctive urge to retaliate. Indeed, some argued that this restraint was strongly tainted with apathy, and carried to such an extreme that it no longer represented a virtue in which to take such pride. It should therefore be recorded at this point that, following the attack on the Tel Aviv car park, troops of the Division at Qastina took the law into their own hands for a short time the following night, and damaged some dozen houses and several of their occupants in the adjoining Jewish settlement of Beer Tuvya. This incident, whatever the provocation, could not be overlooked, and the ringleaders were punished. The only other occurrence of this nature in which the Division was concerned was a similar demonstration in Nathanya by troops of 2nd Parachute Brigade following the flogging of their Brigade Major by Jews. The spontaneous outburst of indignation which was featured by the local Jewish Press on these two occasions, and which omitted or glossed over their causes, helped little in restoring a sense of proportion to either side.

THE ANGLO-AMERICAN COMMITTEE

At the time when World War II was ending in 1945, the I.Z.L. produced a slogan that "VE Day for the British is D Day for us."

Although this reflected in the martial sense the attitude of the extremists, it also typified in a more moderate sense the mood of the
Jewish community in Palestine as a whole. Before the war was
even over, all sections of Jewish political thought were engaged
with plans concerning the coming struggle for their homeland. As
it became clearer that most of their aspirations were unlikely to
meet with success, their attitude stiffened, and their hostility to
Great Britain increased. Following several preliminary clashes,
there opened in 1945 a campaign of bitter political endeavour, in
which the Jews strove to portray themselves as an irresistible force ;
in which Britain pledged herself to thwart any illegal aims or prac-
tices and to remain mistress of the situation; and in which the
Arabs, lacking unity of purpose, misled themselves and failed to
command their full measure of respect from the other sides. There
followed two years of relentless effort by Britain for the achievement
of a just settlement of the Palestine Question acceptable to Arabs
and Jews alike. That these labours proved in vain detracts nothing
from the spirit in which the problem was tackled.

Throughout the succession of political developments the Army
maintained a high level of interest. That the Security Forces were
sitting on a powder-keg liable to be detonated by any one of several
parties was only too readily understood. Progress in the political
sphere was, therefore, watched keenly, and interpreted as simply
as possible to all ranks with the object of keeping them informed of
current events.

One of the milestones in this ever-changing political scene was
the brief visit of the Anglo-American Committee, to which passing
reference has already been made. It occurred in March, 1946,
following two months of preliminary work in Washington, London,
and Europe. The commission remained for three weeks in the Middle East, and while in Palestine had the full co-operation of Jews and
Arabs, from both individuals and all political parties. In this in-
soluble problem they received no better advice than from the wise
and diplomatic veteran Jewish leader Dr. Weizmann, who expressed
the hope to them during his evidence that their decision should "take
the line of least injustice."

The Committee left Palestine at the end of March for Switzer-
land, where they deliberated on their report, which of necessity

took the form of a compromise between two widely separated view-points. The report, which was published on 1st May, contained the following salient features:—

    (1) Palestine alone could not meet the immigration needs of the Jewish victims of Nazi and Fascist persecution.

    (2) 100,000 certificates should be authorized immediately for the admission into Palestine of Jews from Europe.

    (3) Palestine should be neither a Jewish state nor an Arab state, and the interests in the Holy Land of Christendom should be recognized.

    (4) The Land Transfer Regulations of 1940 should be rescinded. (These regulations strictly limited Jewish purchase of land and so dealt a severe blow to Zionist land acquisition schemes.)

    (5) Any attempt by either side to prevent by force the execution of these recommendations should be resolutely suppressed.

In the following months no progress was made with the implementation of these recommendations, as a result of which the British Government decided to make yet another effort to bring the Jews and Arabs together. A round-table conference was called for 9th September, but this achieved no more than any of the previous efforts to find a solution, or even an agreed basis on which a solution might be formulated. On one point alone it appeared that the Jews and Arabs were in agreement—that Great Britain should renounce the Mandate and withdraw from Palestine. This without doubt was advocated in order to clear the field for a settlement by force of arms. At the same time, when that course was eventually announced as the unshakeable intention of the British Government, neither the Jews nor the Arabs would at first credit it, and the doubt even persisted in certain quarters after the evacuation was visibly in progress.

CHAPTER V

TRAINING

TRAINING in Palestine was limited entirely by the demands of the operational situation. Because the latter was never quiet for long, such training and exercises as were carried out had to be snatched as opportunities offered, and for this reason little progress was made with the plans for staging airborne exercises in many of the countries of the Middle East.

The air-backing for the Division in Palestine was provided by 283 Wing, R.A.F., under the command of Group Captain R. B. Wardman, O.B.E., A.F.C., until the Wing returned to England in June, 1947. It consisted of two squadrons of Halifax aircraft (644 Squadron and 620 Squadron, later redesignated 47 Squadron and 113 Squadron respectively), and operated from the airfields of Aqir and Qastina, which lay between Gaza and Tel Aviv. The Division was very fortunate in having Group Captain Wardman and his staff looking after the interests of its air training. In spite of calls from elsewhere on their aircraft, and a host of other difficulties, they responded nobly in producing the maximum air-effort for airborne training. Following the departure of 283 Wing, Dakota aircraft were provided by various other Transport Command Squadrons of the R.A.F. based in the Middle East. Even had the Division not been preoccupied in the operational sphere, it is doubtful whether any large-scale air training could have been undertaken, for during this period the R.A.F. was undergoing a reorganization onto a peace-time basis which resulted in a steady decline in the number of flying crews available for training airborne troops. It was therefore in any case, impossible to devote either the thought or the time that had been hoped to this important branch of the Division's activities. However, the training which was carried out at the Airborne Training School at Aqir was of a high standard, and sufficient to ensure that the airborne technique and spirit were kept alive. Parachute courses on a small scale were run during 1946 and 1947, and a total of over 20,000 descents were made. Most of the training consisted of refresher courses for trained parachutists, but in addition a small number of untrained officers and other ranks who were posted to the Division while in Palestine, and who could not be spared to return to England in order to qualify, were given basic parachute courses at Aqir. A great deal of the credit for the results achieved must go to the R.A.F. Parachute Training Instructors; under the leadership of Squadron-Leader Stannard, they did much for the Division.

Apart from the Air Training School, there also existed the Divisional Battle School which opened at Ein Shemer in 1945 and finally closed down at St. Jeans, north of Acre, in 1948. The main feature of the Battle School was its versatility. Its charter was to organize any type of training (apart from air training) for which there was a demand in the Division. This it did with unflagging enthusiasm.

It was never possible to carry out any formation training in the Division as each brigade was, if not actually committed on internal security duties, at least in reserve and liable to be called upon at short notice for some operation. Thus the most ambitious form of training to be undertaken was the rare battalion, and more frequent company, air exercises which took place outside Palestine in such places as Cyprus, Transjordan and Iraq, which were all visited by units of the Division. Several more ambitious exercises farther afield were also planned, and among these was a projected visit of a small force to Hassani airfield at Athens in which anti-tank guns were to have been dropped by parachute and the troops taking part were to have co-operated with the Greek Army. The plans for this exercise were well advanced when it had to be dropped owing to the situation in Palestine. Projects were also in hand for visits to Aden, Tripoli and other British Middle East garrisons, but of those visualized, only one actually took place and that was Exercise "Gordon" in May, 1946, in which a large battalion group was flown from Palestine to Khartoum.

The object of Exercise "Gordon," which took place from 4th to 8th May was threefold. Firstly, to show the flag, secondly, to practise a parachute battalion group in an air transported role over a long distance, and thirdly, to practise communications over long distances.

The troops taking part consisted of 3rd Parachute Battalion, "A" Company 8th Parachute Battalion, and detachments of other arms. The Battalion landed in Halifax aircraft on Khartoum airfield after a 1,200 miles non-stop flight from Qastina in Palestine. The Company, on the other hand, was dropped by parachute from Dakota aircraft after staging midway the previous night at Wadi Halfa. Their journey was about 1,400 miles. Three gliders towed by Halifax aircraft also took part in the exercise, and landed on Khartoum airfield loaded with jeeps and trailers containing heavy equipment.

The tactical setting of the exercise was of considerable historical interest as it led to an engagement with part of the garrison of Khartoum, representing a Dervish Force, on the site of the Battle of Omdurman.

The exercise was well worth while, although it was marred by the high casualty rate incurred in the parachute drop. Many valuable lessons on the employment of airborne troops in hot climates were learned as a result of this exercise, though no immediate advantage could be taken of the experience gained, as it was the only exercise of its type to be carried out.

The casualties amounted to 1 killed, 3 major injuries and 74 minor injuries (cuts and scrapes) out of a company of 108. There were no casualties in the 3rd Battalion. A thorough investigation into the causes revealed four factors which contributed towards this casualty rate. Some were unavoidable, others were unforeseen owing to the lack of airborne experience under similar conditions. Firstly, owing to bad visibility from the air caused by a dust haze, one stick was dropped short of the dropping zone, and they fell among buildings. This accounted for all the major casualties. Secondly, shorts were worn instead of trousers, and smocks were dispensed with on account of the heat (the temperature was about 110° F. in the shade). This lack of protection was largely responsible for the minor injuries which were incurred while the troops were being dragged by their parachutes in the wind. Thirdly, it appeared that the rate of descent was faster than normal, which was thought to be caused by the thinner density of air, owing to the heat and also possibly by strong down currents. As a result, on landing, the troops were momentarily stunned by the impact and possibly the effect of the heat, and therefore failed to apply the correct anti-drag drills until it was too late. Many were dragged for several hundreds of yards. Fourthly, the wind, which was approaching the borderline for safety, but was considered safe, increased suddenly as the drop was in progress, and at the actual time the troops landed was possibly gusting at 25 m.p.h. This by itself would not in normal conditions result in a heavy casualty rate, but combined with the other factors it was instrumental in causing the injuries on this occasion.

There is no denying that the drop marred an otherwise enjoyable exercise, and one which had the makings of an outstanding success. Naturally, keen concern and disappointment, owing to the casualty rate, was felt by those who had planned it, but the greatest danger was that of a drop in confidence among the parachute troops, which could have followed. The reverse was, however, the case, and following a talk from the Divisional Commander to those who took part, in which he explained why he believed such high casualties had been suffered, the C.O. of the 8th Battalion reported that morale was higher than ever.

The exercise, however, was not without its lighter side. Major Dover, commanding the Parachute Company which dropped on the airfield, landed in some telephone wires from which he was suspended for some time before he could release himself. While in this state of helplessness, a fuzzy-wuzzy opportunist seized his chance of making away with the pair of boots which were hanging so temptingly within his reach. The mobility of parachute troops is dependent on many factors.

The return journey with one exception was accomplished safely on 8th and 9th May after the troops had spent a day off duty in Khartoum as the guests of 8th Battalion The Royal Warwickshire Regiment. The mishap on the return journey occurred when one of the gliders had to be cast off in the desert by its tug aircraft. This was caused by the failure of one of the engines of the aircraft from overheating, and signs of a second doing likewise. The glider landed safely 130 miles south of Wadi Halfa. The crew was rescued thirty hours later by an Anson aircraft which landed alongside, and a party of the Sudan Defence Force eventually collected the jeep and equipment. During the period which the crew spent in the desert they were supplied by parachute with all the necessary supplies, some miscellaneous comforts, and a cartoon, showing Major Tipper, the first pilot of the glider, vainly scanning the sandy horizon for signs of rescue.

THE FIRST KIDNAPPINGS

On 18th June, 1946, in a course of a week of violence by the Hagana, I.Z.L. and Stern Gang, there occurred in Tel Aviv a new development in lawlessness—the kidnapping by the I.Z.L. of five British officers. The scene was lunchtime in the Tel Aviv British Officers' Club, and the hold-up was carried out without difficulty, for at this time all troops when not on duty were unarmed.* One of the officers was struck on the head, carried to waiting cars outside, and taken off, together with the other four, to prepared hiding places.

The object of the raid was to get hostages to hold against the two Jews who had been captured in the arms raid at Sarafand on 6th March. These, in the meantime, had been tried by a military court and sentenced to death on 13th June. The sentence was subject to confirmation by higher authority, and the I.Z.L. adopted this method in order to secure a commutation—a practice which was to be repeated as time went on, and which had far-reaching effects. Of the five officers, three were from the Division, the fourth was from a static R.E.M.E. unit, and the fifth from the R.A.F. The last two were taken to a separate hiding place, and on the way they were transferred to an ingeniously fitted lorry which carried a large, shallow, wooden chest with stretchers inside. The chest lay hidden under a load of concrete slabs, access to which was gained by lowering one of the sideboards of the vehicle. This suggested that the vehicle had been prepared to pass through military or police check-posts on the way to its destination.

The two officers, who had been kept together, were released four days later in Tel Aviv. They had not been treated with violence but had been kept shackled with chains by hands or feet, and part

---

* The theory was to avoid provoking the population with armed troops in their midst, possibly appearing to some as reminiscent of occupation forces. Many attempts were made during each lull in dissident action to revert to this state of only having troops armed when on duty, but the idea in the end had to be abandoned. Thereafter all troops were armed at all times when outside their camps.

of the time had been permanently gagged. They had been constantly guarded by four armed Jews. The reason for their release was probably twofold. Firstly, it was thought that the Hagana and Jewish Agency had exerted considerable pressure on the I.Z.L. to release all officers, as otherwise, they feared drastic action by the Government against the Jewish leaders and institutions. Secondly, the energetic British reaction in the shape of numerous searches entailed a great risk in keeping the officers prisoner. By releasing two of them, the risk was reduced, a compromise was offered to the more moderate organizations, while the three remaining officers still provided a very effective bargaining counter.

The remaining three officers were held captive for another twelve days (by which time the death sentence on the two condemned Jews had been commuted), and were released on 4th July. Their treatment had been similar to that of the others. In order to pass the time they had been given books of Zionist propaganda to read, and their captors also took every opportunity of explaining their extremist views. The interest of the captives soon flagged, however, and in any case they were not in a very receptive frame of mind as far as this subject went. Nor was it quite the ideal setting for the conversion of dubious material to a new outlook on extreme Zionism.

The manner of their release was interesting. They were first chloroformed and then placed in wooden boxes in which they were taken from their hiding place (which was discovered the following day in Tel Aviv), and were finally dumped unceremoniously at a street corner. On recovering consciousness the officers broke their way out of their "coffins" and found themselves free. They reported that of the hundreds of passers-by at the time, none took the slightest notice of them, as though this sort of event was an everyday occurrence. This small point illustrates how the Jew-in-the-street in Palestine avoided at all costs becoming involved in anything which might lead to his being obliged to give evidence against a dissident organization.

OPERATION "AGATHA"

It was by no means due to the kidnapping of the five officers by the I.Z.L. that Operation "Agatha" was launched, although it was

VEHICLE IN WHICH KIDNAPPED BRITISH OFFICERS WERE
TRANSPORTED BY JEWS.

CONTENTS OF AN ARMS CACHE FOUND AT DOROT, A JEWISH
SETTLEMENT IN THE NEGEV.

undoubtedly one of the reasons, and possibly the final straw which brought it about. Between 1st November, 1945, and the end of June, 1946, the illegal Jewish armed organizations had conducted a campaign of terror, sabotage and murder; 47 incidents of a major nature had resulted in the death of 18 officers and men of the British Army, while another 101 had been wounded. The Palestine Police had also suffered proportionate casualties. Apart from the bloodshed, sabotage to the value of over £4,000,000 had been carried out. During this period, every means short of drastic action had been taken, and numerous warnings given, in order to bring the extremists under control, but the situation, far from improving, had in fact worsened.

Accordingly, the High Commissioner was authorized to take such steps as he considered necessary, and the plans for Operation "Agatha" were drawn up. It was directed principally at certain known leaders of the Jewish community, suspected of condoning, if not actually being implicated in, the action of the various Jewish organizations which had been responsible for all the bloodshed and sabotage. It was also concerned with the collection of more evidence from various Jewish Headquarters, on which further action, if necessary, could be based.

The operation was countrywide, and involved a high proportion of the whole Field Force stationed in Palestine. There were four objects. Firstly, to occupy the Jewish Agency in Jerusalem for a brief period, in order to search for incriminating documents. Secondly, to arrest certain members of the Jewish political bodies, who were considered either to have been implicated in recent terrorist activities or to have been responsible for inciting the people to violence. Thirdly, to occupy certain buildings in Tel Aviv suspected of being Headquarters of Jewish illegal armed organizations. And lastly, to arrest as many members as possible of the organization "Palmach." Any searches for arms would be incidental, and it was not anticipated at the outset that any thorough searches would be possible.

The Divisional Commander received his initial orders from the G.O.C. Palestine on Sunday, 23rd June, and the operation was timed to start at 0415 hours on Saturday, 29th June. The tasks given to the Division were the same as those mentioned above, less the one concerned with the Jewish Agency in Jerusalem. These tasks were broken down and assigned to 1st, 2nd and 3rd Parachute Brigades. The most important targets were given to 2nd Parachute Brigade (now commanded by Brigadier J. P. O'Brien Twohig, C.B.E., D.S.O.), which was stationed in the Lydda District, and was responsible for Tel Aviv. This Brigade was given a list of addresses of suspect Jews who were to be arrested. In the north, 1st Parachute Brigade was to search six settlements of which Ma'barot, lying between Nathanya and Hadera, was the most important. 3rd Parachute Brigade in the south was to search Givat Brenner and No'ar Oved.

As was the case in all similar operations, the biggest problem was that of security of information. This has already been touched on, and it requires little imagination to realize the difficulties of keeping the entire civil population from suspecting that anything was in the wind until it was too late. As security was of such importance, it is worth mentioning some of the means employed in this particular operation to prevent any leakage, and which in fact did enable complete tactical surprise to be achieved. To start with, all conferences were held away from Headquarters, as the commanders and their cars would have been very noticeable as they arrived. To make it even safer, senior officers arrived at the chosen rendezvous dressed without their distinctive red hatbands. All correspondence was dealt with on a system by which all letters concerning the operation contained an inner sealed envelope marked with a code word, and only officers on a restricted list were allowed to open or read the inner letter. As time went on, the list had to be increased as more officers were introduced to the parts of the operation which would concern them. Normal life was carried on as far as possible up to the last minute. For example, the Jerusalem Horse Show, which was fixed for 28th and 29th June, was allowed to continue, although on the second day it was of course completely disorganized. Briefing of troops was left until the last possible moment the previous night, after they had been confined to camp. A number of persons concerned in the operations received sealed orders to be opened shortly before, or at H hour. Detention camps were prepared under the pretext that they were required for illegal immigrants, and as a ship was expected at about that time this worked well. These were the main security measures taken in advance. Many others had to be resorted to on the brigade and unit level, in order to mislead the force of more than 17,000 troops which was involved, and so prevent any one of them from unwittingly disclosing information.

An important step was the cutting of all civilian telephone communications throughout the affected parts of the country between 0345 hours and 0515 hours on the first morning. Small parties from Divisional Signals, escorted by detachments of the Glider Pilot Regiment, moved quietly through the night in jeeps and took the civilian exchanges by surprise. They put the boards out of action for the necessary periods, and kept their staffs under guard. In addition, the telephone lines leading to the settlements which were about to be searched were cut as a further precaution.

As a result of the very elaborate planning, the operation achieved all its objects. One of the most gratifying results of the degree of surprise attained was the absence of any form of prepared resistance, and in consequence casualties on both sides were much lower than might have been expected. In Tel Aviv a large number of small parties of troops and police drove unobtrusively up to the houses assigned to them, while farther afield, cordons were thrown round the settlements about to be searched. In the first case the troops knew exactly whom they wanted and they held their descriptions. In the second, they were provided with lists, and in many cases photographs, of known or suspected Palmach members, but they had little idea which of them they might find, or where. It was up to the police to carry out the specialized work of screening. Some of the Jews on these occasions openly compared our troops and their methods with those of the Gestapo, from which so many of them had suffered during the war. Moreover, it must be admitted that the technique of these sudden swoops may have had its similarities: the knock at the door in the early morning and so on. But inwardly they cannot have entertained these thoughts seriously. The troops and police were interested only in those whom they had reason to believe were connected with the campaign of violence which had reached such proportions. Moreover, those who were arrested were treated with the greatest humaneness, and while under detention they were administered under conditions of which no one could be critical. If this had not been so, and the Jews had really had reason to fear our troops, it is very doubtful whether the same degree of arrogant vituperation would have been met. Nevertheless, on occasions too numerous to mention our troops were openly insulted in the most profane strains, and in the settlements were often met with violence which could only be met with violence, and passive resistance which could only be broken by force. It was altogether a disagreeable business, the more so because the law-abiding section of the community, which was the vast majority, so frequently sided openly with the thugs. Had they realized what a cancer they had in their midst and been determined to cut it out, relations with the troops would have been so different. They had been largely friendly in Palestine during the war, and it was certainly not in the interest of the soldiers deliberately to stir up hatred, and so kill any hospitality which otherwise might have been offered. But expressions such as "Gestapo" and "English bastards," spat out with such venom, could hardly be ignored indefinitely, and without doubt were sometimes answered in kind—but not often. A rather pathetic example of the lengths to which this inseminated hatred was carried was the organized demonstrations by the children of the Jewish settlements, who were lined up in front of the troops engaged in operations. Encouraged by their elders, they indulged alternately in a vulgar form of spitting drill and the singing of a song in Hebrew called "Kalanyot." This song, specially reserved for Airborne troops on account of their distinctive headdress, contained a line which referred to "the red poppy with a black heart." For British troops, who are renowned for their love of children, this was particularly unmerited.

The operation ended on 1st July and the number of persons taken into custody was 2,718, which included 56 women. Of that number, 571 were released within a week, and the majority of the remainder were freed in the following months. Although many of these were arrested for the reasons already explained, a high proportion was detained because of resistance offered to troops during the operation, or simply for refusing to give their names to the police. They hoped that by so doing the whole plan would break down and become administratively unworkable. This was far from the case, however, and the bluff having been called, the same trouble was never experienced to any comparable extent again. The Division sent 636 persons to the detainee camp at Latrun. Of these, 135 were suspected Palmach members, 161 (including 10 V.I.Js.) were taken in the specified Tel Aviv addresses, 23 resisted search or arrest, 271 refused to give their names or show their identity cards, 2 were unable to prove their identity, 1 was armed, 31 were curfew breakers, and 1 was dressed as an Arab, and as the occasion appeared not to warrant it, he was therefore highly suspect.

The operation certainly achieved some purpose in that it obliged the Hagana and Palmach to be very circumspect in the planning of any further offensives, and from this time onwards their efforts against the British were confined within very narrow limits.

Jewish casualties in the Divisional area amounted to 25 injured (15 slightly), all of which were sustained in the settlements by those who offered resistance. Not one of these casualties was caused by firearms, although in the course of the operation the Airborne troops had occasion to fire 25 warning shots.* There was some unavoidable damage done when buildings and safes had to be forced, but the use of explosives or other means of entry were only resorted to after efforts to find the owners or the keys had failed. A small number of illegal arms were found, but these only totalled 11, together with some assorted ammunition. The astounding arms discovery took place in the settlement of Mesheq Yagur near Haifa, which was searched by 2nd Battalion The Cheshire Regiment from 1st Infantry Division. The search developed following an early success there, and after several days had been spent in the settlement, nearly 600 assorted weapons had been found together with about half a million rounds of ammunition and quarter of a ton of explosives. This small arsenal was distributed between 33 caches which were dispersed about the settlement in such diverse

---

* The practice of firing warning shots is contrary to generally accepted military teaching on Internal Security Duties. There are many reasons advanced against it which were thoroughly explained to all ranks undergoing instruction on their arrival in Palestine in 1945. However, gradually the practice came to be applied in certain situations, and before long it was officially recognized that on occasions, after taking into account the mood and intent of the crowd, warning shots were justified before the extreme measure of shooting to kill. Undoubtedly, because of this the lives of many who heeded the warning were saved who otherwise would have been killed by deliberate fire, and the opinion was widely held that the practice was fully justified. There were no cases in which crowds took heart from the ineffectiveness of the first shots—they were more inclined to disappear like magic, which was exactly what the military set out to achieve.

places as nurseries and cowsheds. Much of it was hidden below ground. It was difficult to tell who were the more surprised, the Jews, whose ingenuity had not been quite good enough, or the troops who were awed by the sight of a find of such unexpected proportions. As it was the first really successful arms search, troops of other formations, including 6th Airborne Division, visited the scene in order to see for themselves the various devices by which the weapons had been concealed, so that in the event of further searches of this type they would have some idea of how to set about the task. A great deal of resentment was registered by the Jews at the thorough way in which this operation was carried out, and it received much publicity in the Press, but the arguments were most unconvincing on why the search should be unjustified, nor was a solution found subsequently by either side as to how such searches could be thorough and yet inflict no damage to property. It was inevitable that the damage should be considerable, but allegations that it was ever wanton, were unfounded, vicious, and can be utterly discounted. Another stock allegation which followed almost every search was of looting by the troops. To assert blandly that this never took place would be equally ridiculous. In this type of operation opportunities will inevitably come the way of the light-fingered from time to time, whatever precautions are taken. Furthermore, when feelings are running high and insults and abuse are lavishly imparted, consciences are subjected to an elasticity which may catch them off their guard. But looting was neither general nor frequent. All troops were searched at the conclusion of every operation and during the searches they were employed by units and sub-units under the command of officers or full-rank N.C.Os. At the end of each operation clearance certificates were obtained if possible from householders or prominent members of the local Jewish community. The object of false claims of looting was to obtain either propaganda value or easy compensation. In many cases looting there was, and proven in the end to be the work of the less scrupulous members of the Jewish community. At small risk to themselves they would break the curfew under cover of darkness and enter shops and houses which they knew to be empty.

CHAPTER VI

THE KING DAVID HOTEL

DEVELOPMENTS in Palestine after the end of the Second World War showed a gradual but steady decline in a situation which started as difficult and ended as impossible. This downward course, which culminated in the relinquishment of the Mandate, could be simply traced by reference, among other things, to each new atrocity in the programme of the Jewish dissident groups. Such a landmark was the outrage at the King David Hotel. "Outrage," like "terrorist" and other similar words, became very overworked in Palestine, but here in Jerusalem, on 22nd July, 1946, there was indeed an outrage.

On that day, soon after noon, a party of between 15 and 20 Jews, dressed as Arabs, entered the King David Hotel, in which were housed the Secretariat of the Government of Palestine and Headquarters British Troops in Palestine and Transjordan. At that time the building was still in partial use as a hotel, which was to the advantage of the gang as they were likely to attract less attention than if it had been entirely occupied by military and government offices. Acting the part of an Arab working party, they unloaded from their lorry several milk churns filled with explosive, and placed them in the basement of the wing of the hotel occupied by the Secretariat. A British officer who became suspicious, and started to investigate, was shot and subsequently died, and a policeman stationed at the tradesmen's entrance suffered a similar fate. The Jews after igniting the fuses bolted from the building as the alarm was given, and though several were shot and wounded by the guards as they withdrew, they made their escape. There was no time to evacuate the building, and the charge exploded with devastating effect. Many were killed instantly as the whole wing of the building subsided about them; others were trapped and many more were injured.

As this took place in Jerusalem, 6th Airborne Division would normally not have been implicated, for it was outside its area of responsibility. However, as there were at that time no Royal Engineers stationed in Jerusalem, and they were urgently required, 9th Airborne Squadron, R.E., under command of Major E. W. J. Cowtan, M.C., was ordered up that afternoon in order to undertake the rescue operations.

The Squadron, which was just back from a period of training at the School of Military Engineering in Egypt, was stationed at Qastina, forty miles away, but they turned out and reached Jerusalem in record time. As they entered the city through the Jewish quarter on the western side they had to force their way through improvised Jewish road-blocks, and whilst so doing were stoned and booed. But the troops by now, after much practice, had become used to that sort of reception. On these occasions, and they were all too frequent, the British soldier displayed a composure and dignity which revealed something far deeper than training and discipline.

By 1600 hours they were hard at work in the rubble. The task was a race against time, and not until all hope of saving further lives had been abandoned, days later, did they relax their efforts. Day and night the rescue operations went on with the Sappers working like men possessed, for deep in the wreckage, could occasionally be heard sounds which encouraged them to fresh exertions. At 2200 hours that night the Squadron was formed into three shifts, and for the next three days each shift worked 16 hours on and 8 hours off. Even so, some men refused to rest until, on the point of exhaustion, they were ordered to fall out. It is recorded that one Sapper drove his bulldozer for thirty hours without leaving the wheel, which is remarkable.

Out of the wreckage the Squadron raised six survivors, the last being freed seventy-one hours after the explosion. Owing to the danger of falling masonry and further subsidences, the use of mechanical equipment had to be very limited until it was considered that none remained alive under the debris. The remainder of the operation took a further week, and by the time the work was finished, 91 bodies had been recovered and 2,000 tipper loads of rubble had been removed. The stench which accompanied the work, which was carried out in the sweltering heat of mid-summer,

TROOPS OF 9TH AIRBORNE SQUADRON, R.E., ENGAGED IN RESCUE OPERATIONS AT THE KING DAVID HOTEL, JULY, 1946.

DEMOLITION OF OVERHANGING MASONRY BY DIVISIONAL R.E.
FOLLOWING THE ATTACK ON THE KING DAVID HOTEL.

can be imagined and it added considerably to the trials of those engaged.

This magnificent effort did not go unrecognized, and congratulations and thanks were poured on the Squadron. One of those most impressed with the manner in which the sappers set about the task was General Barker, G.O.C. Palestine, who himself had been inside the building at the time of the explosion. Major Cowtan, who had been in charge of the rescue operations throughout, was later awarded the M.B.E.

A point of lasting interest occurred at a stage in the operation when it became necessary to demolish a great weight of overhanging masonry which was endangering those working below. The amount of explosive required was calculated from the formulæ with which Sappers are provided, but as it appeared a little excessive it was halved, the officer in charge being prepared to carry out a further demolition if necessary. But the freaks of blast sometimes baffle even Sappers, and the explosion was so effective that a second charge was quite unnecessary. To this day it remains a matter of the keenest academic interest among the experts when they think of what the effect would have been had the full charge been used.

On the day following the outrage, 8th and 9th Parachute Battalions were moved to Jerusalem to take part in searches for the perpetrators. There was an amusing sidelight as the two Parachute Battalions, after debussing, marched off in file past men of the 52nd Light Infantry and The Royal Ulster Rifles, who until recently had been part of the Division. Some of the latter were posted on roof-tops to cover the troops carrying out the search, and many good-natured cracks were made at the expense of the parachutists. "Look, here come the Red Devils, what a fine body of men !" And then, pointing to the most diminutive man present who was sweating under the weight of a Bren gun: "Did you ever see such physique ?" Needless to say, other equally apt comments were thrown back at the brown berets above.

During the course of the day they found one dead Jew and another wounded, both of whom were presumed to have taken part in the attack. Thirty-seven other Jews were arrested, but, as in so many cases, it was impossible to prove complicity. This was one of the difficulties under which the Palestine Police continually laboured, and the reason for it was simply that witnesses could never be found. In such cases, under the authority of one of the Military Commanders, they could only confine the suspects in detention camps. While this treatment prevented the same individuals from doing any further harm, it did not amount to justice, and many who were guilty of murder or attempted murder were never convicted.

Two days after the attack on the King David, the British Government published a White Paper on the connections between the Jewish Agency and the so-called "terrorist organizations." Coming as it did at such an inconvenient time, this was a great shock to the Yishuv. Moreover, in the light of it, such expressions as "dastardly crime" and "abominable outrage," which had figured so prominently in the Jewish Palestine Press in connection with the act, looked far less convincing. Having said this, it would be unjust to omit mentioning the genuine praise in one or two of the Jewish papers for the men of the 9th Airborne Squadron, R.E., who evoked such admiration from all who saw them.

The consequence of greatest moment, however, as far as the Jews in Palestine were concerned, came exactly a week later in the shape of Operation "Shark." It was the largest-scale operation of its type ever to take place in Palestine, and as such it deserves a description as full as space permits.

OPERATION "SHARK"

The fact that at last the Lion was roused was obvious to all. The repercussions of the attack on the Secretariat were expected to be potent, though it is doubtful whether many anticipated exactly what form the counterblast would take. For some days the lower levels of the Army were as much in the dark as the civilian communities, on the line which was being followed in high places, but they did not have to wait long. In the meantime, the Arabs had reacted violently to this latest and most ruthless outrage; indeed, there was a danger of their taking steps which might lead to communal disturbances, unless the British reaction satisfied their ideas of justice. They had not hesitated (as ever in this connection) to condemn us for our "weakness, leniency and unpreparedness."

The Jews for their part, waited uneasily to see where and how the storm would break.

Operation "Shark" was something new. It was also bold, for had it not worked our prestige would have crashed. But boldness was called for, and so it was decided to do a thorough search of every house and every person in the whole of Tel Aviv for members of the I.Z.L. and the Stern Gang. There was evidence that at least some of the perpetrators of the King David outrage had taken shelter there. This city of nearly 170,000 inhabitants presented a problem quite unlike any which the Army had yet tackled; moreover, once the decision was made, there was no time to be lost. There existed no blueprint of how to set about an operation of this type and magnitude, and the few days available for its planning were vital ones. 6th Airborne Division was to carry out the operation, and the Divisional Commander was promised whatever additional troops he considered necessary for the task. The total came to four infantry (or parachute) brigades, three independent battalions, and three cavalry regiments, backed by the full weight of the supporting arms and services of 6th Airborne Division.

This impressive force had to be prepared, briefed, and concentrated round Tel Aviv without any rumour reaching the ears of a single inhabitant. These phases alone presented a formidable problem, and at the risk of giving the security aspect of these operations too much prominence throughout this record, some mention must be made of the difficulties encountered prior to Operation "Shark." Unlike Operation "Agatha," the entire force was to be concentrated on the same target, thus there was far less chance of deceiving the wary through the movement of units in all directions. In addition, it only required a hint to leak out, and the thugs, whom it was hoped to take by surprise, would have a choice of the remainder of the country in which to take refuge. A further difficulty was that the opposition were already on their toes and prepared for such a visitation. They only required to know the day. These aspects of the problem were only too apparent, and more care than ever had to be taken in order to avoid the fatal slip which would render the whole plan abortive.

The operation was planned to open before first light on the morning of 30th July, and it was anticipated that it would take five to

F

six days to complete. The first phase obviously was to get a continuous outer cordon into position round the town under cover of darkness. It would prevent the escape of the thugs into other parts of the country, and until a curfew was enforced they would do no harm in moving about inside the cordon. The next stage was to impose a complete house curfew and to establish inner cordons, which had the effect of splitting the town into a number of independent sectors. In fact, each brigade group was given roughly a quarter of the town to cordon, search and administer. Although no difficulty was anticipated in imposing and maintaining the curfew, it would not be practicable to confine the population to their houses for the best part of a week. The next problem, therefore, was how to enable the inhabitants to do their essential shopping of foodstuffs from time to time without jeopardizing the plan and providing loopholes for the thugs to slip through the net. It was proposed to solve this by maintaining the curfew without a break for thirty-six hours, thereafter to subdivide brigade sectors into further watertight compartments by establishing additional temporary cordons. For two hours in the evening of the second and each subsequent day, it was planned to allow the population to circulate freely within their own limited areas. It only remained to ensure that the essential foodstuffs would be available within these areas during the short periods when the curfew was to be lifted.

In the early hours of D Day (Tuesday, 30th July), the four brigade columns started to move out of their widely dispersed camps. 1st Parachute Brigade came from near Nathanya, 2nd Parachute Brigade from the Lydda District, 3rd Parachute Brigade from the Gaza District, and 2nd Infantry Brigade, one of the brigades of 1st Infantry Division, came from the Hadera Area. Simultaneously the brigades converged by four different routes onto Tel Aviv. As far as it could be ascertained, surprise was complete, and the outer cordon had slipped quietly into position ahead of the main columns before the alarm was given. The remainder of the force passed through into the city as the first glow of dawn began to appear and the curfew was imposed before most of the inhabitants were awake. One furtive individual was surprised by the outer cordon as he tried to slip out into the open country. He was also seen to hide a bundle of papers in a hedge before doubling back into

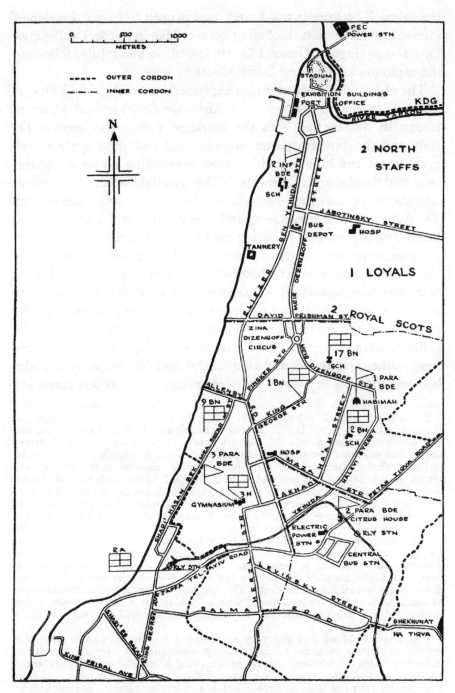

OPERATION "SHARK," TEL AVIV.

the town. The bundle was found, and proved to be a collection of interesting documents, including certain Hagana orders and notes. One was a Hagana General Order issued on 22nd July, following the explosion at the King David Hotel.*

The object of the operation as expressed in the Divisional Operation Order was as follows : "6 Airborne Division and attached troops, in conjunction with the Palestine Police, will cordon Tel Aviv and the Jewish quarter of Jaffa, and will thoroughly search every house and building with a view to checking up on all inhabitants and detaining any suspects." The essential feature of the operation therefore, was that every house, attic, cellar and basement in Tel Aviv had to be searched, and every inhabitant old or young, healthy or infirm, had to be screened by the police.†

There were three stages of screening. The first was by the searching teams which went methodically up each street. Each household was first assembled in possession of their identity cards, in one room, while the rest of the house was searched, probably in the presence of the householder. Then all except the aged and the children were escorted to the Battalion screening teams. Here they were further segregated, and all doubtful ones (the majority of males between the ages of 15 and 60) were taken to the expert screening

---

* "Hagana General Order issued on 22nd July, 1946, at 11 p.m. subsequent to the explosion at the King David. It is to be anticipated that the Government will take action as a result of the I.Z.L. activity today. For the time being until further orders, the previous instructions re armed opposition to searches are not to be put into effect. The special armed squads who are camped in the vicinity will return to their settlements and will stand down until further orders. Only in the event of the military finding arms will you retaliate with action by armed parties. This should be done in such a manner that action is taken at least one kilometre distant from the scene of finding the arms. If searches are made for terrorists, the mukhtar should reply that there are no terrorists in his colony and that the Yishuv has already denounced the King David outrage. No further blockades will be placed at the gates of settlements. This is to demonstrate the opposition of the Jews to what occurred in Jerusalem. The military should not be goaded or exasperated. No member will assist in the search. No identity cards will be produced; false names should be given. The mukhtar will not assist in identification. Widespread searches are anticipated with a view to the arrest of known active leaders. Every precaution should be taken. Suspects will not sleep at their permanent addresses."

† It was an old trick of gangsters and wanted men to adopt the guise of a cripple or patient in order to escape being questioned. In several operations including "Shark," Medical Officers in searching a hospital or clinic suspected bogus cases, and after examination exposed them as such. Some suspects even went to the extent of feigning broken limbs, and having plaster casts applied, in order to avoid facing a police screening team.

teams at Brigade Headquarters. Here a team of C.I.D. officers, provided with photographs and descriptions of wanted men, and in many cases familiar with the better-known fanatics and gangsters made a thorough examination of each individual. All suspects and persons who were unable to give a satisfactory account of themselves were sent to the detention camp at Rafah under military escort. Among those who were brought forward was a prominent member of the Stern Gang. He was disguised as a Rabbi, having also grown a long black beard, but he failed to deceive the screening team. A police officer, without quite knowing why, suspected him of being spurious, and after much interrogation started to go through the hundreds of photographs. A slight similarity was observed in the photograph of a clean-shaven man who had escaped a few years before from Latrun detention camp. The sergeant who had been responsible for his previous arrest was called for, and, using a clever ruse, confirmed the identification. Approaching the suspect from the rear, he called out his underground nickname. The reaction which this produced removed all doubts, and the man was arrested and ultimately deported to Eritrea. The sergeant who was responsible for his arrest was murdered by the Stern Gang in Haifa a few months later as he left his house. Such were the risks knowingly accepted by the British police who served in the C.I.D.

In the course of the operation, which was completed without a hitch in four days, approximately 100,000 persons were screened at battalion level and about 10,000 at brigade level; 787 were detained and sent to the detention camp at Rafah. There, further thorough screening continued with the object of releasing any innocent persons who had been detained. Apart from this side of the operation, some other interesting discoveries were made. Altogether five arms dumps were found, and the most sensational of these was discovered in the basement of the Great Synagogue, where, in addition to an assortment of weapons, ammunition and military equipment, there were also discovered £50,000 of forged bearer bonds, forging equipment and the black mask recognized by the kidnapped officers as having been worn by one of their guards. The weapons captured in the caches amounted to some 176 rifles and pistols, 4 machine guns, and 23 mortars. There were also 127,000 rounds of small-arms ammunition and a large quantity of explosives.

The attitude of the civilian population on the whole was reasonable, and at times positively co-operative. Some even got a certain amount of amusement out of it and went to and from the screening cages quite cheerfully. But even so, it was quite clear where their sympathies lay when those who were to be detained were driven off in lorries to Rafah. An interesting sidelight was the way in which many tradesmen took advantage of the conditions to start a Black Market in bread and other foodstuffs. The prices in some shops rocketed, while many of the first-comers among the customers bought more than they required, and then went to the back of the queues and started retailing their purchases at greatly increased prices. There they were bought by those who feared that the supply might fail before they could be served in the shop.

From the military standpoint, undoubtedly some of the most valuable lessons learned from the operation concerned the administrative side, which presented the ugliest problems. The majority of these were foreseen and allowed for by careful planning, but others arose suddenly and had to be solved through the elasticity of existing arrangements and improvisation. Neither previous experience nor the time available for planning, allowed for all the problems to be anticipated. If the life of a city of this size is to be brought to a standstill by a complete curfew, there are certain essential public services which still have to continue, unless the consequences can be faced. For example, babies must have their fresh milk daily, surgical operations have to be performed, the population has to be fed, the power stations must be kept working, the water supply has to be maintained and the sewage must be disposed of. If any of these fail, there is an immediate effect on the health of the community which leads to an increase in the normal death rate. As these effects had to be avoided at all costs, the essential services had to be maintained, while for different reasons various other activities also had to continue. For example, those who died from natural causes had to be buried, and as far as possible had to be afforded funerals with proper rites, attended by their close relatives. It was apparent therefore that a proportion of those operating all these and various other services would have to continue their work. This was arranged for, and hospitals, power houses, etc., were placed under military guard while their staffs continued to function, assisted where necessary by the Army. Some of these services were able to continue with the minimum dislocation, but others which were unadaptable to the peculiar demands of the operation had to be improvised. In the latter category came the methods employed for the distribution of the two necessary basic foods—bread and fresh milk. Both these commodities had to be collected from outside the town, brought through the cordons, concentrated at supply centres, passed on to retail points and finally distributed to the inhabitants. The organization of this was undertaken by Headquarters South Palestine District (Commander, Brigadier G. P. R. Johnston, C.B.E.), which bore much of the brunt of the administrative burden.

The operation, which required tremendous endurance from the troops, finished at 1500 hours on 2nd August. In a special message to all who had taken part, General Cassels pointed out that the operation had been an outstanding one in many respects. " . . . It was clear from the beginning that it was going to be a long, difficult and laborious task involving great tolerance and cheerfulness on the part of everybody concerned. It was impossible to foresee every contingency and a great deal had to be left to the initiative and commonsense of the individual. The fact that the search was completed far quicker than I had ever hoped and with virtually no incidents of any kind speaks volumes for the great work, good spirit and example of every one of you.

"I consider that this was one of the most difficult operations that I have ever had to undertake and its scope was, I believe, more ambitious than any similar operation ever staged. It has now been completed expeditiously and well. There is absolutely no doubt that we have achieved very considerable success. This is entirely due to the great loyalty and support that you have given me throughout. . . ."

There was no doubt that the praise of the Divisional Commander, which reflected the opinion held in all responsible quarters, was very thoroughly deserved.

The following troops took part:—

    Headquarters 6th Airborne Division.
    2nd Infantry Brigade Group.
        2nd Battalion The Royal Scots.

1st Battalion The Loyal Regiment.

2nd Battalion The North Staffordshire Regiment.

The King's Dragoon Guards.

Detachment of 200 all ranks The Glider Pilot Regiment.

1st Parachute Brigade Group.

    1st, 2nd and 17th Battalions The Parachute Regiment.

    12th Royal Lancers.

    1st Battalion The King's Shropshire Light Infantry.

2nd Parachute Brigade Group.

    4th, 5th and 6th Battalions The Parachute Regiment.

    6th Battalion The Gordon Highlanders.

    1st Battalion The Hertfordshire Regiment.

3rd Parachute Brigade Group.

    3rd, 8th and 9th Battalions The Parachute Regiment.

    3rd The King's Own Hussars.

    6th Airborne Divisional Royal Artillery.

Arms and Services 6th Airborne Division.

THE OPPOSITION

At this stage it is time to discuss the factors which enabled the dissident groups to remain not only in being, but thoroughly active during the post-war years when all the efforts of the Security Forces were concentrated on their elimination. Because these reasons were not understood by the public, there were frequent (and under the circumstances, almost excusable) observations made in uninformed quarters on the degree of success which the "terrorists" achieved in their operations. That they were bold in conception, well planned and daringly executed is not to be disputed, but that does not explain why these gangsters could carry out one operation after another apparently with such immunity.

It is therefore worth digressing to review accurately the causes which contributed to this state of affairs. When these factors are balanced against the results which the Jewish dissident groups achieved in their campaign of violence it is hoped that the Army and Police will be given the credit for restricting the successes of these gangsters as thoroughly as they did. Moreover, it is fully maintained that the initiative was never lost by the Army, certainly where the 6th Airborne Division sector was concerned, and there is no reason to suppose that it was lost elsewhere. Local initiative might be gained temporarily by the Jews in a particular short-lived operation, such as the dislocation of railways, but the situation was inevitably restored and the dissidents forced to take a new line. When all the results of the dissidents' activities are analysed, therefore, it is quite apparent that what they achieved fell far short of what they attempted, and what was popularly believed. The administration of the country was never seriously upset, rail communications were never permanently cut, and road communications were restricted only by night.

When attempting to summarize what they did achieve, some of the issues become bound up with political opinion, which is outside the scope of this record. Undoubtedly the extremists were instrumental in bringing about a fresh crisis in the fundamental problem of Palestine, and the developments in that direction eventually resulted in the termination of the Mandate. But it might be equally well stated that this issue was inevitable, either with or without the influence of the extremists. Returning therefore to the material results, these would appear to be largely confined to sabotage which, with a few exceptions, never became embarrassing.

The foregoing views are designed to put into clear perspective what the extremists gained and what they did not. Let us not minimize the loss of life which without doubt was the most serious problem at the time. In retrospect also, it appears that apart from the main political issues, security of our own troops lay on a plane of importance by itself. In this field both soldiers and police were at a serious disadvantage. From time to time there was an undercurrent of talk on reprisals—not in blood but by more moderate means, though for one reason or another they were never adopted. Opinions on this point, however, lead again towards a problem with an overwhelming political bearing which lies as far outside the charter of this book as it lay at the time beyond the control of the soldier on the spot.

Before passing on from this vexatious subject, however, let us summarize some of the reasons which enabled the opposition to remain a constant threat to security.

1. At no stage during the whole period under review did the

Jewish community, either individually or collectively, show any desire to co-operate with the Security Forces in this problem. Moreover, on occasions too numerous to mention they actively assisted the dissidents to escape detection. It is worthy of mention that there was not one case in the Divisional area during the whole period under review in which one member of the Jewish community was prompted by his or her conscience to come forward and give evidence against a known criminal. It need not have been done openly ; in fact it was quite possible for information to pass without the least danger to the law-abiding citizen. Here is the greatest factor of all, for it is well known that in all forms of guerilla or underground warfare, if the partisans have the undivided support of their kinsmen, the work of occupation forces is increased beyond calculation.

This attitude of the community was the subject of repeated representations by senior officials and officers of the Government and the Army to the Jewish leaders. The answers varied. The most popular excuse was one of ignorance ; the dissidents were no more known to the community than they were to the Security Forces. When this was refuted, the fear of reprisals by the dissidents served as the next best reason for withholding information.

The foregoing paragraphs should not be interpreted as meaning that the more moderate members of the community were in favour of the dissidents—in the majority of cases they were opposed to their methods, if not always to their motives. The fact remains, unfortunately, that their conscience was divided in favour of their countrymen, however lawless the latter on occasions might be.

2. The acts of violence were committed by a relatively small proportion of the Jewish community. This made it harder to justify collective punishment, which might have had the desired results.

3. The standard of training for the type of operation in which they specialized was of the highest order. Their older members had received their initial training in many cases in some Regular Army, or had seen previous service in an underground movement during the late war. In some cases they had been trained as saboteurs by our own instructors for operations against the Nazis. All this weight of experience was passed on to the younger generation, who soon became a credit to their instructors in the art of gutter warfare.

4. There was no means of identifying members of the Jewish dissident organizations. They were free to adopt whatever disguises they chose, and frequently appeared perfectly dressed as soldiers, policemen or Arabs. Often when operating in Jewish areas it profited them to use no such deception, and with their task completed they mingled back into the crowd as quickly and unobtrusively as they had appeared. Thus in one way or another they were free to move about without fear of attracting attention to themselves on any occasion.

5. Because of their ability to move freely in most places there was nothing to prevent the most thorough reconnaissances from being carried out. Their information was invariably accurate, and to this end they made a painstaking study of the habits of our troops. If it could not be done in the role of a bystander, there were ways and means of gaining admittance into camps and defended areas in the guise of a technician, tradesman or labourer. If for obvious reasons access to a chosen objective was closed to all Jews, they frequently had Arabs at their disposal who for a consideration would undertake the reconnaissance for them. Thus they were never at a loss for accurate information—possibly the most vital prerequisite for success in this type of operation.

6. The scale of arms and equipment for underground warfare can be a limiting factor—the Arabs suffered from this disadvantage in their rebellion of 1936. Here there was no such handicap ; arms only required money, and of that there was no shortage; without doubt the dissident groups were almost lavishly equipped for their tasks.

7. The lack of an adequate reliable guard force for the security of all V.Ps. entailed a large number of commitments being accepted by the Army or Police (British personnel). Such dissipation reduced the force available for mobile and offensive operations, thus assisting the Jewish law-breakers to evade capture.

It would be possible to expand further on the factors which enabled the extremists to gain local superiority on the scene of their operations. However, the reasons already given should show clearly that the British soldier started at such a disadvantage that it is quite remarkable he did his duty so efficiently.

CHAPTER VII

THE SEARCHES OF DOROT AND RUHAMA

DURING 1946, the immigration issue in Palestine continued to occupy Jews, Arabs and the Government alike. The Jews had formed a vast organization in Europe which aimed at flooding the country with immigrants and creating an impossible position for Britain, who was restricting the flow to 1,500 a month. Throughout the year thousands of immigrants had been arriving in Palestine, only to be transferred to camps where they would remain until their turn came for admission under the quota. On 13th August, therefore, the Government was obliged to announce that all future arrivals would be transferred to Cyprus or elsewhere, and housed in camps "until a decision can be made as to their future." The first batch was embarked at Haifa for Cyprus the same day, while everyone waited for Jewish official (and unofficial) reactions; for it had always been said that the Yishuv would fight on the issue of immigration. Continued opposition could be expected from the extremists, but it was not known what line the Hagana would take. With some of their leaders in Latrun, with the knowledge that the Army was prepared to unearth their arms (as they had done at Mesheq Yagur) and to use force if necessary in doing so, and taking into account the stakes in the political field, it would have been a rash move for the Jews to have committed the Hagana at this juncture.

As time went on it became clear that the Hagana was not to be involved in a general offensive either in the open or underground, and it continued to confine its activities to problems immediately relating to illegal immigration. On 21st August, for example, three "frogmen" of the Palmach blew a large hole in the bottom of the *Empire Rival*, one of the ships used in the recent deportations, while she lay at anchor in Haifa Bay. The military answer came in the shape of searches at S'dot Yam and elsewhere, and, though not directly connected with this incident, 6th Airborne Division was very soon after given the task of searching for arms two Jewish settlements in the Negev. The settlements chosen were Dorot and Ruhama, which lie close together in barren country some ten miles east of Gaza and which were known to be centres of Hagana activity. At a time when Hagana opinion was divided over their best course of action, it was hoped that by demonstrating that we were in a position to cripple them by arms-seizures as and when we chose, a steadying influence might be exerted. These hopes were well founded, and during the next two years the Hagana repeatedly revealed by their actions that they were very conscious of this chink in their armour.

The searches of Dorot and Ruhama, Operations "Bream" and "Eel" as they were known, were carried out by 8th and 3rd Parachute Battalions respectively, with 9th Airborne Squadron, R.E., under command. The colonies were both small ones supporting populations of about 235 and 170, and were known to be centres of illegal armed training and to have a large number of concealed arms. The troops arrived under cover of darkness and established at dawn on 28th August cordons which remained in position round the settlements for six days. On the first day, all male inhabitants were screened by the police, and, as was expected, a number of strangers who explained that they had come "to assist with the harvest" were revealed in the process. No resistance was offered, and before long it was found possible to raise the curfew, except by night, and allow most of the normal activities of the settlers to continue while the search progressed.

The searches started off on orthodox lines with the use of mine detectors and prodders, and a careful examination of all buildings which might contain hiding-places. It was a matter in which the troops employed had to use all their intelligence and imagination, as considerable ingenuity was invariably used in the construction and concealment of arms caches. For the first two days, work went on with meagre results, though signs were not lacking which suggested that there were arms, particularly the spent cartridge cases lying about and the practice rifle range at Ruhama. It was beginning to look as though the task was a failure when late on the second day there arrived a team of ten metal-detecting dogs with their section of C.R.M.P. dog-handlers. The Division had been asked if they would like to try them in this unusual role, and had accepted the offer with little hope or interest. How could dogs it was argued, hope to find arms where mine detectors had failed? They had a preliminary trial on the evening of the second day, watched by some faintly amused troops, but were apparently tired after their long journey and were soon taken off the work in order to be fresh for the next day.

The following morning the dogs made finds in each of the settlements. Their modus operand! was very simple: They scented keenly the ground over which they were cast, and if they scented (or sensed) metal they sat down on the spot and were ultimately rewarded with a lump of meat. In both cases on this occasion the detection of an arms cache was made on ground which had already been thoroughly covered by the Sappers with their mine detectors. At Dorot it was in a henhouse with a floor of concrete slabs on which a cross-bred Labrador Retriever sat before unbelieving eyes. The concrete was raised with the aid of a compressor drill, and the earth below was dug out to a depth of four and a half feet before the roof of a cache seven feet deep was reached. In it were stored some fifty assorted weapons, including heavy mortars and machine guns, together with many thousands of rounds of ammunition. They had been there for some considerable length of time, and how they were detected at such a depth remained a mystery to all but the dog. In Ruhama there was a similar discovery. Alongside the site of a new building a large pile of gravel concealed the entrance to a deeply buried cache. At this the dogs pointed, and after it had been removed they indicated the exact position of a circular steel drum which was eventually found buried under five feet of earth. It contained a large collection of weapon parts, magazines, mines, explosives and military equipment.

From this rime onwards the dogs dominated the remainder of the operation, which progressed entirely according to their moods. At times they were uninterested, and the heat made them useless in the middle of the day, so for the rest of the searches two battalions and a number of units from supporting arms and services were dependent on their canine whims. Whether they shot their bolt on the first day or whether there were no more arms to be found was uncertain, but for the next three days they worked (when they felt inclined) and found nothing. Some further empty caches were found, but it was doubtful whether they had yet been in use as such, and the operation was ended on the morning of 3rd September when the troops returned to their camps and the dogs to their kennels.

While 3rd Parachute Brigade was busy in the Negev, 2nd Parachute Brigade, at the request of the police, had cordoned and searched Latrun Civil Detention Camp, in which all suspects were held under the Defence Regulations. Following Operations "Agatha" and "Shark," the camp had filled up so rapidly that the camp staff were no longer entirely in control. The operation, which was called "Weedout," had four objects. Firstly, to identify all detainees; secondly, to extract nine V.I.Js. and transfer them to Jerusalem; thirdly, to carry out a thorough search of the whole camp for arms, ammunition, escape apparatus and signs of tunnelling; and lastly, to carry out certain structural alterations inside the camp. These tasks were successfully performed on 29th August, and during the course of the search a number of miscellaneous escaping tools were found and confiscated. It was an unfortunate fact that in Palestine escapes from gaols and detention camps were far too frequent. The main reason was probably the insufficiency of reliable and trustworthy camp guards. It was a police responsibility, but there were insufficient trained policemen to carry out the task. As a result, numbers of Arabs and Jews had to be employed in varying duties in which, by reason of their partisanship and disaffection, they were a constant menace to security.

THE PROBLEMS OF RAILWAY PROTECTION

It has already been pointed out how easy it can be in certain circumstances for a small force of determined saboteurs to carry out attacks against a railway system. Whenever more spectacular results were unattainable, the illegal Jewish organizations in Palestine could always fall back on railway sabotage. While the Stern Gang preferred to carry out occasional mining operations with their usual object of taking the heaviest toll of British lives, the I.Z.L. were prepared to conduct an intensive campaign of sabotage with the object of dislocating the railways and terrorizing the train crews. In November, 1946, both organizations turned their attentions again in this direction, and during the first three weeks of that month, carried out 21 attacks against the railway. Some were successful, some were thwarted, but together they caused 6 deaths and 22 injuries among the Security Forces and the railway staff. It was not surprising that the Arab engine-drivers and firemen, who had already refused to operate at night, eventually struck on 19th November and refused to work at all until a satisfactory form of military protection was guaranteed. With the approach of the citrus season, in which some millions of cases of fruit had to be moved to the ports, there was no time to be lost in restoring the confidence of the train crews and persuading them to resume work.

The technique of the saboteurs was either to mine the railway by night in order to blow up trains the following morning, or to blow up the permanent way so that no trains could operate until repairs were completed. The former was the more effective means, but the latter was simple, and entailed less risk as it took less time. When the railway was mined with the object of blowing up a train, the mine had to be very carefully hidden under the ballast in such a way as to be unnoticeable to a patrol at first light. The majority were pressure mines exploded by the weight of a railway engine or armoured patrol-trolley, but occasionally there was the electrically operated type similar in principle to that which was used so largely on the roads. These entailed an operator remaining under cover at the end of a length of wire leading from the mine, and pressing a switch or button at the moment he wished to detonate the mine. The advantage of this method lay in the ability to blow up any particular part of a train, and it held a great appeal for the Stern Gang, who specialized in blowing up troop trains. Unfortunately, if the entire railway system had to be inspected every morning before a train passed over it, several hours of running-time had to be wasted before it could be declared open. However, on this occasion in November, 1946, that in fact was what had to be done for several weeks in order to keep the railways functioning at all.

It was appreciated by the G.O.C. Palestine that with all available troops deployed on the railway by day, complete protection could be guaranteed to the train crews after the line had been proved

RAILWAY SABOTAGE.

each morning. It was realized of course, that a much smaller force patrolling the line by night would probably be just as effective, but the Arab drivers insisted on guaranteed safety, and this could only be promised by the first method. Another strong factor was the psychological one of showing the crews lots of soldiers obviously deployed for their protection. This also appealed to their sense of importance, and under these conditions they agreed to start work on 22nd November.

This operation, in which the Army became involved for a period of several weeks was called "Earwig," an apt name, for the large number of troops which were strung out along the line bore a certain resemblance to that insect. It was both an unprofitable and an unpleasant operation in which the troops had to leave camp well before dawn each day, and return in the dark after a boring and tiring day on the line, during which they watched perhaps half a dozen trains pass. Nor was it much of a rest to be left in camp, for there too, there were guard duties to be done. Apart from the battalions kept in reserve, the whole Division (including supporting arms) was deployed in this dreary operation over a length of seventy miles of track. This was divided into red, amber and green sectors according to the locality and degree of danger, and each sector had a different density of troops. In the red stretches, posts were established every few hundred yards and were linked by patrols. The line in these areas was also patrolled by night. Each day started with intensive patrolling and an examination of the permanent way, in which the troops were assisted by Arab railway gangers. These men knew their stretch of railway so intimately and had such good eyesight that they could tell at once if the ballast had been interfered with during the night. As soon as a mine was spotted or suspected, the Sappers were called up to carry out the detailed investigation and its subsequent disarming or destruction.

No one would question the fact that the real dirty work went to the Royal Engineers. In this month alone (November, 1946) two officers of the Divisional R.E. were killed and one officer and two other ranks were wounded while dealing with railway mines. It so happened that the Jews had devised a new type of anti-handling device which they started to fit to their mines, and it was while dealing with one of these, and not knowing it to be booby-trapped, that Captain J. M. Newton lost his life on 17th November. Later the same day another mine was reported on the railway between Lydda and Tel Aviv, and Captain G. S. Harris of 1st Airborne Squadron, Royal Engineers, was detailed to investigate. For the manner in which Captain Harris completed his task he received a Commendation for Gallantry from the G.O.C. British Troops in Palestine, in the following words : " . . . Captain Harris knew of the fatal accident that had already occurred, but at this time no additional technical information was available. The charge was almost completely buried in the ballast. Captain Harris worked for half an hour until he was able to attach a cable to the mine to pull it clear. During this period he succeeded in obtaining the new type of firing mechanism. Throughout, Captain Harris worked alone, dictating his actions to his driver, who was at a safe distance. The charge was eventually exploded. During the previous six weeks, Captain Harris had been responsible for dealing with several mine incidents. At all times his work was of the highest standard and he showed great personal courage. The G.O.C. wishes to place on record his appreciation of this act of gallantry. . . ."

On the following day another mine, probably of the same type, was reported on the railway near Petah Tiqva, and Captain S. Adamson was detailed to investigate. Unfortunately, the Arab who had found it was unable to explain exactly where it was, and, like the others, it was likely to be very skilfully hidden. While he was looking for the mine, Captain Adamson must have trodden on it, and he was killed by the explosion. Another officer and a Sapper who were with him at the time were seriously wounded. Ultimately it was forbidden to attempt to neutralize these mines and they were destroyed *in situ*.

The scale of effort which the Army made available for railway protection in Operation "Earwig" had the desired effect, and the Stern and I.Z.L. saboteurs, finding that they were unable to continue the offensive, turned their attention to other things. This was fortunate indeed for the troops, who were particularly stretched in this operation, for after about two weeks it was possible to reduce the numbers so employed, and eventually reversion was made to a system of periodic patrols only.

CHAPTER VIII

FINALE IN THE SOUTH

FROM the beginning of November, 1946, until the Division shook the dust of Southern Palestine off its feet nearly three months later, when it changed places with 1st Infantry Division, which was in the north, there was little rest for the troops. The dissidents' campaign of railway sabotage which was brought to such an abrupt end by Operation "Earwig" was followed, after a short pause, by an almost equally sharp attack on the roads. This was a constant menace during this difficult period and will be discussed later. Suffice it to say that fortunately it never reached proportions in which it was necessary to enforce a system of protection comparable with that of the railways. This particular outburst which included widespread attacks on other objectives, ended on 5th December with the blowing up of part of South Palestine District Headquarters, landlords and close neighbours of the Division.

The Stern Gang claimed responsibility for the attack which was carried out by means of an "explosive vehicle," a method of sabotage which became more and more popular as time went on and was copied in the closing stages of the Mandate by the Arabs, who used it against the Jews. The Arabs, however, often lacked the finesse which was necessary to achieve the best results, and were apt to disregard such important factors as the quality of their fuses, or the detailed planning which characterized the efforts of the real experts.

The merits of the method lay in its simplicity, its devastating effects and the avoidance of many of the preventive measures designed by the Security Forces for use against other forms of attack. The technique was easy. Following careful reconnaissances and thorough planning, a hold-up would be staged in which a suitable vehicle (preferably W.D.) was stolen, and its driver, usually a Jew or Arab, held under guard possibly until the operation was complete. The vehicle was driven to a suitable hiding-place, where it was dis-

85

guised and loaded with an explosive charge which was hidden under some innocent-looking load, or similarly concealed. It was then driven to the chosen objective by its operator, who was, if necessary, dressed in the appropriate military or police uniform, and provided with all the necessary documents. There it was parked with some suitable pretext in a position from which it could do the most damage, after which the driver disappeared in order to "report his arrival," "slip into the N.A.A.F.I. for some cigarettes" or "enquire where he might fill up with petrol." If those who were left at the "business-end" were lucky, some observant person might soon see a tell-tale wisp of smoke coming from the fuse, and give the alarm before the devastating explosion took place. In spite of every precautionary measure, these murderous attacks continued to take their heavy toll of lives and property.

In the case of the attack on South Palestine District Headquarters, there was little departure from the normal procedure. The driver of the vehicle was questioned by the sentry, who engaged in a short conversation with him, and the vehicle exploded fifty minutes later. Rarely did the operators allow themselves more than a few minutes in which to escape, but on this occasion it was necessary for the Stern gangster to get well clear of the cantonment. The explosion caused damage over a wide area and resulted in 1 officer and 1 other rank being killed, and 23 all ranks and 5 civilians being wounded.

There followed a lull during the middle of December while the dissidents were prevailed upon to hold their hand during the 22nd World Zionist Congress at Basle, at which, so far as many were concerned, Britain, and no other, was to appear as the villain in the drama of the Holy Land.

On 13th December the Division reluctantly said "Good-bye" to General Cassels, who, after a particularly trying ten months in command of the Division, had been selected to attend the next course at the Imperial Defence College. It was fortunate, however, in being able to welcome back General Bols, its late commander, who arrived from England on 6th January. Another change in commanders had taken place a month earlier, when Brigadier F. D. Rome, D.S.O., arrived on 15th November to take over command of 3rd Parachute Brigade from Brigadier G. W. Lathbury, D.S.O., M.B.E.

Christmas was spent by the Army in an atmosphere of uncertainty; while the lull had not yet been broken, there were signs of it soon coming to an end. The reasons for this assumption take the narrative back to 13th September. On that day the Ottoman Banks in Tel Aviv and Jaffa were raided by the I.Z.L. The attacks were only partially successful, the raiders succeeding in stealing little more than £4,000, a fraction of what they had hoped for. In the Jaffa attack they became involved in a gun-fight with the police, as a result of which 13 of the gangsters, of whom 3 were wounded, were captured. One Arab policeman was killed, another wounded, and 2 cilvilians were killed and 10 wounded. One of those captured during the raid was a youth by the name of Benjamin Kimchin, who was eventually tried in December for his part in the raid during which he had discharged a firearm and carried bombs. He was sentenced as a result to 18 years' imprisonment and 18 strokes of the cane, and had he been a year or two older he would have been sentenced to death.

On 17th December the sentence was confirmed by the G.O.C. Palestine, but before the latter part of the sentence was carried out, the I.Z.L. threatened in broadcasts and pamphlets distributed in the Divisional area that they would also subject to flogging any member of the Army who fell into their hands if the sentence on Kimchin was carried out. Justice was done with little delay and nothing happened until 29th December. On that day, after dark, the Brigade Major of 2nd Parachute Brigade, on his way to visit some picquets in Nathanya, was held up, kidnapped and taken into the open country, where he was stripped and flogged. At the same time, in Tel Aviv and Rishon-le-Zion, three British N.C.Os. were subjected to the same treatment.

To say that feeling was high among the British Forces is almost an understatement. All ranks were immediately confined to barracks to prevent any further similar incidents and to guard against the possibility of retaliatory action by the troops. With one exception, in Nathanya itself, there was no retaliation—an achievement in restraint which was fully recognized by the Jews and which thoroughly mystified the Arabs. The opinion of the latter (not without self-interest) was summed up in the paper *Al Difa'a* under the headline "The Terrific Insult," and the question "Who was

Benjamin Kimchin anyway, that a British Major and three sergeants should be whipped for his sake ?"

There was, however, one compensation for the forces of law and
order, which were being called upon to endure so much.
Immediately following the incident at Nathanya, a road-block
manned by troops of 1st Parachute Brigade at Wilhelma, north of
Lydda, succeeded in halting a car containing five I.Z.L. members,
which had already eluded two other blocks farther north, and which
tried to do the same a third time. After shots were exchanged,
in which one of the occupants was mortally wounded and a soldier
was slightly wounded, the other four occupants were captured and
found to have in their possession an assortment of arms and two
rawhide whips. They were later tried and three were eventually
hanged.

As was to be expected, these incidents were followed by the inevitable searches, screenings and arrests. On the other hand, the Jewish
authorities also reacted characteristically with expressions of horror,
indignation, and condemnation of the perpetrators. These were to
be expected with exactly the same regularity as the outrages themselves, but on this occasion it was apparent during the ensuing
operations that the saner-minded members of the Yishuv realized
that there was a limit to which British tolerance could be stretched.
As a result, less hostility than normal was shown towards the troops
in the execution of their duty.

The dissidents themselves, however, were full of self-justification
and stated that they would refuse to stand by and see their "soldiers" imprisoned and flogged like natives. "We are Jews, not
Zulus." This opinion, moreover, was by no means confined to the
extremists; many of the moderate members of the community overlooked the original murderous offence when putting the ultimate
responsibility for the incidents onto the Government for the inflic-
tion of "such mediæval punishment."

On 30th December 1st Parachute Brigade, with 8th Parachute
Battalion and 3rd Hussars under command, started to search the
Yemenite quarter of Petah Tiqva in Operation "Prawn." During
the search for members of the Stern Gang and I.Z.L., a small arms
cache came to light, and by the end of the operation the following
day, 939 civilians had been screened, of whom 19 were detained.

While this was in progress, 2nd Parachute Brigade, with one squadron of 12th Royal Lancers under command, was searching in Operation "Noah," the south-eastern quarter of Nathanya. In the course of two days 1,923 persons were screened, of whom 24 were arrested. The Mayor undertook at the start to co-operate with the Army during the search, but later asked if he might be released from this undertaking. On 31st December, 3rd Parachute Brigade, with one company of 2nd Battalion The King's Royal Rifle Corps under command joined in the campaign with a search of the Yemenite quarter of Rishon-le-Zion—Operation "Ark." During this search, 262 people were screened and 18, including a prominent member of the I.Z.L. by the name of Karpinkes, were arrested. In Karpinkes' house was found a list of fellow-members which was of great interest and use to the police. These three operations brought to a close the Division's activities of 1946. During that year service casualties amounted to 49 killed and 122 wounded, of which 6th Airborne Division had 20 killed and 61 wounded.* The police casualties totalled 28 killed and 34 wounded. In the same period the "terrorists" lost 25 killed and 46 wounded. It is also worth mentioning that 30 terrorists were tried on capital charges before military courts for using or carrying firearms or explosives. Of these, 19 were sentenced to death, and in each case the sentence was commuted by higher authority to life imprisonment. No captured members of the Jewish dissident groups who were tried by military courts between October, 1945 (when the Division arrived in Palestine), and the end of 1946 suffered the supreme penalty. This was another of those things which took some explaining to the troops.

The New Year saw a continuation of the series of searches. Parts of Tel Aviv, Rehovot, Sht Hat Tiqva and Montefiorre were searched during the first three days by the Parachute Brigades, each Brigade taking a part. A further 9,000 people were screened and 130 detained. The searches went off in very much the same way as the others, and in all cases either the Mayor, President of the Local Council, Town Clerk or Chief Councillor was interviewed by the Brigade Commander, informed of the object of the search, and invited to assist in the identification of criminals. In every case they agreed to help, but their co-operation went no farther than the

---

* Plus 13 minor injuries not included in the above totals.

prevention of resistance to the searches, and the signing of certificates at the end, which stated that no damage, or only specified damage, had been done to property, and that they had no complaints against the manner in which the search was carried out or the conduct of the troops.

On the occasion of all searches the Press was given a free hand to attend and go wherever they chose under escort. This was often a problem; for when dealing with recalcitrant extremists who understood the value of propaganda, it was easy for a Press photographer to take shots of British troops seemingly meting out brutal treatment to all and sundry. Much depended on the tone of the captions which appeared in the Press. Unfortunately, there appeared to be no means of forcing even a local paper to give a fair and accurate account of an operation. The result was that in a large section of the local Press, and various organs of the world Press, some particularly distorted and vicious anti-British propaganda was regularly featured. From time to time, official communiques were issued, and the local papers to which they were submitted were obliged to print them, but this hardly compensated for the perpetual virulence of certain sections of the Press. On some occasions it was debated whether or not to exclude the Press from a particular operation, but this idea was normally rejected for it would inevitably have been misconstrued in some quarters. The British Press was perhaps a little slow in the early stages in presenting a true picture of the problems which the Army was facing, but after a time this was rectified. Thereafter the balanced reports produced by the majority of British papers were one of the few compensations to the troops in their unpleasant work.

While the New Year searches were still in progress, the dissidents staged a series of attacks on the night of 2nd January. In the South Sector there were four incidents, three of which were cases of road mining in which 8 other ranks of 4th and 5th Parachute Battalions were wounded. In one case a 3-ton truck, travelling in convoy and preceded by two armoured cars, was blown up, thus dispelling the theory held by some that only a lone vehicle was liable to meet this fate.

The fourth incident was an attack by the I.Z.L. on Citrus House in Tel Aviv, which was occupied by Battalion Headquarters and one company of 1st Parachute Battalion. At 1810 hours the opposition opened heavy automatic fire on the Headquarters from surrounding buildings, to which the troops made a spirited reply. This type of fighting was understood, and provided a welcome opportunity for the troops to hit back. The object of the attack was obscure, but whatever it was, it failed completely. At one stage an attempt was made to attack with portable flamethrowers (in use for the first time), armoured cars parked outside the building, but the initial shots of liquid failed to ignite, and the fire which the troops directed at the operators compelled them to jettison their cumbersome apparatus and retire hastily. The engagement lasted for half an hour, after which the attackers withdrew. Casualties included 1 Jewish policeman killed, 2 other ranks of 1st Parachute Battalion slightly wounded, and 1 Jewish policeman and a Jewish N.A.A.F.I. female employee wounded. Casualties to the opposition were not known.

An interesting point which came to light the next day was that the plans for the attack had been known beforehand among the inhabitants of Tel Aviv. One such indication of this was when a N.A.A.F.I. employee, wounded during the attack, was heard to reproach herself by saying "My husband told me not to come to work tonight."

On 6th January there began a new type of operation against the dissidents in the South Sector which was called Operation "Octopus," and proved to be very successful. It consisted of a series of very small-scale raids by small forces of police and troops on certain known "black-spots." It was backed with some accurate intelligence, and therein lay the reason for its success. Hitherto, the Security Forces had too often been groping in the dark, and many of the large-scale operations achieved results which were out of all proportion to their scope. Operation "Octopus," on the other hand, very soon got the dissidents in such places as Rishon-le-Zion, Rehovot and Petah Tiqva very much on the defensive, and that led to a marked reduction in their activities. In the space of ten days, some ninety people were arrested and a much higher proportion of this total than usual was retained in custody.

During this period, there were great hopes that the Jewish authorities were at last actively opposing the dissidents, and much prominence was given in the Jewish Press to the measure of control which was then being exerted on the extremists by the Jewish Agency. Moreover, there had been signs for some time that the Yishuv was becoming more anti-terrorist (though no more pro-British). However, a lull which had lasted for a week was shattered on 12th January with the blowing up of the Haifa Central Police Station. The attack, which was as audacious as any, was carried out by one man who drove a utility van into the compound behind Police Headquarters. His behaviour aroused immediate suspicion, and on being challenged, he succeeded in evading the shots fired at him and escaping through the gate. The alarm was sounded, but, before the building could be cleared, the van blew up with devastating results. This attack also exploded the still-born theory of Hagana and Agency control over the extremists. Again the Jewish Press, the national institutions and many notable citizens whipped themselves into a frenzy of anti-terrorist condemnation, but still the one thing that mattered was withheld—co-operation with the Government and its forces.

The move north, to which the Division had looked forward for so long, started on 18th January, and was completed, except for part of the Divisional Artillery and the R.A.S.C., which followed soon after, by 22nd January, on which day at noon the Division assumed responsibility for the North Sector from 1st Infantry Division. In the south the Division handed over the Gaza District to 3rd Infantry Division, which came up from Egypt less one Brigade Group. The remainder of the area was taken over by 1st Infantry Division. On 24th January, 2nd Parachute Brigade sailed from Haifa for England in H.T. *Alcantara*. There the Brigade was to rest and reorganize for a short time before moving to Germany in order to make up some of the ground in Airborne training which had been lost in Palestine. It was emphasized, however, that although separated by such a distance from its parent formation, it remained in every sense part of the Division.

In leaving the south, the Division had to bid farewell to 12th Royal Lancers, 8th Battalion The Royal Tank Regiment, 1st/6th Battalion The Queen's Royal Regiment, 2nd Battalion The King's Royal Rifle Corps and 2nd Battalion The Royal Ulster Rifles, which units had all carried out excellent work under command of the

Division for some time past. Otherwise there was not a single regret —the move was regarded as one into another land where the country would be pleasant, living conditions improved, and the inhabitants friendly. The feelings of the Division were aptly summed up in the remark of one of its soldiers: "They've had us, and we've had them, now let's move on."

PART TWO

NORTHERN PALESTINE
JANUARY, 1947—MAY, 1948

CHAPTER IX

ARRIVAL AND DEPLOYMENT IN NORTH SECTOR

FOR a week the narrow roads of Palestine were crowded with endless columns of transport while the Army played a game of general post. The war had been over for nearly two years. Units had cast aside their light scales of stores and baggage which at one time they had been able to move in one lift. Now it took all their own vehicles and a number of attached ones to ferry their impedimenta from one station to another. To add to the complications of the Divisional changeover between 1st Infantry Division and 6th Airborne, 3rd Infantry Division (less certain units) arrived from Egypt to take over the Gaza District, which entailed an alteration in the organization of sectors of responsibility. A new area, the Central Sector, was formed, consisting of Samaria, Lydda and a small part of Haifa District, which became the responsibility of 1st Division. Gaza District became the South Sector, Jerusalem remained as it was in the hands of 9th Infantry Brigade, and the North Sector comprised Galilee and the larger part of Haifa District.

With 2nd Parachute Brigade about to embark for the United Kingdom, there was no difficulty in disposing the other two brigades in the new area. 1st Parachute Brigade was assigned to Galilee, 3rd Parachute Brigade to Haifa, while the 3rd Hussars went to Afula, and the Royal Artillery was widely dispersed throughout the Sector. Divisional Headquarters took over from Headquarters, 1st Infantry Division in the Carmelite Monastery at Stella Maris, which overlooks Haifa from the western spur of Mount Carmel. Of the two brigade areas, Galilee was expected to be the quietest and pleasantest, while Haifa was regarded as a potential trouble spot, although it compared very favourably indeed in this respect with Tel Aviv.

The country was quite different from that to which the Division was used in the south. In the place of the monotonous expanses of orange groves and flat coastal plain, parts of it fertile and

97

parts barren, here was a wonderful change with hills and scenery. Mount Hermon rose majestically in the background, sparkling in the sun with her covering of snow. From Metulla, the northern-most extremity of Palestine, one overlooked the Jordan Valley, with Lake Huleh at one's feet and the Sea of Galilee beyond. All this and countless other lovely places acted as a tonic to those who had seen enough of the south. Some were fortunate enough to live on Mount Carmel, and from there, looking out across the Bay of Acre, enjoyed one of the finest views in the world. Towards the end of the Mandate, when the task of the British Army grew more difficult and unpleasant, the serenity and beauty of these views never lost their attraction and remained a source of great pleasure.

Before the move took place, commanders were faced with the problem of future relationships between the troops and the Jews in the north. As must be abundantly clear by now, the Division and the inhabitants in the south had very decided views about each other. Even had there been a complete change of outlook on the part of the latter, it is probable that relations had deteriorated too far for matters to be righted in a hurry. But in the north, 1st Division had by no means suffered from the same complaint, and it was most desirable that the Division should not destroy any good will that existed in these parts towards the Army. To this end some very serious propaganda was launched within the Division, which un-doubtedly had its effect. It would have had more but for the force of circumstances. No sooner had 3rd Parachute Brigade arrived and settled down in Haifa, than it had to impose, with the assistance of 2nd Battalion The East Surrey Regiment and "B" Squadron 3rd Hussars, a curfew on Hadar hak Carmel, the main Jewish quarter of Haifa. The cause was the kidnapping by the I.Z.L. of Judge Windham from his District Court in Tel Aviv on 27th January, 1947, who, together with another Briton, Mr. Collins, was held as a hostage against a "soldier of the I.Z.L." by the name of Dov Gruner, who was under sentence of death. Following the post-ponement of the death sentence on Gruner, the Judge, and later Collins, were released. In the meantime, however, curfews were imposed by night in a number of towns throughout the country, and road checks carried out by day in order to assist in the search for the missing Britons. The curfew in Haifa, which was imposed

CARMELITE MONASTERY, HAIFA, IN WHICH HEADQUARTERS,
6TH AIRBORNE DIVISION WAS ESTABLISHED, 1947-8.

VIEW OF HAIFA FROM DIVISIONAL HEADQUARTERS.

Facing page 98

on the nights 27th/28th and 28th/29th January, caused no trouble apart from a number of curfew breakers who were detained and later fined. But troops and civilians both felt that it was perhaps an unfortunate start for the new garrison in Haifa. For several reasons the Arabs in this respect never presented the same problem. Firstly, Britain was indirectly supporting their cause, by no means as they would have wished, but nevertheless she was, for various reasons, generally in opposition to the Jews, and this suited the Arabs. Secondly, they were in no way organized to make trouble, even if, like the Jews, they would have liked to back their threats with force. Thirdly, neither the British soldier nor the Arab ever used to take each other too seriously. Both have a wonderful sense of humour, and, on occasions when trouble was developing, this invaluable asset very frequently saved the day. That is also why even later on, when tempers were getting frayed, the British Commander on the spot, providing he could find the Arab who had caused or was about to cause trouble, was so often successful in retrieving the situation.

The Division found itself faced with a number of important tasks in the north. Haifa, as the principal port of Palestine, had to be protected against sabotage, which became an ever-increasing commitment as time passed. Close by were the oil installations—the refinery of the C.R.L.,* the pipeline and storage plants of the I.P.C.,† and the installations of Shell and other companies. These, too, being the principal British interest in this part of the world, had to be looked after as far as manpower would permit. To assist in these tasks, 2nd Battalion The East Surrey Regiment and a squadron of Arab Legion were placed under command, although in a few months the former unit was required elsewhere, and its tasks then devolved on 3rd Parachute Brigade. Also in Haifa there was the standing commitment of all transhipments of illegal immigrants who arrived in large numbers at irregular but frequent intervals from various parts of Europe. This task was handed to the Royal Artillery, which from then (January, 1947) onwards handled all these operations until the Royal Navy took them on just over a year later.

---

* Consolidated Refineries Limited.
† Iraq Petroleum Company.

H

In Galilee 1st Parachute Brigade, with its Headquarters at Nazareth, had a large district, with the towns of Acre, Safad, Nazareth, Beisan and Tiberias to look after in the event of trouble. Apart from the general charter of maintaining law and order, its principal commitment was the prevention of smuggling and illegal immigration over the northern and eastern frontiers which bordered on Lebanon, Syria and Transjordan. Placed under the Brigade's command for this purpose were the Cavalry and Mechanized Regiments of the Transjordan Frontier Force. Its second task was the protection of the I.P.C. pipeline from the River Jordan to Haifa Refinery, and responsible for this, also under command of the Brigade, was 3rd Mechanized Regiment, Arab Legion. The third specific task was the prevention of illegal immigration from the sea, which entailed periods of coast watching from time to time, and was the responsibility of the two Parachute Battalions which were stationed on the coast north of Acre. The other Parachute Battalion was stationed at Rosh Pinna, north of Tiberias, and was responsible for taking action if necessary in Safad, a town particularly prone to communal riots. Finally, stationed at Tiberias, and also under command of the Brigade, were 1st King's Dragoon Guards, who left for North Africa in the spring and were relieved by 17th/21st Lancers, who remained in Palestine until the final evacuation.

In Haifa, Divisional Headquarters found a new situation on arrival. There, North Palestine District Headquarters was a very small increment-staff which joined up with the Headquarters of whatever field formation was in command of the sector at the time, while yet another body, Headquarters Haifa Base, existed to command a number of the base installations and static units. It seemed to the Division that this arrangement could be improved upon, and eventually permission was granted for the two static Headquarters to combine as Headquarters, Haifa Sub-District, which later became Headquarters North Palestine District. There was one other novelty for the Division, which was also an honour and greatly appreciated, for in Stella Maris was situated the Headquarters of the Royal Navy in Palestine under the command of Commodore A. F. de Salis, D.S.O., R.N. In the following year and a half the Division saw a lot of the Royal Navy and benefited

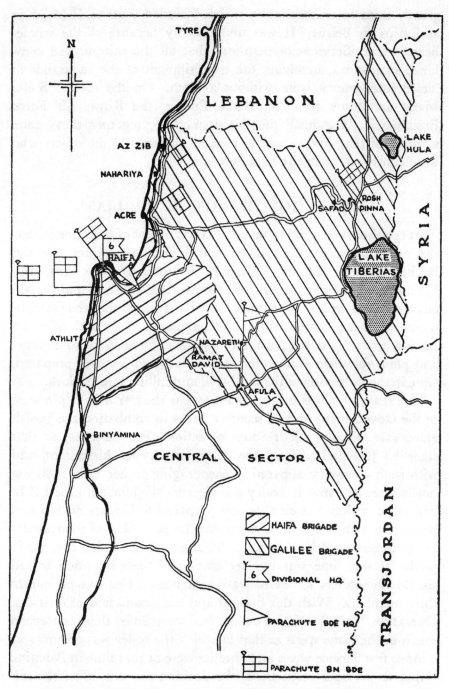

DIVISIONAL LAYOUT IN NORTHERN PALESTINE, 1947.

greatly from their hospitality, which included visits to H.M. ships and trips to Beirut. It was undoubtedly because of the whole-hearted inter-Service co-operation, that all the complicated com-bined operations, involving the transhipment of the thousands of illegal immigrants, went without a hitch. On the roof of Stella Maris lighthouse flew the White Ensign, the Royal Air Force Ensign and "Pegasus," the Divisional flag; together they made a proud display and served to remind all ranks of the others who were contributing to the common task.

EVACUATION OF BRITISH CIVILIANS

At 1400 hours on 31st January, the Government of Palestine broad-cast an announcement on its decision to evacuate all non-essential British civilians resident in Palestine. To quote from the broadcast, "It has been decided that British women and children and certain other civilians will be evacuated from Palestine so that the Govern-ment and armed forces will not be hampered in the task of main-taining order." Such a possibility had been foreseen for some time, and plans for their evacuation, which had been secretly prepared, were in the possession of the local civil and military authorities.

The reason for this drastic measure was the growing helplessness of the Government and its security forces in combating the Jewish extremists without full freedom of action. For example, at that stage no Jew had suffered the death penalty for his crimes, and with such clemency apparently encouraging rather than reducing lawlessness, a change in policy was clearly called for. But the I.Z.L. had already shown itself able and prepared to kidnap Britons and hold them as hostages, and there was the possibility of their tactics being applied to British women. A current threat which they made public at this time was the declaration of their intention to kill six British soldiers for each death sentence carried out on one of their members. With this background the evacuation of civilians, Operation "Polly" as it was called, was accepted by those concerned much in the same spirit as that in which the order was given.

As so few Service wives and families were at that time in Palestine owing to previous restrictions, the decision did not affect the sol-dier personally; indeed he welcomed it as a sign of the firm measures which appeared at last to be on the way, and of the decks being cleared for action. While this belief persisted, and it was widely held by both soldiers and civilians, it remained as much a source of hope to the soldier as it was of portent to the Jews. But in spite of the steady deterioration in an already desperate situation, the gloves remained on during the following months.

The notices of evacuation were served on 1st February to all those classified as "non-essentials." They were asked to prepare themselves and their families for evacuation under Army arrangements within forty-eight hours. They were given detailed instructions on measures to be taken for guarding their houses and property, and advice on various other domestic problems. The scale of baggage authorized per head was one suitcase, two blankets, and rations for one day, and in addition each family was allowed to bring a perambulator.

Altogether some 1,500 civilians mostly women and children, were evacuated from Palestine, approximately one-third of whom came from the North Sector and were administered during this period by the Division. The plan provided for a number of collecting centres to which the evacuees were brought in military transport. From there they were taken to the Concentration Centre in Peninsula Barracks, Haifa, at that time occupied by 9th Parachute Battalion. This unit moved out into a temporary tented camp in order to make room for the evacuees, and a camp staff to look after the latter was provided by the Divisional Training Centre under the direction of Lieutenant-Colonel J. H. Marriot, M.C.

One of the features of the operation was the tremendous amount of trouble taken by all the Services to try to make this difficult period a little more bearable for those who had been removed so abruptly from their homes. It was assumed that the evacuees would not expect more than the barest necessities, so that every improvement that could be made on that standard would be appreciated. The Divisional R.A.O.C. which was commanded throughout in Palestine by Lieutenant-Colonel R. J. Meech, M.B.E., excelled themselves by providing everything that ever came out of a Quartermaster's store, and much more besides. The R.A.M.C. and the Divisional Provost Company were no less helpful and understanding, and the R.A.S.C. drivers contributed handsomely towards the success of the operation. For this display of human consideration, which was so far outside the soldier's normal routine, a very genuine gratitude was shown. To the countless personal tributes were added the thanks and congratulations of His Excellency the High Commissioner and General Barker, G.O.C. Palestine.

The evacuation itself took place between 5th and 8th February by rail from Haifa to Maadi in Egypt, and during that time a special effort was made in the protection of the railways by a system of intensive day and night patrolling in order to ensure a safe passage. This was the responsibility of 8th Parachute Battalion. Farther south the evacuees from Jerusalem and the other parts of the country concentrated at Sarafand, and were evacuated thence either by rail or from Aqir by air. There followed for them an unpleasant wait of two or three weeks in Egypt before the majority were embarked at Port Said for England.

Concurrently with "Polly" occurred Operation "Cantonment," the object of which was to concentrate within safe areas all remaining British civilians and all outlying minor units which were either too exposed to attack or for some reason unable to look after their own security. The effect of this process of concentration was to create a large demand for accommodation in the selected "fortresses," and the only way in which this could be overcome was to requisition civilian property on a very large scale. A small amount became vacant through the evacuation of British civilians, but this only served a fraction of the need, and it became necessary to requisition all Jewish and majority of Arab houses in each fortress. The measure was in no way punitive, but there undoubtedly was a certain amount of partiality in the selection of the houses to be vacated, and the reason for this lay in the bearing it had on the security of the fortress. The Arabs presented no threat in this direction and for that reason alone they received a certain amount of preferential treatment. The Jews, however, remained unconvinced by this theory which also affected the Army's choice of tradesmen and contractors. The largest fortress in the North Sector stretched for nearly a mile along the western end of Mount Carmel from Stella Maris up to Central Carmel.

For the Division it was a hectically busy period. Having only just arrived from the south, it hardly knew its new area before it was faced with two vast administrative operations, the repercussions of which affected every unit. It was also a time in which all security measures had to be rigorously overhauled. The new fortresses all needed a system of defence, and in the main one on Mount Carmel 3rd Parachute Battalion had to move in and take over this commitment. But, without doubt, the hardest-worked people of all were the cipher personnel and switchboard operators of the Divisional Signals Regiment. Their job was never an easy one, but on this occasion they surpassed their own high standards in dealing cheerfully and efficiently with the immense volume of work which descended upon them.

By 10th February this latest step in security precautions had been completed. At the time it was anticipated that it might be possible to revert to more normal conditions within six months, "after the situation had been brought under control." Unfortunately, however, that hope was never realized, and the fortress system continued in use until the final British evacuation.

THE LONDON CONFERENCE

The drastic and unexpected moves of the Government of Palestine in early February left the Yishuv bewildered and speechless, though the latter state could not be expected to last for long. Such action could only be the prelude to strong repressive measures in the event of continued terrorism, and there was much speculation on the shape which those measures might take. Interest, however, was by no means confined to events in Palestine, for, only a week before, the London Conference had reopened after an adjournment of nearly four months. In order to bring the political background up to date it is necessary at this point to recall certain previous events.

Following the failure to implement the recommendations of the Anglo-American Committee of Enquiry, which were made public in May, 1946, another Anglo-American Committee of experts drew up a Federal plan for Palestine. This plan, which was put forward as a basis for discussion between Jews and Arabs, proposed to divide Palestine into four provinces: Jewish, Arab, The Negev, and a district around Jerusalem and Bethlehem. This was announced in the House of Commons on 31st July and was intended for discussion at the forthcoming London Conference due to assemble in September. In fact, however, it was turned down by both Arabs and Jews before then, and the Conference, when it eventually assembled, did so without Jewish representation. After a fruitless three weeks the British and Arab delegates decided to adjourn until December in order that the British might study certain Arab proposals, and that the Arabs might represent their States in the forthcoming session of the General Assembly of the United Nations. On 1st October, however, just as the conference was about to end, a Jewish delegation assembled in London in order to enter into unofficial talks with the British Government. These talks, which helped temporarily to clear the air, ended early in November. The British Government emphasized throughout that, if terrorism did not stop in Palestine, every military weapon would be used to crush it, "with all that that implies." The Jewish authorities were told that they had until 16th December, the date on which the London Conference was due to reassemble, in which to demonstrate their willingness and capabilities. The Government furthermore refused to increase the quota of Jewish immigrants allowed into Palestine while terrorism lasted, but they did undertake as a measure of good will to release the Jewish leaders in detention at Latrun.

As time passed, the reassembly of the London Conference was adjourned until January, in order that it would not clash with the 22nd World Zionist Congress at Basle, due to start on 9th December, or the extended session of the General Assembly of U.N.O. At Basle, however, the Congress voted against Jewish participation in the London Conference and the latter reopened on 27th January, 1947, with no Jewish delegation, but with very powerful representation of the Arab Higher Executive of Palestine in addition to the Arab States. For the second time, however, there was a Jewish shadow delegation, which sat on the fence and remained outside the Conference, conducting unofficial talks with representatives of the British Government. At the Conference yet another plan was put forward by the Government, which proposed a system of autonomy, with Jewish and Arab majorities in certain areas where they already existed; a five-year trusteeship with the prospect of independence for Palestine at the end of that time; and an increase in Jewish immigration to 4,000 per month for a period of two years.

But this plan, like its predecessors, was rejected by Jews and Arabs alike (the former still expressing their views from outside the Conference). After every effort had been made, therefore, to find a basis for discussion—a basis for settlement was even more remote— the British Government announced its intention to place the problem before U.N.O. In his statement to the House of Commons on 18th February, 1947, the Foreign Secretary said: "But if the conflict is to be resolved by an arbitrary decision, it is not a decision which the British Government are empowered as the Mandatory to take. The British Government have themselves no power under the terms of the Mandate to award the country either to the Arabs or to the Jews, or even to partition it between them. . . ."

The decision was welcomed by the Arabs, who were already well represented in U.N.O., while the Jews were faced with a hard struggle in order to get support for their case. They had never wished for the problem to go before U.N.O. and the decision came as something of a shock to them. Once committed, however, they turned all their energies to the preparation of their case, and from this stage they never lost hope or relaxed their efforts.

In the meantime, there had been another important and significant development in Palestine. Following Operations "Polly" and "Cantonment," the Chief Secretary of the Government of Palestine addressed a letter to the Jewish Agency and Vaad Leumi in which he called upon all responsible national institutions to heed the danger of the existing security situation, to co-operate with the Government in eradicating terrorism, and to communicate their intentions in this matter to him within seven days. The replies from both the Jewish Agency and the Vaad Leumi were in the negative, the latter arguing that the Yishuv could not be expected to become informers and spies to the Mandatory Government whose action to frustrate the aspirations of the Jews had contributed to the growth of the terrorist organizations. The attitude thus shown suggested little likelihood of an improvement in the security situation, although at that time expectations of strong British action were still prevalent.

CHAPTER X

ILLEGAL IMMIGRATION

AFTER moving north in January, the Division was confronted for the first time at close quarters with the problems of illegal Jewish immigration, and on 9th February carried out its first transhipment operation at Haifa. During the following twelve months, it carried out twenty-two of these operations, which in many ways constituted the most unpleasant of all the varied tasks which came its way.

Migration to Palestine from Europe and parts of North Africa was a matter upon which every Jew in the country was agreed. Whatever the consequences, immigration had to go on at the fastest possible rate and by every available means. At the same time, for reasons of which they were equally convinced, the British Government was just as determined to prevent unlawful entry of Jewish refugees into Palestine. The resolution with which these two conflicting policies were carried out became the main cause of Jewish bitterness against the British.

Reference has already been made to the organization which was formed and developed in Europe for the purpose of bringing Jews to Palestine. That this organization was vast and very adequately backed is apparent when considering the number of immigrant Jews it succeeded in moving to the Promised Land. The Division, however, was only concerned with one of the many stages in their long and arduous travels—their reception in Palestine and re-embarkation for Cyprus.

The immigrants' ships, which varied in size from 100 to 5,000 tons, were of all types; they sailed from various ports in southern and eastern Europe, and made their way to Palestine with the hope of being able to slip through the blockade and land their passengers secretly at points where their reception and dispersion were prepared. Occasionally, with one or two of the smaller ships, this plan succeeded, and the Security Forces would then be deployed in searching for them before they became too widely separated. The possibility, then, of ships being able to beach, made it necessary for the Army to maintain at certain times a beach-watching organization, which would summon forces to cordon the areas in which any landings were observed before the immigrants could disappear into Jewish towns and settlements far afield. These duties, which were carried out in the Division's sector by the Parachute Battalions, were toilsome and boring, and incidentally never achieved the desired object. But a far more unpleasant task was that which involved the supervision of transhipments which took place at Haifa, and which came about following the interception of the Jewish ships at sea.

The ships were normally spotted by long-range aircraft of the R.A.F. operating from Palestine, which directed destroyers and other ships of the Royal Navy until they made contact. H.M. ships then shadowed the Jewish ships until they neared the coast. By international law H.M. Navy was unable to board until within the three-mile limit, and this gave them little enough time in which to gain control of the illegal ships. Only on one occasion did they fail to prevent a ship beaching in this manner and that was in the case of the *Ulua*, an ex-U.S.A. corvette, which succeeded in reaching the shore at Haifa before the boarding party had gained control. These naval boarding parties had a dangerous and unpleasant task, as they were almost always opposed, and in gaining control of the ships they caused and suffered casualties in fighting which was often severe. Once they were in control the ships were towed into Haifa Port for transhipment of the immigrants by the Army. It was necessary always to tow them because the last thing which the Jews did before submitting to the boarding parties was to sabotage the engines and throw overboard the wireless.

The transhipment operation was a complicated affair organized by the Headquarters of the Divisional Royal Artillery and carried out by their own units, assisted where necessary by all the Services. The port was previously closed in order to prevent interference from outside, and in Haifa itself the Parachute Brigade responsible for the town's security, deployed troops to prevent disorders which could so easily arise out of protest meetings. Apart from those taking part in the transhipment operations, only Press representatives were allowed into the port, and of these there were always a number, some friendly, some hostile. Unfortunately, there was apparently tremendous scope for propaganda on behalf of the Jewish cause on these occasions, which resulted in frequent demonstrations and opposition to the troops for the benefit of the Press. The attitude of the immigrants and their degree of resistance during the transhipment depended on several factors. Of these probably the most important was the instructions which they had previously received from the Jewish organization sponsoring the ship. Another consideration was the outcome of the naval boarding operation; if casualties had been sustained by the Jews in that phase there was rarely any serious opposition later on. But, as there was no means of gauging what their attitude would be to transhipment, the troops had to be prepared for the worst. The first phase of the operation was for an Army boarding party to relieve the Naval one. When this was done and all was ready to transfer the passengers to the transport ship, or ships, on the same quay, the climax of the operation had been reached, and at this stage any further will to resist was manifested. Then also were made various exhibitions for the benefit of the Press. If casualties had been suffered during the boarding, these were displayed, including the dead. The length to which the striving for propaganda was carried is illustrated by the example of the exhibition on one occasion of a one-year-old child who had died at sea several days previously, with the statement to the Press: "The dirty Nazi-British assassins suffocated this innocent victim with gas." The *sotto voce* remark, "It's not against you, it's for the Press," made by one of the more moderate passengers to some of the troops, hardly compensated for this satanic lie.

On happier occasions it was obvious from the start that the Jews had no intention of causing trouble, and with sighs of relief the troops replaced their steel helmets with berets, discarded their truncheons, and were soon carrying children down the gangway in their arms, and assisting the aged, infirm and sick onto the quayside. There, the sick were taken to the first-aid post, all passengers were sprayed with D.D.T. as a precaution against certain diseases, and all their baggage, normally limited to one piece per person, was searched for arms, ammunition, explosives, illegal literature and escape apparatus. Through the neglect of this precaution on an earlier occasion a transport was seriously sabotaged by an

TRANSHIPMENT OPERATIONS BY NIGHT.

BEACHING OF ILLEGAL JEWISH IMMIGRANT SHIP *ULUA* AT
HAIFA, 28TH FEBRUARY, 1947.

DIVISIONAL BOARDING PARTY TAKING OVER CONTROL OF
ILLEGAL JEWISH SHIP FROM THE ROYAL NAVY.

SEARCHING OF IMMIGRANTS' BAGGAGE.

explosive charge after it had disembarked its passengers in Cyprus. Other precautions also had to be taken, and one of these concerned the sick and wounded immigrants. They were the first to be disembarked from their ships, and were then transferred to ambulances which took them to hospital in Haifa. These ambulances had to be escorted and the wards in hospital had to be provided with armed guards day and night in order to frustrate attempts by the dissident organizations to kidnap the patients and later set them free inside the country.

Although the behaviour of the immigrants from each ship varied, there were several constant factors which were noticeable on all these occasions. One of these was the fanatical, and, at times, almost pathetic attitude of the immigrants towards Palestine—"their land." That this may have been strengthened and developed by artificial means is not to be denied, but even allowing for the effects of organized propaganda, it was still apparent that one and all they valued their admission into the Holy Land more than anything else in the world. The realization of this vital concept by all who witnessed it made the tragic situation of these would-be immigrants the more real and vivid. Perhaps this was why even the bitterest and most unjust accusations, and the determined physical resistance, were so soon forgiven and forgotten by the troops against whom they were directed.

Another thing common to all operations was the appalling condition of the ships. It was to be expected that, as they were only required for one voyage, after which they would be liable to confiscation, the oldest and most dilapidated ships would be chartered; but into these hulks was loaded a mass of human beings who lived in conditions of hardship and filth during their voyage which confound description. Tiers of communal bunks were built into every inhabitable compartment of the ship, and even so there was not lying space for all. On the *San Miguel* nine persons were confined in a space of six feet cubed. In many of the ships there were nearly two persons per gross registered ton, and, by comparison with conditions in British troopships (which are by no means luxurious), this represents a state of congestion approximately ten times greater. In such conditions the passengers lived for perhaps a month, after which many were too weak to walk off their ships unaided.

At the end of each transhipment, the empty ship was inspected for time-bombs, which might sink it before it could be removed from the jetty, and then towed to the "graveyard" alongside the breakwater, where it joined an increasing and unsightly collection of other hulks. In the meantime, the British transport (or transports) with the immigrants on board, under a guard provided by the Division, and one of H.M. ships as escort, sailed for Famagusta in Cyprus. Here the I.J.Is. (Illegal Jewish Immigrants) awaited their turn for admission to their Promised Land. It might be wondered why this complicated procedure was not avoided by towing the ships direct to Cyprus. The reason lay in the risk of one of them foundering while on tow, with a consequent loss of life which would almost certainly have been heavy.

ROAD MINING

At the end of February, 1947, Palestine experienced a further paroxysm of lawlessness and violence. The Yishuv had not welcomed the British decision to place the problem before U.N.O., and the dissidents used the occasion for a renewal of their campaign. The Government's reply was to impose for a period of two weeks a state of Statutory Martial Law in parts of Jerusalem, Tel Aviv, Ramat Gan and Petah Tiqva. This threat alone had a very marked effect on the Jewish community in Haifa, and, though its implementation was widely expected, it never materialized in the north. There were, however, at the beginning of March several further road mining incidents which lost the Division a number of lives. In fact, a high proportion of the Army's casualties occurred in this way, and the highly efficient technique of the opposition presented the Security Forces with one of their most difficult problems.

Mines were practically never laid *on* a road, except when the gangsters wished them to be seen for a particular reason, such as to hold up a pursuit or cause a diversion to a main attack. In such cases one of several types of box mines was used; they were perfectly obvious and frequently accompanied by notices of warning in English, Arabic and Hebrew. The mines would be laid in one or more rows across the road, and usually a proportion of them were dummies. But the type which caused most of the casualties was laid on the verge of the roads, and either dug into the camel track or disguised as perfectly innocent objects. There they were electrically detonated by one or more operators at the end of a length of wire, who took cover some way from the road and pressed a button on an exploder box at the exact moment a vehicle was passing the mine. To simplify the procedure, the operators would place the mine in line with some conspicuous object, such as a telegraph pole or lone tree, to act as an aiming mark. The mines themselves varied slightly in construction, but a type which became almost universal was the "kilostone" or "kerbstone" type. A mine of this variety was first used in this role on 2nd December, 1946, on the Jerusalem–Jaffa road against a jeep of 2nd Forward Observer Unit (Airborne), in which all four occupants were killed. Previously, a mine of similar design had been used in Jerusalem in October of that year and was fixed to a lamp standard disguised as a litter box. It was placed in position shortly before a military check-post was due to arrive at that point to impose the evening curfew, and was fitted with a delayed-action mechanism. Fortunately, it failed to explode owing to a fault in the primary charge, though mines laid in other parts of the city the same night exploded as planned by the opposition and caused casualties.

Specimens of the kilostone type were later found during search operations, and dissected for examination by the Divisional Royal Engineers. They were found to be constructed in the shape of a kilostone, or white kerbstone, such as was used to mark the verges of some roads in order to assist drivers. In a rear compartment they contained a charge of some 25-lbs. of mixed explosives, in front of which was packed a similar weight of small steel rivets to act as shrapnel. The finished article was painted white, sometimes even coated with plaster of Paris, and was very difficult to tell apart from the real object. The force with which the rivets were blown out of the mine was sufficient to penetrate all but armoured vehicles, and the blast usually blew them off the road and frequently set them on fire. The effect was lethal providing that the detonation was correctly timed when the vehicle was opposite to the mine, and if the blast and rivets both failed to cause death, the resultant fire was likely to do so.

Counter-measures and precautions were never wholly successful.

The mines could be laid in a matter of seconds and operated either by day or night, and, though at times vehicles were ordered to move in pairs, this did not render them proof against attacks of this kind. Some drivers used to move on the crown of the road, when traffic allowed, in order to be farther from the explosion, and some used to drive fast with the hope that they would present a more difficult target, preferring of course to be caught by the C.R.M.P. in preference to the "terrorists." Another school of thought advised against this practice, as the blast was in any case liable to cause the driver to lose control, and a crash at 65 m.p.h. (Airborne jeeps) into a cactus hedge was hardly a more preferable fate. Whether the exponents of fast driving were responsible or not is unknown, but the gangsters eventually improved their technique by laying two mines some fifteen feet apart, and this allowed them the necessary margin of error when competing with fast-moving vehicles. They chose to destroy, if possible, a lone vehicle which allowed them time to escape, either on foot or by car; and incidentally ensured that no assistance was readily at hand to help any wounded soldiers. Many died from injuries and burns sustained in this form of attack.

One of the favourite places for minelaying was on a very steep bend half-way up Mountain Road, Haifa, which became known as "Dead Man's Corner." Here all vehicles had to slow down to a crawl, when they were particularly vulnerable. As soon as the mine was detonated, the operators made use of an easy line of escape past the nearby Jewish houses into Hadar hak Carmel, where they disappeared. No evidence was ever available from the many spectators; the nearest to it was on an occasion when a Jewish witness was about to describe the operators to the police, but was prevented with threats by her neighbours, and described in the process as "a . . . traitor."

"Dead Man's Corner" was eventually rendered practically safe by the erection of a vast protective barrier of dannert wire and an anti-personnel minefield which prevented interference with it. In addition, this road was also patrolled and picqueted from time to time by troops of the Parachute Regiment. Elsewhere the white kerbstones were sometimes removed as a precaution, though this made little difference.

Every unit in the country was exposed to these dangers, but

RESULTS OF ROAD SABOTAGE.

naturally those whose duties took them on to the road the most were likely to suffer the heaviest casualties. Whether it worked out this way is not easy to say, but within the Division the unit which suffered most was the Provost Company. These men carried out their duties, which were frequently dangerous, with a good humour, efficiency and determination of which the Division was rightly proud. Another unpleasant job was that of the Royal Corps of Signals line parties. Their duties took them out on to the roads by day and night searching for faults and sabotaged communications. On occasions severed cables would also be booby-trapped, and when this was suspected a Sapper had to accompany each line party in order to give the necessary specialist assistance.

As in the case of the "explosive vehicle," the Arabs eventually copied the Jewish method of road mining, again not always with the same success, although they were reputed to have "experts" from many different countries who were instructing them in the art of using explosives, with the ultimate object of out-bombing the other community. But in this particular branch of the art, their operators were inclined to detonate their mines long before the selected victims had drawn level, which, if not damaging, must at least have been very frightening. A story was told in Beisan of how an Arab explained such an error of judgment which led to a Jewish vehicle escaping destruction. The fellahin, unfamiliar with electricity, had allowed a considerable margin of time for the completion of the circuit and had "aimed off" accordingly.

One of the difficulties with which commanders were constantly faced in Palestine was in knowing when to relax and when to increase security measures for the safety of their troops. At times all might be quiet for several weeks, and then suddenly, without warning, a number of vicious attacks would take place. It was obviously impracticable to maintain security restrictions at a constant level whatever the prevailing conditions, so the stringency with which they were applied used to vary from time to time.

It was not until 19th June, 1946, that the order was published for all ranks to be armed at all times when out of camp or barracks, and to walk out in twos by day and threes by night. On one or two occasions this was cancelled and everyone would go back to the beginning as in a game of Snakes and Ladders. Only six months

I

previously an order had been circulated which ordered officers on long journeys "to have a weapon in their vehicle," and that was more of a precaution against highway robbery by Arab banditti than anything else. But gradually as time passed, more and more restrictions were introduced, which eventually took the form of three "security states"; "Red," "Amber" and "Green," one of which would be in force at all times according to the prevailing situation. These formulæ, which were for ever changing, became the basis of a host of other minor precautionary measures, and altogether they were the cause of endless exasperation. Unfortunately, nobody could ever think of a more practical scheme, which suggests that after all it was perhaps the best way of doing it.

PROTECTION OF THE OIL INDUSTRY

A danger which the Jewish dissident groups had always to bear in mind was that of incurring the displeasure of the Yishuv to a point at which the latter might be forced into taking action against them. This could happen if their activities against the British were likely to have a harmful or embarrassing effect on the general community. They were therefore ill-advised to continue their operations when the barometer of Jewish public opinion had reached the danger mark, and this restriction on their activities was responsible for many of the lulls which occurred periodically. But there was one means by which it was always possible to get their acts of sabotage and murder accepted without loss of prestige; there was never any lack of support for acts of retaliation to British countermeasures against illegal immigration, and that is why so many acts of sabotage coincided with a transhipment operation at Haifa. The destruction of the Shell Oil installations on 31st March, 1947, is one example, and the wrecking of the Area Cash Office and part of Barclays Bank in Haifa on 28th February, 1947, is another.

It was during the transhipment of immigrants from the *San Filipo* that the most serious and costly act of sabotage against the Oil Industry was carried out in March, 1947. The ship had previously broken down fifty miles from Haifa, and developed such a dangerous list that in order to prevent her capsizal, 700 of her 1577 passengers were transferred to H.M.S. *Charity* and H.M.S.

Octavia. The Royal Navy was later referred to by an Arab newspaper as " . . . receiving its passengers with the greatest hospitality
at the expense of the Palestine Government," while a Jewish paper
commented on " . . . the cruelty involved by the attitude of the
authorities to the refugees. . . ." This, incidentally, is a typical
example of how the Government and its security forces so often
incurred the displeasure of Arabs and Jews simultaneously.

At 0130 hours on the morning of 31st March, while the transhipment of immigrants was in process in Haifa harbour, a small party
of I.Z.L. saboteurs cut their way through the wire perimeter fence
round the oil storage tanks of the Shell Company just outside
Haifa. By means of three explosive charges expertly placed against
the sides of the tanks they caused a large escape of oil which was
immediately set on fire by the ignition charges placed for that purpose. The fire raged for four days and spread until it had destroyed
ten of the thirteen storage tanks in the compound, and more than
20,000 tons of oil. The damage was estimated at some £500,000
and the effect of the loss of so much oil made the defence of all
remaining stocks a matter of prime importance.

The result was that troops of the Division moved in for a short
time to undertake the close protection of the remaining stocks of oil,
until the security measures which were the responsibility of the oil
firms had been improved and put into effect. The close protection
of the oil installations was never before (and never subsequently)
the responsibility of the Division, which was normally only responsible for maintaining a mobile reserve in the area for the purpose
of taking offensive action against dissidents. To have used troops
there in a purely defensive role would have reduced still further
the slender forces available for mobile operations, and in any case
the "oil area" was so vast that the few troops which might have been
spared would have been as a drop in the ocean. The troops which
did assist in the task of close protection from time to time were those
of the Transjordan Arab Legion, who were lent by their country
in order to assist the British forces in their many tasks. In addition
to patrolling the entire length of the pipeline from the River Jordan
to Haifa during most of this period, they also provided troops for
the defence of the oil installations. The work which they did and
the reputation which they gained while so employed compared

favourably with their fine war record. They were first and foremost soldiers and proud of their calling, and their professional pride, efficiency and sense of humour commanded the respect and affection of all who served with them. As in the case of the railways, whenever the I.Z.L. were at a loose end there was always the pipeline to attack. It was so easy to blow up (as the Arabs found during their rebellion of 1936-39), and so very difficult to guard effectively. But the Legion stuck to the task and without their services the losses in oil would have been very much greater.

Rather more ambitious as forms of sabotage were the periodical attacks carried out in and around the oil area at the terminal of the pipeline, of which the effort against the Shell plant in March, 1947, was the most successful. Although they occurred less frequently than the almost routine attacks on the pipeline, they were of greater consequence. But improving the standard of security in the oil area at Haifa, which represented one of the greatest centres of oil industrial activity in the Middle East, was no easy task. The Army for its part insisted that its responsibility lay in the overall maintenance of law and order throughout the country, and that from spring, 1947, onwards, the number of British troops which could be spared for the defence of the oil area was sufficient only for a counter-attack force. The Companies would have to enlist, with the assistance of the police, a force of T.A.Cs. (Temporary Additional Constables) for use in guarding their installations against attack from outside and sabotage from within; the latter danger being just as real as the former. The Army would always advise in matters of security, and in fact undertook this duty seriously; one Parachute Battalion was eventually affiliated to each major oil firm in order to give that assistance.

The argument of the oil firms was equally reasonable. They pointed out that their task was to produce and market oil. In the abnormal conditions which obtained in Palestine at that time they could not be expected to raise and maintain a dependable force of armed watchmen competent to defend their installations. Furthermore, they stressed repeatedly that as theirs was the major British interest in that part of the world, which affected not only their own prosperity but also that of the nation, the Forces of the Crown should accept the responsibility for its safety. If the troops were not

RESULTS OF OIL SABOTAGE.

available on the spot, it should be only a matter of adjustment necessary to produce them. In the end the Government gave a ruling in favour of the Army, although the latter continued to provide assistance in excess of its commitments until the final withdrawal of the Arab Legion. It would be wrong to omit mentioning that in spite of the two widely separated viewpoints in this vital matter, the greatest co-operation existed between the soldiers and civilians concerned who had to deal with the difficulties as they arose on the spot.

As far as the troops were concerned, oil protection duties were a poor job. Situated on the least attractive side of Haifa, part of the installations lay unpleasantly close to the municipal rubbish dump, which rotted, smoked, and stank until the most important thing in life for those committed to this task became the direction of the wind. Nor were the tented camps ("J" site for one) in which they lived any inducement to remain so employed a day longer than necessary. Those who took their turn were 3rd Hussars, 66th Airborne Anti-Tank Regiment, R.A., 2nd Battalion The East Surrey Regiment, battalions of The Parachute Regiment and, of course, the Arab Legion.

CHAPTER XI

THE CASE OF DOV GRUNER

OF all the individuals, British, Jewish, Arab and others, who were connected with Palestine during the post-war years, few received more publicity than a certain Jew by the name of Dov Gruner, a member of the I.Z.L., who in the space of three months became world famous.

At noon on Saint George's Day, 1946, a Jew disguised as a British Army sergeant entered the Police Station at Ramat Gan, a town just outside Tel Aviv, and told a policeman that he was bringing in a number of Arabs who had been caught thieving. He then led in about ten men dressed as Arabs "escorted" by two "soldiers." A police corporal had just started to interrogate the prisoners when the whole gang produced arms from under their clothing and held up all within sight. However, one Jewish constable was able to lock himself in the wireless room and at considerable risk to himself operated the wireless while under siege, and sent out a call for reinforcements.* Meanwhile, the gang had forced the armoury and was beginning to load arms and ammunition onto their truck outside. In so doing, they were harassed by four policemen who engaged them from the roof and other vantage points, and eventually the arrival of police reinforcements compelled them to make a hurried withdrawal. They took with them 30 assorted weapons and 7,000 rounds of ammunition, but left behind one dead and two wounded, one of whom was Dov Gruner. Others were hit in the truck as they drove off. Police casualties amounted to one killed and two wounded.

Dov Gruner recovered in hospital, was tried by a military court some eight months later, and sentenced to death on 2nd January, 1947. As soon as this was announced the I.Z.L. threatened that if the sentence was carried out, they would execute a British officer

---

* He was later decorated for his gallantry.

in reply. However, first of all the sentence had to be confirmed by the G.O.C. Palestine, and it was anticipated that there would be an attempt at kidnapping in the event of a confirmation. Accordingly, instructions were prepared for the adoption of precautionary measures which would come into force if required. Troops were to be warned of the danger and ordered to walk out off duty in fours; they were to be confined to their camps after dark except for operational reasons, and all Jewish cafés and cinemas were to be placed out of bounds. On 24th January the sentence was confirmed and the precautions were put into force. As a result the I.Z.L. found themselves unable to kidnap any soldiers but decided to capture two British civilians, Judge Windham and Mr. Collins (as already mentioned), whose detention was easily achieved.

Then started the period in which Gruner's fate became a matter of world-wide interest. 27th January was a day of great activity which started with the kidnapping of the Judge, continued with frantic efforts on the part of the Jewish authorities to secure his release (they understood only too well what might happen if they failed to do so), and finished with the announcement that the sentence of death on Gruner was suspended in expectation of an appeal by him to the Privy Council. Whether the I.Z.L. would have been forced to release the two Britons had they not had the face-saver of the suspension of sentence is a matter of opinion, but the Judge was released the following day and Collins the day after. As might be expected, the I.Z.L. were not slow in claiming a victory, and they coupled with their boasting a further threat that they would execute seven Britons if the death sentence was eventually carried out on Gruner.

For the next two and a half months the Jewish community conducted a campaign with the single object of gaining a reprieve for Gruner. The condemned man himself observed an attitude of disinterestedness throughout the proceedings and refused to sign appeals on his own behalf, arguing that he had committed himself to the "cause" and did not recognize the authority of his judges to try him. Although it might be described as fanaticism, his conduct throughout his year in custody, four months of which was spent in the condemned cell, was that of a very brave man. A number of appeals on behalf of the condemned man followed: no sooner had one appeal been turned down than another was undertaken. They were made by relatives and prominent personalities to the Palestine High Court and to the Privy Council, and while they were being pursued, three other Jews, those captured on the night of the flogging incidents, were also condemned to death.

On 16th April, 1947, almost a year after he was arrested, Dov Gruner and his three compatriots were hanged at Acre Prison. The precautions which accompanied and followed the execution, during the burials (at Safad) and in the general maintenance of law and order, had to be very extensive, because the fate of the condemned man had become an issue of great importance to the Jews throughout the country. As a result of the measures taken by the Security Forces there was no immediate reaction by the community, nor was the I.Z.L. able to carry out its threats of kidnapping and subsequent execution. But the evil that terrorists do lives after them. A spate of attacks by the extremists was inevitable, and of those which followed the most successful was the mining of the Cairo-Haifa train on 22nd April. This was carried out by the Stern Gang just south of Rehovot, and resulted in 5 soldiers being killed and 23 wounded, and a further 7 civilian casualties. To add a final bestial touch, the gangsters responsible machine-gunned the wreckage of the train before escaping by car. In eighteen other minor attacks which were carried out by the I.Z.L. and Stern Gang during the preceding five days, the Security Forces suffered 30 further casualties. But, in spite of their threats, the I.Z.L. were unable to kidnap any soldiers, though that development and its brutal sequel was to come some months later. As far as was known they had only made one attempt on this occasion, and that was in Tel Aviv on 24th April, when they found that the Briton whom they had kidnapped was also a Jew, and released him of their own accord. Further attempts were foreshadowed, however, in an I.Z.L. broadcast made at that time which stated: "We will no longer be bound by the normal rules of warfare. In future every combatant unit of I.Z.L. will be accompanied by a war court of the Jewish Underground Army. Every enemy subject who is taken prisoner will immediately be brought before the war court, irrespective of whether he is a member of the Army or civil administration. Both are criminal organizations. He will be tried for entering illegally into Palestine, for illegal possession of arms and their use against civilians, for murder, oppression and exploitation; there will be no appeal against the decision of the people's court. Those condemned will be hanged or shot." If justification were needed for Operation "Polly" it could be found in this broadcast. The I.Z.L. may not always have been able to put their threats into practice, but they never bluffed.

ATTACK ON ACRE GAOL

It has been mentioned that the dissident groups in Palestine rarely acted without first taking into consideration the effect their action would be likely to have on the community, and so on their flow of recruits. They were also worshippers of the spectacular and theatrical, and any reverse which they suffered from time to time had, if possible, to be avenged severalfold. In this respect the execution of Gruner and his three fellow-members of the I.Z.L. presented that organization with a challenge which they could not ignore. As an immediate reprisal they joined with the Stern Gang in a series of attacks which have already been described. But the I.Z.L. attempted at first nothing ambitious, such as the Rehovot train attack carried out by the Stern, although it was rumoured strongly in Intelligence circles that something was in the wind, and whatever it was would involve a large number of their "field personnel."

The operation which eventually materialized was carried out on 4th May, less than three weeks after the executions. It is doubtful whether even in this time the complicated plans could have been drawn up, rehearsed and carried out, which suggests that perhaps the operation had been planned for some time and the Gruner case provided the ideal background and excuse for putting it into force.

The town of Acre, which is almost wholly Arab, has a long and interesting history which can be traced back intermittently for 3,500 years. Renowned as the last stronghold of the Crusaders, its fortifications still remain intact, and in the citadel itself was situated the central prison of Palestine, which contained over 600 criminals in the proportion of three Arabs to one Jew. Among the Jews was a large number of Stern Gang and I.Z.L. members, serving long sentences for acts of murder and other lesser crimes. Here, also, Dov Gruner and the others had paid the supreme penalty for their crimes. The Gaol, therefore, was selected by the I.Z.L. as the objective for what was to be their most ambitious attack since the King David Hotel was blown up. It was probably the most carefully planned operation of any they undertook, and its reconstruction later showed that those taking part had an accurate knowledge of the prison buildings and the routine observed in them. The attack, which was carried out with the assistance of some of the locals and with the probable connivance of some of the prison staff, was executed by a force estimated at forty strong, of which a small proportion represented the Stern Gang. They assembled in the area from all parts of Palestine, mostly in captured or disguised military vehicles, with the passengers dressed in the correct uniforms and provided with the appropriate papers. One vehicle was on an important dispatch run to Beirut under command of an "officer," who carried British identity documents, a work ticket correctly completed, a movement order which gave his route from the south of Palestine and his dispatch for the "Officer in charge of the Docks" at Beirut.

At about 1600 hours the assault party approached the prison, which lies in the centre of the town, and by means of ladders scaled the side of the Turkish Baths which lie adjacent to the prison. From there they reached the outer prison wall at a point pre-selected for demolition. Entry was gained by the use of three charges totalling some 130 lb. of explosives, which were placed against two windows in the vast wall. These were successful, and the assault party entered through the breaches and repeated the process on an iron door which barred their way into the inside of the prison. At this time a large number of prisoners were exercising in the prison yard. At least some of the Jewish prisoners knew of the plan beforehand and had received instructions on how they were to leave the prison, where they could find transport waiting for them, and what routes to follow for their escape into the country.

The Arabs, most of whom were in ignorance of the plan, took panic at once, as was hoped, since it added to the general confusion which was further increased by the throwing of grenades into the lunatic section of the prison. The guards were either overcome or forced on to the defensive, and were unable to prevent a mass escape through the breached walls of 214 of the 460 Arabs and 41 of the 163 Jews in the prison at the time. As the Jewish prisoners reached the waiting transport they were armed so that they, as well as the attackers, might fight their way out if necessary.

Meanwhile, covering parties of Jews had been engaged in mining all the main roads leading to Acre, which they anticipated would be used by troops of the Division who might be expected to arrive some time after the initial explosions. Their own withdrawal would take place by way of tracks previously reconnoitred. In all, thirty-four box mines and two shrapnel "kilostone" mines were used, one of the latter being detonated on the Haifa road against a three-ton truck in which five soldiers were injured. They even went to the extent of carrying out a diversionary attack with mortars on the camp of 2nd Parachute Battalion three miles north of Acre. They anticipated that this unit would be the first to send reinforcements, and planned to forestall them. In this surmise they were wrong, and it was 1st Parachute Battalion, eight and a half miles north of Acre, whose turn it was to provide an immediate reserve in this eventuality. As soon as word reached the Battalion of the attack a platoon was despatched, and, in spite of the mines which it met and had to clear on the way, reached the prison in thirty-five minutes. There, although the initial mass escape had already happened, it was able to assist the prison staff in restoring order in the prison and preventing any further escapes. But, as was so often the case, the unexpected took a hand in the proceedings in the shape of three small bathing parties from 1st Parachute Battalion, The Divisional Battle School and Divisional R.A.S.C., who, at the time of the explosions, were on the beach half a mile east of the town. The mines on that side of the town had been laid on a bridge farther still from the town, so these troops were within the mine belt.

As soon as the explosions were heard and the columns of smoke were seen coming from the direction of the prison, the picquet responsible for the protection of the 1st Parachute Battalion bathers, under its Commander, Corporal J. Powell, went into action in their White scout car. On the way into Acre they were held up by terrorists dressed as British troops (R.E.), who, acting their part perfectly, put them on to a false trail. However, the picquet was soon overtaken by a truck full of gangsters who opened fire on them with automatic weapons as they passed. The picquet replied from the vehicle and took up the chase following closely on the heels of the opposition. An exciting running fight developed as the two vehicles raced out of Acre on the Haifa road. They soon came to the R.A.S.C. bathing party covering the road, but they, unable to tell friend from foe, had to watch them speed by without joining in the fight. The red berets in the rear vehicle were seen to be getting the upper hand though, and dead and wounded started to fall out of the gangsters truck. As the two vehicles approached the next block, manned by bathers of 1st Parachute Battalion and the Battle School, the gangsters' truck crashed off the road and those in it who had not been killed or wounded, scattered in all directions. Some went down to the beach where another truck was waiting for them. This had been there during the afternoon with gangsters disguised as soldiers bathing next to the troops. What the object of this small party was could not be found out for certain, but possibly it was expecting only a small military bathing party and had orders to engage it with fire and prevent it from interfering with the general withdrawal. At any rate it was still there when the other vehicle tried to break through the road-block, and it succeeded in getting away with a number of gangsters on board.

At this stage, Private A. McCormack and Private C. G. Thorne, both of 1st Parachute Battalion, who with several others had been exchanging fire with the gangsters, saw the second vehicle escaping from the beach and chased after it. On the road which ran close by they commandeered an Arab car, pursued the truck and eventually caught up with it in some cornfields. The Jews, who had dismounted from the vehicle, engaged the two soldiers with a Bren gun; but the latter closed with the Bren gunner, and after killing him turned the weapon on the remainder of the party. There followed another brisk fight which ended with McCormack marching off five wounded gangsters to the police station, while Thorne, together with an officer, recaptured three escaped Arab prisoners who were seen making off for the open country. The Bren gunner they had killed was dressed as a British R.A.S.C. Captain and was later thought to have been in command of the operation. For their outstanding display of initiative and courage, McCormack and Thorne were both decorated later with the British Empire Medal.

SCENE OF THE ACRE GAOL BREAK, 4TH MAY, 1947.

It took some time to sort out the confusion, but it was eventually established that the bathing parties had killed 8 Jews (4 attackers and 4 escapees) and one Arab escapee, and captured 13 Jews, of whom 8 were wounded. British casualties were 8 wounded, 5 of whom had been blown up by the mine on the Haifa road.

While this spirited action had been going on, 1st Parachute Brigade, at that time under the command of Lieutenant-Colonel T. C. H. Pearson, D.S.O., was busily deploying troops on a cordon round Acre, and road-blocks as far afield as Safad and Beisan. The following day Acre and various other places were searched, but with disappointing results. The majority of those who had escaped were never recaptured.

The effect of this serious gaol break was a general improvement in the security of prisons throughout the country and the provision of better communications between the Army and the police, by which reinforcements could be summoned more quickly in future. The fundamental handicap, however, remained—the presence of disaffected prison staffs, which, because of the shortage of British police, had to include a high proportion of Palestinians. However highly developed the Army's co-operation with the police might have been, that by itself could not, and did not, prevent further escapes from time to time. Some months later another mass escape, on a very much smaller scale, happened again at Acre, which resulted in further drastic measures. So this remained to the end a constant source of worry to the Army, which, though not responsible for the security of prisons, was called upon to provide reinforcements and initiate counter-action whenever an escape took place.

THE UNITED NATIONS SPECIAL COMMITTEE ON PALESTINE

In replying to Britain's decision to lay the Palestine Question before U.N.O., a special session was arranged, the opening meeting of which took place at Lake Success on 28th April. After a few days of preliminary discussion it was decided to appoint a Fact-Finding Commission, to which the Arab States were in strong opposition, claiming that the facts about Palestine were already too well known and the need was for action. While delays were incurred, they argued, the Jews were continuing with their illegal immigration. What they felt but did not state was their fear that every day that passed the Jews were becoming stronger, and the same was not true of the Palestine Arabs. There followed two weeks in which some disagreement between member nations came to light, and further committees had to be appointed for detailed examination of various associated problems. Also during this time, both the Jewish and Arab cases were briefly put to the Assembly by their own spokesmen. The session ended on 15th May with the adoption of recommendations for the composition and terms of reference of the United Nations Special Committee on Palestine. U.N.S.C.O.P. as it became known, which was to visit Palestine the following month, was to consist of a delegate from each of eleven United Nations member states, and by a large majority it was decided that none of the Great Powers should be represented. The Commission was given a free hand to visit any countries which were connected with the Palestine problem and was given instructions on various factors to be taken into consideration during the investigations. Finally, it was to submit a report to the General Assembly not later than 1st September, which was to contain such proposals as it considered appropriate to the solution of the problem.

There followed a period of intense political activity on the part of both Jews and Arabs. The former with little to lose and everything to gain, redoubled their efforts and prepared for the reception of the Commission with a case as detailed and convincing as it was possible to produce. The Arabs, on the other hand, again divided within themselves, could not agree on what attitude they should present. In the end the counsels of the Mufti prevailed, and the Arab Higher Committee representing the Arabs of Palestine decided to boycott U.N.S.C.O.P. That this decision was likely to do them far more harm than good was realized only too clearly by the far-seeing members of the community, but the desire to demonstrate solidarity, combined with the fear of reprisals, forced the more balanced minority to remain silent. Their case was finally put on their behalf by the Arab States during visits of the Commission to Lebanon and Transjordan.

U.N.S.C.O.P. arrived in Palestine on 14th and 15th June, and started work on the 16th, when it was presented by the Government with a survey of Palestine consisting of strictly factual evidence. The purpose of this preliminary meeting was to give the members of the Commission an elementary knowledge of the country before it set out on a two weeks' tour of Jewish and Arab areas.

The Jewish case, which opened on 4th July, was noteworthy for its thoroughness, and included the views of all political and quasi-military bodies. Even the I.Z.L. and Stern presented their impassioned appeals in writing, though these were possibly too far-fetched to command serious attention. But the more moderate views as expressed by the Jewish Agency, and notably Dr. Weizmann, were in favour of partition, and powerful arguments were presented in support of that solution. The Jewish Agency's case, which, apart from the larger issues at stake, was designed to portray the progress of the Jews, the decadence of the Arabs and a miscellany of British shortcomings, contained the following passage in reference to the Huleh Concession*: "Buffaloes wallowed in the mud, mosquitoes swarmed and carried the poison far and wide, Arab babies died like flies. Fellahin eked out a miserable existence out of mat-making; Englishmen in high boots splashed through pools of water shooting wild duck. . . ." The final reference made at the expense of the resident British sportsmen, many of whom were serving with the Division, though possibly meant to be taken seriously, was greatly appreciated by the "cranks" concerned.

The hearing of the Arab case began in Beirut on 22nd July when the views of the Arab States were put by the Lebanese Minister for Foreign Affairs. He explained that the policy of the Arab States was based "on the fact and conviction that the Zionist political programme and its expansionist scheme, policy and aims for the domination not only of Palestine, but of certain other additional areas in the neighbouring Arab countries, constitutes a threat to peace in the East." The solution they proposed was to regard all Jews who had lawfully obtained Palestinian citizenship as equal in rights to the Arabs, and to establish an independent national Government based on proportional representation. This, of course, would have placed the Jewish minority in a comparatively power-less position.

---

* The scheme for the development of the Huleh Basin by the Palestine Land Development Company.

U.N.S.C.O.P. left Palestine on 25th July for Geneva, where it worked out its findings and compiled its report, which was published on 1st September. The Commission had been unable to agree on the presentation of a unanimous plan, so had produced a number of recommendations agreed by all its members, backed by two alternative solutions—the Majority Plan and the Minority Plan.

The first five of the unanimous recommendations were as follows:

(1) The Mandate should be ended at the earliest practicable date.

(2) Independence should be granted as soon as possible.

(3) There should be a transitional period preceding the granting of independence.

(4) The Administering Authority should be responsible to the United Nations during the transitional period.

(5) That the sacred character of the Holy Places and religious freedom should be preserved.

Very briefly, the Majority Plan provided for the partition of the country by the setting up of independent Jewish and Arab States with the city of Jerusalem under international control. The two States were to become independent after a transitional period of two years. Provisions were also made for amending the existing laws relating to immigration and land transfer restrictions. The proposed state boundaries had been worked out in detail. This was the plan eventually adopted by U.N.O. in November.

The Minority Plan advocated a federal system, with a Jewish State, an Arab State and the Federal Capital of Jerusalem. These proposals were also backed by a number of detailed recommendations, including the definition of State boundaries.

The reaction of the Jews as a whole towards the Majority Plan was one of concealed elation, while the Arabs denounced both plans in the same vein as that which they had adopted so consistently towards all previous proposals other than their own. Britain, meanwhile, withheld her judgment—she was soon to take a decision which was to have its own far-reaching effects.

CHAPTER XII

THE I.Z.L. HANG TWO BRITISH SERGEANTS

THE events during the six weeks which U.N.S.C.O.P. spent in Palestine certainly enabled that body to see for itself the difficulties under which the Mandate was being administered, and to feel the atmosphere of strain and strife which affected all communities so deeply. The day after its work began the discovery by the Hagana of a tunnel, probably constructed by the Stern Gang, under Citrus House, the Military Headquarters in Tel Aviv, forestalled an outrage of "King David" proportions. The Hagana was fortunate indeed in being presented with such an ideal opportunity of demonstrating their efforts in support of the law and for the prevention of bloodshed, while the dissidents in turn denounced them as "Adolf Bevin's Militia."

The Stern Gang, however, was determined to demonstrate its characteristics to U.N.S.C.O.P., and, ignoring the repeated advice of the moderates, launched a campaign of murderous attacks on the Security Forces in which a number of troops were killed and wounded. A typical episode occurred on the evening of 28th June in Haifa when the Astoria Restaurant, in which a number of officers of the Division were dining, was attacked. Two young Jews in a taxi drew up opposite the restaurant, and after dismounting, fired tommy-guns through the windows at the officers inside. Captain M. C. Kissane of 9th Parachute Battalion was killed and two other officers were wounded. The remaining officers, who escaped injury, took up the fight and forced the gangsters to withdraw. The taxi was hit repeatedly as it drove off and before it had gone far was abandoned by the Jews, who escaped down a side street after at least one of them had been wounded. The offensive action of Major E. A. D. Liddle of Divisional Headquarters was particularly prominent throughout this engagement, and he was later decorated with the M.B.E.

After a number of other similar attacks in Jerusalem, Haifa and Tel Aviv there took place the bloodiest of all the gangsters' acts—the kidnapping and subsequent murder of two British sergeants by the I.Z.L. On 16th June, sentence of death had been passed by a military court on three Jews who had participated in the attack on Acre Prison. Almost a month later, in the early hours of 12th July, two British Field Security N.C.Os., Sergeants Paice and Martin who were on duty in Nathanya and in company with a Jewish clerk, were held up by five armed Jews and driven off to a secret hiding place. The same day, 1st Infantry Division cordoned the area around Nathanya, and intensive search operations were started which lasted for two weeks. During this time a "Controlled Area" was defined encompassing Nathanya and a large tract of country round it, in which Martial Law was imposed. Numerous searches were also undertaken in some twenty other places farther afield. Although these operations resulted in the arrest of a number of suspects and the finding of some arms, the object was not achieved; the missing N.C.Os. could not be found.

At 0700 hours on 27th July, Operation "Tiger"—the imposition of Martial Law in the Nathanya area—was concluded. On 29th July the British authorities, unable to bow to the blackmail of the I.Z.L. even though British lives were at stake, had no alternative but to allow the sentence of death on the three Jews to take its course. Two days later, on 31st July, the two British N.C.Os. were found hanging from a eucalyptus tree in a wood one and a half miles from where they had been kidnapped. They had been dead for about two days. The area for some distance round was mined and as one of the bodies was cut down it exploded, having been booby trapped. In this explosion, a British officer was severely wounded.

The feeling of revulsion which affected every member of the Government and Security Forces in Palestine cannot adequately be described. To some extent it was also felt in Britain and throughout the world, but it is only natural that those on the spot were most deeply affected. The entire Arab world, and many Jews, were equally shocked at this, the most bestial act in the long list of Stern and I.Z.L. crimes. It almost goes without saying that nothing ever led to the arrest of the perpetrators.

A few days after these murders, the I.Z.L. posted notices in Hebrew on walls in Haifa, of which the following is a literal translation:

ANNOUNCEMENT

The two British spies, MARTIN and PAICE, who were under arrest by the Underground since 12 July 47, have been put to trial, following the enquiry into their criminal anti-Hebrew activities.

MARTIN and PAICE have been accused of the following crimes:

1. Illegal entry into our homeland.
2. Membership of the British criminal-terrorist organization known as "British Army of Occupation in Palestine" which is responsible:
    for depriving our people of the right to live;
    for cruel, oppressive acts;
    for tortures;
    for the murder of men, women and children;
    for the murder of prisoners of war;
    and for the deportation of Hebrew citizens from their country and homeland.
3. Illegal possession of arms, intended for the enforcement of oppression and despotism.
4. Anti-Jewish spying, disguised in civilian clothes.
5. Conspiracy against the Hebrew Underground, its soldiers, bases and arms, the arms of freedom.

The court has found the two guilty of all charges and sentenced them to die by hanging on their necks until their soul would leave them.

The request of the condemned men for clemency has been rejected.

The sentence has been carried out.

The hanging of the two British spies is not a retaliatory act for the murder of Hebrew prisoners of war, but it is *an ordinary legal action* of the court of the Underground which has sentenced and will sentence the criminals who belong to the criminal Nazi-British Army of Occupation.

We shall revenge the blood of the prisoners of war who have been murdered by actions of war against the enemy, by blows which we shall inflict on his head.

The Court of Irgun Zvai Leumi,
In Eretz Israel.

This announcement, typical of hundreds of others, demonstrates with shocking clarity the mentality and outlook of those with whom the British Army was engaged. These warped members of the community were the enemy in the campaign so aptly described by Mr. Churchill as "the squalid war against the Jews."

THE *PRESIDENT WARFIELD*

It was anticipated by the military authorities that it would be unlikely for the visit of U.N.S.C.O.P. to pass off without the arrival of an illegal immigrant ship and its accompanying volume of propaganda. It was no surprise, therefore, to hear in July that the largest ship so far to attempt running the blockade was on its way from France. The ship was an ex-American river steamer of some 4,275 tons called the *President Warfield*, which was subsequently renamed by the Jews *Exodus* 1947. She had called at a small French port, Sete, near Marseilles, with false papers, and there had embarked about 4,500 prospective Jewish immigrants for Palestine. How it was possible to do this within the law or without arousing the suspicions of the authorities is of little concern to this narrative, but it was later reported that the ship had sailed on the night of 11th July against the instructions of the French authorities.

The Royal Navy was not slow in finding the ship, which was shadowed for the remainder of the voyage. It was clear at the start that any boarding operation off the coast of Palestine would be a hazardous affair, since not only was the ship much larger than her predecessors, but she had been specially prepared to resist boarding. All round her upper decks was built a continuous wooden barricade which was strengthened with barbed wire and wire netting. Round this ran a steel pipe fifteen feet above the water line which was fitted with steam jets at one foot intervals, and connected to the ship's boilers. These defences, used in conjunction with showers

ARRIVAL OF THE *PRESIDENT WARFIELD* AT HAIFA, 18TH JULY, 1947.

of missiles and the avoiding tactics of the ship, were calculated to forestall any attempts by boarding parties to get her under control.

The challenge was accepted, however, and a force of British destroyers, with the cruiser *Ajax* in attendance, succeeded in putting a boarding party of fifty on board the ship as she crossed the three-mile limit south of Gaza. Because of the barricade round the *Warfield* the boarding party could only gain a foothold on her by way of the destroyers' bridges, and this was a dangerous process. Nevertheless, after almost beaching in Egyptian territory, and opposing the boarding party with all means except firearms, the *Warfield* surrendered and steamed under escort up to Haifa. During the fighting on board three Jews were killed and a number injured. Many of the boarding party were also injured, of whom three were later admitted to hospital. While the ship was approaching the coast and trying to run the blockade, an interesting feature was a broadcast from her for the benefit of the Jews on the mainland. This helped much, as was intended, in whipping up the support and sympathy of the Yishuv.

The ship arrived in Haifa at 1630 hours on 18th July. The normal reception as for other transhipment operations had been arranged, and the British transports *Ocean Vigour*, *Empire Rival* and *Runnymede Park* were waiting ready to receive the immigrants. The operation, organized as usual by the Division, was carried out smoothly, and incidentally was watched by Judge Sandstrom, Chairman of U.N.S.C.O.P. By 0530 hours, 19th July, the transhipment was completed, and the ships sailed with their naval escort an hour later. Once they were at sea the news, which until then had been known to very few, was released that the convoy was not bound for Cyprus as usual, but for the south of France, where the immigrants had originally embarked. The announcement had repercussions not only on those directly implicated—the British and the Jews—but throughout the world. From this point onwards the operation became largely a political one. Much happened between the convoy leaving Haifa and the end of the voyage seven weeks later, but the cause and effect of the decisions made cannot be fully described, as so much of it went on behind the scenes. It is only possible therefore to trace the events as they affected the troops who were concerned with this unusual and unpleasant task.

Each of the ships had an Airborne guard of rather over 100 all ranks on board. In the *Ocean Vigour* and *Runnymede Park* the guards were provided by 87th Airborne Field Regiment, R.A., and were under the command of Major R. L. Ellis, R.A., and Captain A. C. Barclay, R.A., respectively, and in the *Empire Rival* by troops of 1st Parachute Battalion, under the command of Major M. C. Gray. In command of all troops engaged was Lieutenant-Colonel M. I. Gregson, M.B.E., R.A. Owing to the demands of security which had prevailed in Haifa before the departure of the ships it had been extremely difficult to prepare everything for a voyage which would last at least ten days. If it had become known among the Jews that they were about to be returned to Europe, the consequences would have been extremely serious; it was therefore vital that there should be no leakage. As a result the troops came aboard ill-prepared for the voyage to France and back, and, naturally, less prepared still for a voyage which eventually took them to Germany.

Although the conditions on board bore no comparison to those on the Jewish ships, nevertheless, to troops who were merely doing a duty which had at the end of it no Promised Land, or even promised leave, the conditions were arduous and intensely boring. Each ship had about 1,500 Jews on board, of whom the women and children were allowed freedom of movement, while the men were confined to their cages and holds in order to lessen the risk of sabotage. Considering the bitterness and disappointment felt by the Jews at being returned to Europe, relations between them and the troops were remarkably good. Many of the Jews who had been fed on propaganda about the evils of British troops were pleasantly surprised to find that they were quite human. Indeed, this mystified them so much as they watched the troops playing with and spoiling the children, that they began enquiring for the ulterior motive. Medical treatment presented a number of difficulties because, although the worst cases had been taken off at Haifa, many others came to light in the course of the voyage. Each ship had a Medical Officer and small staff and these were assisted by qualified Jews who volunteered for the duties. The ships' hospitals were almost always filled to capacity, but fortunately no epidemic broke out on any of the ships.

When the convoy arrived at Port de Bouc, near Marseilles, on 28th July, it was anticipated by all on board that the French had agreed to accept the Jews and that all the necessary arrangements had been made for their disembarkation. Nor was any serious difficulty foreseen from the Jews on board; they appeared resigned to their return to Europe and were not preparing to oppose their disembarkation. Unfortunately, however, it was possible on the arrival of the ships in France for the Hagana to start a propaganda campaign by means of launches fitted with loudspeakers, and through visitors who came aboard in various guises. But for the threats issued by the Jews ashore and the more fanatical ones on board, many of the passengers would undoubtedly have walked willingly off the ships, but in face of the organized opposition, they faltered and eventually remained.

As a result of this propaganda a mere handful of sick persons disembarked, and for over three weeks negotiations between British, French and Jews were carried on. The French announced their readiness to accept the Jews if the latter were prepared to land voluntarily, but they would not do so otherwise. Finally, on 21st August, the British Government announced that the Jews had been given forty-eight hours in which to decide whether they would disembark at Port de Bouc or be taken on by sea to the British Zone of Germany. To this ultimatum there was no response, and on the following day the convoy sailed. During the few weeks spent anchored off the coast of France all the troops were granted brief periods of shore leave and were able to bathe, which did much to relieve the boredom. The next port of call was Gibraltar, where the convoy had to remain for a few days owing to boiler trouble with one of the ships. There, more shore leave was granted, the troops were fitted with warmer clothing and some of the garrison came on board to assist with the guard duties while the ships remained there.

As soon as all was ready, the convoy left on the last lap of the journey, and it finally reached Hamburg on 8th September. During the final stage it became obvious that a proportion of Jews at any rate would resist all attempts to disembark them at Hamburg. Even so, feeling towards the troops did not rise appreciably; moreover, relations had been so good throughout the voyage that many

Jews stated their conviction that these troops would never obey an order to use force on them. In spite of good-humoured attempts by the troops to convince them otherwise, many of the Jews continued with this wishful thinking. Others, who were prepared for the worst, apologized in advance for the resistance which they were determined to put up at Hamburg, and explained that its object would not be directed at the troops, but their Government. However, neither of these approaches, nor any other, made any impression on the troops. When the time came for the disembarkation they were confronted with a hard core of resistance in two of the ships and before the operation was completed a bitter battle had taken place. The Jews used all sorts of weapons and every missile they could lay their hands on. The ship which organized the most resistance was the *Runnymede Park*, in which a number of the companion ways into the holds were demolished, and the Jews placed themselves in a state of siege. It was necessary to bring on board reinforcements of C.R.M.P. and troops of the Sherwood Foresters, and gradually, one by one, the immigrants were ejected. The futility of this bitter resistance was apparent to many of the Jews as well as to the troops who had to deal with them, but its cause lay far deeper than the influence of a few fanatical ringleaders. *The Times*, of 10th September, pointed a very straight finger at some of those concerned behind the scenes: "The responsibility lies upon those who planned the expedition in the *President Warfield* as a political manoeuvre, upon those who permitted it to leave the shores of France, and upon those who used their influence to ensure that the hospitality proffered by the French Government was contemptuously rejected."

When the operation was over, and the troops were on their way to England for two weeks' well-earned leave before returning to Palestine, telegrams of congratulation, having been forwarded from several sources, were received by the Divisional Commander. The following extracts are typical of them all:

From C.I.G.S. to C.-in-C., Middle East Land Forces:

"The disembarkation of the Jews at Hamburg went very well and the fanatical resistance of those on board the *Runnymede Park* was especially well handled. Lieutenant-Colonel Gregson and the escort from 87th Airborne Field Regiment have been particularly mentioned by G.O.C. Hamburg for their good work. Please convey my congratulations to all concerned when they return to you."

From the Secretary of State for Foreign Affairs to C.-in-C., British Army of the Rhine:

"Please convey an expression of my personal appreciation to all concerned and in particular to the O.C. escorts on board the three transports and the troops under his command."

Fortunately, this operation never had to be repeated. If it had been, the lessons learned during this trip would have made the task infinitely easier on subsequent occasions. But even with all possible improvements made to the standard of living, and the provision of many comforts, it could never have been an attractive duty.

CHAPTER XIII

BRITAIN WILL LAY DOWN THE MANDATE

THE reactions of the Yishuv to the return of the *Warfield* passengers to Europe were first of incredulity and then of violence. Had the arrival of this ship occurred at a time which was otherwise peaceful, the consequence might have been less serious. But unfortunately there were other reasons for agitation. The decision of U.N.S.C.O.P. not to visit the Jewish detention camps in Cyprus, the impending execution of three of the Jewish criminals taken at Acre, and the kidnapping and likely murder of the two British N.C.Os., were all *casus belli*.

When the *Warfield* made its broadcast as it neared the shores of "The Promised Land," and rumours circulated in Haifa of a bloody engagement with the Royal Navy, a wave of resentment grew in Haifa. As might have been expected, the Stern Gang took the lead in the inevitable wave of violence when they carried out one of their "orthodox" attacks against the police. On 9th July three Jews armed with automatic weapons shot two British constables in the back at point-blank range in the middle of Hadar hak Carmel, the main Jewish quarter of Haifa, and then escaped. This is an easy technique, and by choosing the right moment and making the correct preparations there is little reason why it should not always succeed—providing, of course, that no one who sees it will interfere or inform the police. Wounded and dying men shot in these attacks were frequently left on the pavement until another patrol arrived, while onlookers "passed by on the other side."

Following so soon after the attack on the Astoria Restaurant and the subsequent warning to the Mayor, and taking into account the already tense situation, the Divisional Commander decided to impose for an indefinite period, a house curfew by night in Hadar hak Carmel. The following day, 20th July, strong mobile and foot patrols operated in Hadar, and at 1700 hours the full weight of 3rd Parachute Brigade with 3rd Hussars, two troops of 17th/21st

Lancers, and sub-units of Divisional R.E. and R.A.M.C., cordoned the area and imposed a curfew which was strictly enforced. On the first night 93 curfew breakers were detained, of whom 35 were tried and fined the following day. However, as each night passed it became easier to   the curfew, and the numbers of troops em-ployed on this duty were reduced.

The curfew, however, by no means prevented the extremists from carrying out a wide variety of attacks, although it undoubtedly handicapped them. In the early hours of 21 st July, the Palmach attacked two installations which they supposed contained radar apparatus and were therefore used against illegal immigration. One of the attacks, on a wireless station near Ahuzzat on Mount Carmel, was successful, the installation being destroyed with explosives. The four Palestinian police on guard duty were all wounded. The other attack was against a similar installation in the area of Divisional Headquarters which lay inside the cantonment on Mount Carmel. Sentries patrolling the perimeter defences of Divisional Headquarters noticed some movement in the dark, put up flares and engaged the Jews who were thus silhouetted. The latter were organized as an assault party of six saboteurs, and a covering party of ten. After much grenade throwing and firing of automatic weapons by both sides, the Jews withdrew leaving one seriously wounded saboteur who died soon after. Their three explosive charges, each weighing some 50 Ib. were abandoned and later disposed of by the Divisional R.E.

Meanwhile the Stern and I.Z.L. were no less active, and for a week an unusually wide range of attacks was made. Road mining was on an intensive scale, of which there were several cases inside the curfewed area. By day the dissidents made their preparations and concealed the mines when there were no military patrols in sight, and then they detonated them by various means at night. Some were pressure mines on the verges of roads, designed against patrols, others were placed in areas occupied on the previous might by a headquarters or military post. These tactics made it imperative that the troops employed should avoid routine behaviour in any form. Patrols had to adopt different routes and timings exactly as in war, and static posts, unless they were occupied continuously, had to move their locations each night. One bomb was thrown from the upper storey of a house at a patrolling vehicle, but as it missed, and the vehicle was armoured, all the damage was confined to the surrounding Jewish property. In cases like this, when the complicity of occupiers could be proved, houses and property were forfeited to the Government, which penalty soon had the desired effect. There were also instances of sniping with silenced small-bore rifles, always a difficult form of attack with which to contend.

Farther afield, incidents of railway mining, oil pipeline sabotage and isolated attacks with automatic weapons on military camps took place. In Haifa harbour the British transport *Empire Lifeguard* was sunk by a charge probably placed by Palmach frogmen. There was also an instance of suspected "suitcase sabotage" in Haifa East railway station, which on this occasion failed in its purpose. The technique, as the name suggests, was to fill a suitcase with explosives and leave it lying inside, or against the wall of any chosen target. Sometimes the suitcase was thrown through a window; sometimes it was brought into a public building quite unobtrusively, and left while the owner found something else to do. After the device had been used a few times, the sight of a suitcase or a bulky parcel lying about anywhere became immediately suspect to the Security Forces. The announcement, however unconcerned, "there's a chap with a suitcase outside," produced an immediate reaction from all present. For every genuine "live" suitcase, there were many harmless or dummy ones, and the Royal Engineers were kept quite busy answering false alarms. The genuine articles, however, in the suitcase line eventually became impossible to deal with. As the suitcase was deposited in the chosen spot by its "owner," he set in operation a delay mechanism and an anti-handling device. If it were then disturbed, the latter would detonate it, and if it were left *in situ*, the former would do the same after a set period. The drill on finding it (often with a wisp of smoke coming from it) was firstly to evacuate the building. Next, depending on taste, the outlook on life of the individuals concerned, and whether there was in fact, or had only been imagined, a wisp of smoke, a plan was made. Usually a Sapper (bless 'em) would approach it, and tie a rope to the handle. From a safe distance it was then pulled. If it exploded the anti-handling device had worked; if it did not explode, either the device had gone wrong or there was none fitted. Thus these rather alarming games progressed and inevitably finished in the same way—with a loud bang.

Towards the end of July the glut of incidents diminished, and on the 30th the curfew on Hadar hak Carmel was revoked. The area affected was one of those in which Martial Law would have been imposed, had it been necessary, in March. It would have been called Operation "Rhinoceros," and quite by coincidence the area when traced on to a map resembled closely the outline of that animal.

In the Galilee District, meanwhile, the situation was largely peaceful as Jews, Arabs, and 1st Parachute Brigade went about their respective activities. Instances in which Arabs caused trouble were still infrequent though occasionally amusing. One which happened this month near Gaza was when an Arab car was checked by the Security Forces and found to contain a load of landmines which, according to the Arab driver, he had contracted to transport for some Jews. The driver was arrested, together with another Arab who at the time was trying to buy the consignment for his own use with counterfeit £5 notes.

On 20th July Brigadier O'Brien Twohig arrived to take over command of 1st Parachute Brigade from Brigadier Bellamy, who returned to England to take command of 2nd Parachute Brigade. As it was only three weeks from the date on which 1st Parachute Brigade was due to take over the Haifa District and all its troubles, it looked as though Brigadier O'Brien Twohig had got the worst of the bargain.

On 19th August command of the Division underwent its final change. Major-General H. C. Stockwell, C.B., C.B.E., D.S.O., arrived from England, where he had been Commanding Home Counties District and 44th (T.A.) Division. General Bols, who had first assumed command of the Division in December, 1944, had commanded it in the Ardennes and Rhine-crossing operations, and had brought it to Palestine, now relinquished command of it for the last time. The Division saw little of its new G.O.C. for about a month; barely had he taken a look round before he put himself on a Parachute Course at Aqir. This he passed with flying colours and returned to Haifa to find a cable from 2nd Parachute Brigade congratulating him on "his elevation to the status of Master-Birdman."

On 26th September, came a sensational announcement from the Secretary of State for the Colonies to the General Assembly of the United Nations Organization. He made the following main points:

(1) Britain agreed that the Mandate should be terminated as soon as possible, and that Palestine should be made an independent State.

(2) Britain would give her support to any plan which was fully acceptable to both the Arabs and the Jews, but would not undertake to implement any policy by force of arms.

(3) In the event of no settlement being found which would be acceptable to both sides, then any recommendation which U.N.O. might have to make should be accompanied by a clear ruling as to how it should be carried out.

Enlarging on this later, the Foreign Office stated that Britain intended to prepare for withdrawal from Palestine immediately after the current U.N.O. debate unless a solution could be found, which was considered most unlikely.

Such a development naturally demanded the closest attention of Arabs and Jews. The former expressed cautious approval, while the latter were caught unprepared for it and expressed more displeasure than satisfaction. There was talk of British "scuttling" and for a time there were signs of panic within the Yishuv. But common to both sides was the refusal to take the announcement seriously. They could not reconcile it with Britain's "imperialistic policy" of which so many were firmly convinced. It was not until repeated assertions by British statesmen and officials had been made in Britain, America (at U.N.O.) and Palestine that eventually the intention to withdraw was accepted as genuine.

THE BIRTH OF THE BARREL BOMB

The symbol of British power in Palestine to the Jewish dissident was the police station. Its occupants were his enemies; its defences defied him and its destruction was his purpose. In the grim duel of wit and courage which developed as the result of this challenge, every round brought with it some advance in technique. The majority of police posts were known as Teggart Forts, and were designed to withstand assault or siege; they were mostly easy to defend, and were not often attacked. Those which were attacked were a less defensible type. They were usually situated in the centres of large towns, where lack of space denied them fields of fire and enabled the opposition to approach them unnoticed. Such a building was the Haifa District Police Headquarters, situated in Kingsway, the town's main thoroughfare. As Haifa figured so prominently in the Jewish illegal immigration campaign which received such frequent setbacks at the hands of the British, the Central Police Station soon became a recognized target for Jewish retaliation. Indeed, the I.Z.L. frequently boasted that they would never allow Police Headquarters to function unmolested for long.

As a result of the introduction of explosive vehicles, suitcase bombs, and tunnelling attacks, the standard of security precautions had been greatly improved on all military and police headquarters and installations during 1946 and the first half of 1947. Barbed wire defences surrounded all vulnerable buildings, and every person not known personally to the sentries was carefully questioned, identity documents were scrutinized, and baggage was searched before admittance was allowed. Parking of vehicles was forbidden within a certain distance, and machine-gun posts and patrols covered these buildings by day and night. As a result of the security measures adopted for the defence of the Haifa Police Headquarters, the I.Z.L. were faced with a difficult problem if they were to carry out their threats of further attacks on that building. In this aim they succeeded, however, by designing an engine of war which not only achieved its object in this particular case, but without doubt was the most ingenious invention produced by any of the dissident groups in the post-war years.

At 0600 hours on 29th September, 1947, a time at which there was little traffic moving in Haifa, a civilian three-ton truck with a peculiarly shaped load, which was covered with cardboard and brown paper, drove along Kingsway. Under the camouflage was a large bomb mounted on a sloping platform. The casing of the bomb was a large steel drum through which ran an axle fitted at each end with a motor wheel complete with tyre, the overall length being some six feet. Inside the drum was a charge of probably between 500 and 600 lb. of explosive. Each wheel rested on an iron ramp to which was fitted a flap in such a position as to prevent the bomb rolling off the truck. Inside the armoured cab of the truck was a lever, which, when operated, would lower the flaps and so release the bomb down the ramps with enough impetus to roll it a short distance. The shock of it landing on the ground would be largely absorbed by the two pneumatic tyres. As the bomb was released, a cord would pull the pin from a device which would ignite a short length of fuse. The truck was armoured in such a way as not to be apparent to a casual examination, and by the working of handles in the cab, armoured plates could be raised into position covering the windscreen and windows. Inside the cab were two members of the I.Z.L. who had been trained in the operation of this secret machine with which it was hoped to destroy Police Headquarters. In front of the truck travelled a civilian car with two other gangsters in it, which might partly shield the truck from view as it approached its objective, and would later be able to escape with the whole party after the truck had been abandoned.

The two vehicles approached the Police Headquarters at a few minutes past 0600 hours without causing undue attention. As they drew level they slowed down to walking pace, and when the truck was close up against the wire security fence on the edge of the road the bomb was released. With the fuse burning it crashed through the top of the wire fence, bounced on to the pavement, and rolled twenty feet until it rested close against the side of the building. As the vehicles accelerated and drew away, the alarm was given. Police guards blew their whistles and less than a minute later came the explosion. The massive building of seven floors, solidly built of stone and reinforced concrete, though still standing, was almost totally wrecked. The crater at its base was six feet deep and twenty-five feet across. Casualties were heavy as the building was also used as a police billet. Nine police and four civilians were killed, and twenty-five police and twenty-nine civilians were wounded. The damage to surrounding Jewish property was very extensive. Those responsible escaped in the confusion. Within a short time troops of 1st Parachute Brigade had cordoned the area and were assisting the police in searching for the criminals, and preventing looting from the damaged shops.

During the following months, the I.Z.L. never again succeeded in using a barrel bomb with comparable results. Counter-measures

THE BARREL BOMB.

Above: The vehicle used in the first attack against Police Headquarters, Haifa.

Lower: Police Headquarters, Haifa, after attack.

against such new methods of attack were never long delayed and it would ultimately have been impossible to have repeated the attack against the Haifa Police Headquarters and most other possible objectives. There were, however, several attempts later which were directed against the Arabs, and which for the most part failed in their object. In February, 1948, a barrel bomb fell off its truck prematurely as the latter was leaving Hadar hak Carmel and approaching Wadi Rushmiya. The Jews escaped and the bomb was detonated where it lay by the Divisional Royal Engineers. Again, so many Jewish windows were shattered by the blast, that it was rumoured the I.Z.L. had big interests in the glass industry. On another occasion in the middle of Haifa a barrel bomb released in an Arab quarter failed to explode and this also was destroyed. The Arabs never attempted, as far as was known, to copy this particular invention.

FRONTIER CONTROL

A principal responsibility which faced the British Army in Palestine was the safeguarding of the frontiers against arms smuggling, illegal immigration, and the possibility of small-scale armed intrusion by Arab bands. In the south and east of the country this was no great problem. In the south the frontier stretched down into the Sinai Desert, inhabited by Bedouin tribes who gave little trouble. On the east side the frontier marched with Transjordan, until 1946 a League of Nations Mandate administered by Great Britain, and with whom the friendliest relations existed. But in the north and north-east, where Jews and Arabs and their land were very intermixed, for a number of reasons the frontiers were open to violation. Here the country marched with Syria and Lebanon, two friendly Arab States which were both co-operative, but which, like the British, had their own frontier control problems. A certain amount of Jewish illegal immigration was known to take place over these frontiers, and at the same time lawless Arab elements took the opportunity of crossing the frontier in either direction to steal or evade pursuit. Disputes between Arabs and Jews, usually over land ownership, were liable to arise in the frontier area from time to time, and the contestants frequently resorted to violence and the

L

use of firearms. It was the task of the police, and if necessary the Army, to uphold the law on such occasions.

Throughout 1947 and early 1948 frontier control in this region was the responsibility of 6th Airborne Division, which had under its command for this purpose the Transjordan Frontier Force. The T.J.F.F. was a British Imperial Force, formed in 1926 and organized on similar lines to the Indian Army. Its Headquarters and base were at Zerka in Transjordan, though its units served mainly in Palestine. The men were nearly all Arabs, of which a high proportion were enlisted in Palestine; the officers were British and Arab. The units under command of the Division were the Cavalry Regiment and the Mechanized Regiment, and until October, 1947, the command of these was delegated to the Galilee Brigade.

On 6th October, the layout in Galilee was changed in order to ease the burden on the Parachute Brigades, which were becoming very stretched operationally,* and to give the T.J.F.F. the opportunity of operating in the field as a force under its own Commander and Headquarters. In consequence there came into being the Frontier Sub-sector, the complete operational control of which was from then onwards handled by the T.J.F.F. The force at this time was commanded by Colonel J. W. Hackett, D.S.O., M.B.E., M.C., who had commanded 4th Parachute Brigade during the war, and who assumed command of the T.J.F.F. from Colonel C. W. C. Montgomery, O.B.E.

It so happened that only a few days after the formation of the Frontier Sub-sector the situation in the north began to deteriorate. At a meeting near Beirut of the Arab League Council, a communiqué was issued referring to "decisions on the measures for the defence of Palestine and the safeguarding of its inhabitants." It was also stated that "the situation demands of the Arab States that they take military measures along the border." These statements were followed by broadcasts from Beirut and Damascus which announced the formation of an Arab League Army, to be composed of contingents of infantry from Lebanon, tanks and armoured cars

---

* The Hadera Sub-sector, which included some well-known "blackspots" such as Binyamina and Zikhron Yaaqov, had been added to the North Sector on 28th September, and this naturally kept a number of troops "tied up."

149

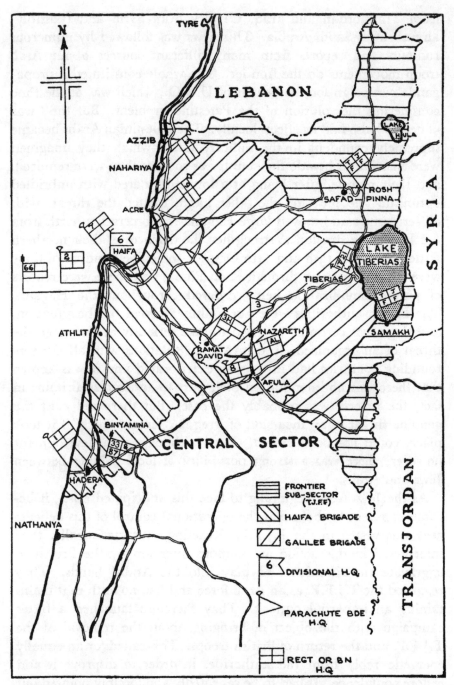

DIVISIONAL LAYOUT IN NORTHERN PALESTINE, NOVEMBER, 1947.

from Transjordan and Iraq, Cavalry from Syria and (possibly) aircraft from Saudi Arabia. This news was followed by numerous rumours and reports from many different sources about Arab troop movements on the frontier. The whole constituted a propaganda campaign for the benefit of U.N.O., which was at the time considering the solution of the Palestine problem. But the "war of nerves" also had its effects locally. The Palestinian Arabs became supremely confident in the military forces which they imagined were massing to invade the country as soon as they were required, and their morale, after being at a low ebb, soared with unbridled optimism. The Jews, on the other hand, treated the threats with all seriousness and moved large Hagana reinforcements north from the Plain of Esdraelon to strengthen the defences of their northern settlements. On 13th and 14th October some five hundred of these were counted moving through Rosh Pinna, and there were reports of partial mobilization being ordered throughout the Hagana. The British authorities were not unduly worried by the situation, and there was certainly no need to take seriously at this stage the threat of an organized Arab invasion. Relations with all the surrounding countries had in no way deteriorated and it was known that there was no intention on their part to antagonize Britain; in fact, the reverse was probably the case. But there did exist the genuine threat of an incursion of irregular forces, which, if it took place, could not be tolerated. Even without such a development however, there was a strong possibility of local trouble between Jews and Arabs.

As the Jews were beginning to face this anticipated crisis, it became apparent to them that the operational control of this delicate area was vested in the T.J.F.F. Reacting characteristically, they interpreted in this action an ominous intention by the British to aggravate the situation and play into the Arabs' hands. They regarded the T.J.F.F. as an Arab force and had no faith in it maintaining an impartial outlook. They therefore launched a bitter campaign with the object of bringing about the removal of the T.J.F.F. and the return of British troops. This called for an equally energetic reply from the authorities in order to disprove it and restore confidence. It had to be repeatedly and forcibly pointed out that the T.J.F.F. was a British Imperial Force engaged in guarding

British frontiers, and in this task they had the complete confidence of their Commanders. The difference of opinion between the British authorities and the Jews might have widened further but for an incident which gave the troops concerned the chance of justifying the support of their Commanders.

On 20th October a T.J.F.F. patrol visiting the Jewish colony at Dan, which lies a mile south of the northern frontier, was informed that a Syrian military post, including armoured cars, was in position on Tall al Qadi, some high ground just inside Palestine. Artillery also had been seen, and the Jewish inhabitants were in a state of some concern. This report was confirmed and the Syrians were kept under observation by the T.J.F.F. while the information was passed back to Divisional Headquarters. The G.O.C. ordered the capture of this post without delay. At dawn on the following day a mechanized squadron and a troop of armoured cars of the T.J.F.F., with a troop of armoured cars of 17th/21st Lancers in support, succeeded in forcing the Syrian post to capitulate without a shot being fired. The ultimatum by the Commander T.J.F.F., followed by a surprise show of force, had the desired effect, and the Syrians were captured with all their arms. As this was witnessed by the Mukhtar of Dan, it went a long way towards restoring the confidence of the Jews in the T.J.F.F., and thereafter the campaign for their removal from the frontier diminished into periodical murmurings. The outcome of this incident also had a salutary effect on the local and neighbouring Arabs. The Syrians were returned to their country the same day.

CHAPTER XIV

DIVISIONAL REORGANISATION

NEWS from the War Office reached Divisional Headquarters in the middle of October, 1947, of the proposal to reduce the Division by one brigade. With this unexpected information came detailed suggestions on how the nine existing Parachute battalions might be reduced to six. Naturally, much thought had been given in high places on how best to effect the reduction. It was desirable to maintain within the Division representation of the various airborne formations which had been raised, and which had founded the traditions of Airborne Forces during the war. The claims of individual battalions also had to be taken into account. After consideration, the Divisional Commander accepted the War Office recommendations as representing the best and fairest course open. In an Order of the Day, which was read out to all ranks of the Parachute Regiment on 5th November, he explained the reasons for the reduction and stated that he shared very fully the disappointment which he was sure was felt by all. At the same time, Commanding Officers explained the proposed new changes in the order of battle.

The plan briefly was to amalgamate 2nd and 3rd Battalions, 4th and 6th Battalions and 8th and 9th Battalions. The 1st (Guards), 5th (Scottish) and 7th (Light Infantry) were the three fortunate units, which by reason of their Regimental affiliations, and the impracticability of amalgamating them, remained as they were. For equally sound reasons it was decided that 7th Battalion would return to England to fill the gap in 2nd Parachute Brigade caused by the amalgamation of 4th and 6th Battalions. The future order of battle therefore would be as follows:

1st Parachute Brigade: 1st, 2nd/3rd and 8th/9th Battalions.
2nd Parachute Brigade: 4th/6th, 5th and 7th Battalions.

The disbandment of 3rd Parachute Brigade would produce a big gap in the North Sector of Palestine, and the next problem was how this could be filled. A plan was produced by higher authority for the formation of an independent infantry brigade which would be commanded by Headquarters 3rd Parachute Brigade. This, however, was soon dropped, and the next plan provided for one infantry battalion only (2nd Battalion The Middlesex Regiment), to offset the loss of 3rd Parachute Brigade. The first of the amalgamations, that of 2nd and 3rd Parachute Battalions, was scheduled to take place in mid-December, and it was arranged that 2nd Middlesex should arrive at the same time. Very soon after, 7th Parachute Battalion would leave for England, and early in January 8th and 9th Battalions would amalgamate. The loss of two battalions was to be accepted unless the operational situation deteriorated, in which case the necessary reinforcements would be made available. All these moves and amalgamations took place as planned.

The reduction in available forces necessitated a reorganization of sub-sectors, which came into force on 16th December. 1st Parachute Brigade remained responsible for Haifa District and were given Acre Sub-district in addition. To deal with the extra commitments, which included watching a further twenty miles of coastline and keeping an eye on Acre prison (which was continually giving trouble), 2nd Middlesex were placed under command. This Battalion moved into Camp 253, north of Acre, from which they were employed on a wide range of tasks until shortly before the end of the Mandate. 3rd Parachute Brigade, now rapidly shrinking, had 3rd Hussars placed under its command and was left with the sub-district of Nazareth only to protect. On the disbandment of Brigade Headquarters in January, 3rd Hussars assumed full operational control of the sub-sector unaided. The T.J.F.F. remained responsible for the frontier sub-sector, which had been extended southwards on 15th November to include Beisan, and 17th/21st Lancers at Tiberias took over the remainder of Galilee.

The main effect of these changes on the private soldier was harder work. Units had larger areas to look after than previously, and particularly with the increase of Arab-Jew clashes, troops were called out far more often than they had been before. But they thrived on it, and much of the work had a new and wholesome excitement about it which raised their morale even higher. Mobility and good communications assumed an even greater importance, since the

very appearance of a mobile column frequently prevented the outbreak of trouble. "Flag marches" organized for this purpose were
undertaken regularly and particularly in the frontier areas. They
were friendly affairs, and the columns, which had a sprinkling of
artillery and armoured vehicles with them, used to stop in the Arab
villages and allow the local inhabitants to examine their vehicles
and weapons. They did untold good.

U.N.O. APPROVES PARTITION

As the tension in the Huleh Valley died down, so did the rest of
the country follow suit. A three-week lull was broken on 12th
November by the Stern Gang, which carried out over a period of
three days a short series of attacks on British Service men and civilians,
of whom 12 were killed and 28 wounded. This recrudescence
followed an engagement between British troops and a party of
young Stern Gang trainees in the Central Sector on 12th November,
in which 5 gangsters were killed and 4 captured, while the troops
had no losses. Otherwise all was comparatively quiet in this respect
during the five weeks which preceded the U.N.O. vote on partition.
For some time much had been heard of Hagana efforts to bring
the dissidents under control, since the former had become highly
conscious of the potential danger which faced any form of future
Jewish administration. From time to time, therefore, sounds of
fratricidal strife echoed up from the underworld, and the rival
organizations sought to gain support from the community by means
of propaganda and pamphlet warfare. A pamphlet issued by the
I.Z.L. at this period probably raised a smile from all sides. "The
Hagana are lying when they accuse us of laying mines in the Nathanya area" it stated; "we haven't laid any there for a week."
There were occasions when the Hagana were positively co-operative with the Security Forces, though they appeared to lack clear
direction in this matter from their higher command. The extent
to which co-operation was carried often rested with the local commanders of either side. As time went on relations slightly improved,
although they never became cordial because Hagana, in British
official estimation, never ceased to be an illegal organization.
Nevertheless, it was an encouraging sign when Hagana members

went to the assistance of British soldiers wounded by Stern or I.Z.L. instead of leaving them lying where they fell. Such behaviour may not have been altogether unrelated to their desire of convincing U.N.O. that they were capable of founding their own state on a sound structure. Certainly much was done in the vital weeks of November which led up to the vote for or against partition to convince the world that, given the opportunity they would be capable of keeping order within their own state, and, if necessary, defending it against aggression from outside.

The news that the partition of Palestine had been approved by the necessary majority in the General Assembly of the United Nations reached Palestine in the early hours of 30th November. Many Jews had waited up all night for the news, and as soon as it was announced the entire Yishuv devoted itself to two days of celebration and thanksgiving. Such elation was only natural, although it was conducted with a certain ostentation which infuriated the Arabs and was partially responsible for the riots and bloodshed which followed.

The Jews had nothing to gain from violence at this juncture and there can be no denying that the trouble which started was the work of Arab hooligan elements. In this respect it might be compared with the Jewish riots in Tel Aviv almost exactly two years previously, with the important difference that on that occasion the trouble was at the expense of British lives and property. But there is equally no doubt that the Jews were not prepared to accept these Arab attacks as the acts of irresponsible elements; reprisals had to follow, and, furthermore, retribution had to be exacted severalfold. Much blood was spilt therefore as a direct result of both sides taking hasty action in the early stages, and thereafter the situation was never wholly restored. It was the unenviable task of the British Army to place themselves between the opposing forces during the ensuing six months in order to maintain some measure of control. It is not only military experience which proves that the third party in a fight frequently becomes the object of the main attention of the other two contestants. The situation which developed on this occasion proved no exception.

Following the spontaneous reactions of the first few days after the announcement, the British authorities eagerly waited to see what the subsequent policy of the Arabs and Jews would be. The Arabs declared that the decision would never be implemented and that they would oppose it by force of arms to the last man. But they also announced that the time had not yet come to resort to violence, and the efforts of all their responsible leaders were directed towards controlling their unruly elements. The wiser ones recognized the dangers of becoming involved with the British, and also the tactical mistake of staging a premature uprising. For a time they were fairly successful, although they never exerted complete control over their fanatical element. Later, they were forced to abandon their efforts as more and more irregulars infiltrated into the country from the Arab States.

The reactions of the Jews were equally pronounced. The Hagana all but came into the open and indeed, had the Security Forces not taken such a firm line, this might have come about. As it was, armed Hagana patrols and sub-units were frequently encountered by British forces, who took all possible steps to disarm them. Another local feature of the difficult months which followed was the frequency with which both Jewish and Arab leaders in Haifa were commanded to attend the Divisional Commander's Orders. They were reprimanded with a severity which normally ensured the orderly behaviour of themselves and their forces for at least several days.

The I.Z.L. more or less called off attacks on British troops and police, except in cases where the primary object of the operation was the seizure of arms. Then they showed themselves as ruthless and regardless of life as ever before. But from December, 1947, onwards the I.Z.L. directed its "war effort" principally against the Arabs. The Stern Gang meanwhile had lost no time in claiming credit for "driving the British out of the homeland." To them the British remained the primary enemy, though they devoted some of their time to particularly bestial attacks on Arab villages, in which they showed not the slightest discrimination for women and children, whom they killed as opportunity offered.

Communal strife started on 2nd December in Jerusalem and Jaffa, and soon spread to Haifa. It took the form of arson, looting and the stoning of Jewish vehicles by Arab mobs, and the occasional episode with grenades or firearms. As armed reprisals by the Jews took place, Haifa began to assume an air of war. Arabs and Jews living in the border areas evacuated their houses and moved back into their own parts of the town. There arose in consequence a no-man's-land between each community into which moved the armed elements of either side. Sniping became a real menace not only for Jews and Arabs, but at times for the British also, whose duty it was to find and deal with the offenders. In spite of all instructions from their own leaders, individual Arabs frequently engaged British troops. This happened either for the purpose of arms stealing, or as the result of troops being mistaken for Jews, or sometimes because Arabs, when they are excited, often cannot resist the temptation of letting their gun off at anything that moves. The same trouble was experienced to a certain extent with the Jews, but for a different reason. In their case, sniping at British troops would normally be practised by the extremists only, and rarely because of mistaken identity; some were still interested in taking British lives when they had the chance. Only one day during December passed in the Divisional sector without one or more incidents taking place, and on some days they were so numerous that it was not possible to record them all. But it was not until 30th December that the first real major incident took place—a communal riot at the C.R.L. oil refinery at Haifa.

It started when I.Z.L. gangsters threw two bombs from a passing car among a large group of Arab employees waiting for transport outside the refinery. This act resulted in 6 Arabs being killed and over 40 wounded, many of them seriously. The casualties were immediately taken into the refinery First Aid Post, on the way to which they were seen and questioned by their compatriots working in the refinery. The reaction of the latter was instantaneous, and within minutes Jews were being beaten to death in all parts of the refinery. The rioting spread so rapidly that there was little which the British staff could do to control it. A small party of police were the first of the security forces to arrive, and, though outnumbered by hundreds to one, succeeded in saving many Jewish lives. Their conduct during the riot, in which they had to deal with enraged Arabs who had gone quite berserk, was very courageous and in the finest traditions of the Palestine Police. Reinforcements soon arrived from 2nd/3rd Parachute Battalion and before long the situation was under control. It was decided to clear the refinery of all Arabs and Jews except the ghaffirs as soon as possible, and they were taken in buses back to their homes, escorted by armoured cars of 3rd Hussars.

Owing to the fact that Arabs outnumbered Jews in the refinery by about four to one, all subsequent casualties were suffered by the Jews, of whom 41 were killed and 48 injured. In spite of the fact that this massacre was the direct outcome of the initial attack by the I.Z.L. which caused some fifty casualties to the Arabs, the Hagana felt itself obliged to carry out a reprisal. The following night the Arab village of Balad es Sheik, which lies three miles south-east of Haifa, was attacked by a strong party of armed Hagana, who entered the village dressed as Arabs under heavy covering fire from the high ground. Firing sub-machine guns and throwing grenades into the houses, they succeeded in killing 14 Arabs, of whom 10 were women and children, and wounding 11. Their own casualties were slight.

No better example than the above could be found of the type of incident, which from this stage onward happened commonly in all parts of the country where Jews and Arabs shared the same locality. As time passed they became more frequent and the burden on the Security Forces grew accordingly.

SYRIAN INVASION

It was not until the middle of December that trouble started brewing in the Frontier Sub-sector. There had been one or two very minor incidents, but nothing of consequence happened until Safad flared up on the 13th. Sniping between Jews and Arabs started after a Jew who had gone into the Arab market disappeared. Firing soon became intense and casualties were suffered on both sides. The police called for military assistance and one troop of the T.J.F.F. with armoured cars in support moved into the town to restore order. Later the same day they were reinforced by a company of 8th Parachute Battalion and a curfew was imposed. From this day onwards, until the final evacuation of Safad by the administration, there was always a company of British infantry in the town. For its size Safad probably gave more trouble than any other town in Palestine. It is built in a very commanding position about 2,750 feet above sea level and was inhabited by some 12,500 people in the proportion of three Arabs to one Jew. A further outbreak occurred on the 21st in which the Parachute company was engaged freely by the Arabs. The latter appeared to be incensed at being prevented from waging their own private war against the Jews. During the firing a corporal was wounded, but in spite of great provocation, the time had still not been reached for really offensive counter-action, and it is recorded that the company fired only eleven rounds of rifle fire during the day. Soon British troops were returning fire with interest whenever they could spot either Arabs or Jews who had engaged them.

On 18th December there was trouble in the Huleh Valley when Jews entered the Arab village of Khissas, near the Syrian frontier, and killed 10 and wounded 5 Arabs, most of whom were women and children, with grenades and machine-gun fire. They withdrew without suffering any casualties after leaving pamphlets stating that the attack was carried out by the Hagana as a reprisal for casualties suffered in Safad, and an incident near Khissas where a Jew had recently been killed by Arabs. The latter event had been in turn a reprisal for the shooting of an Arab by a Jewish Settlement policeman. So the system of one life for another, and often ten lives for another, was fostered. The attack on Khissas, in which 2 Lebanese and 2 Syrian visitors had been killed, resulted in the first hostile invasion of Arab irregulars over the frontier from Syria. The attack did not materialize at once, however, and in the meantime tension grew throughout the length of the Valley.

In order to maintain control of the Valley, Commander T.J.F.F. moved reinforcements up to the middle of the troubled area and imposed a road restriction, hoping to reduce the mobility of both sides and prevent any tip-and-run attacks with the use of transport. The situation, though strained, got no worse over Christmas, and on 27th December the T.J.F.F. were reinforced by 17th/21st Lancers, 1st Parachute Battalion and detachments of Divisional Royal Artillery, Royal Engineers and Royal Army Medical Corps.

One of the problems in the area was the defence of the Jewish settlements which lay close to the frontier, overlooked by high ground from which the Arabs could at least make life very difficult by sniping. A more serious possibility was the elimination of one or more of these colonies by a well-organized attack. The first attempt by a large Arab band to carry out such an attack was on 9th January, 1948, in which the settlements of Dan and Kafr Szold were attacked by two forces of Arab irregulars estimated in strength at 80 and 50 respectively. A troop of armoured cars of 17th/21st Lancers was dispatched to the scene of each engagement, where they both came under sporadic small-arms fire from the Arabs. The Jews, not unnaturally, were quite pleased to see them. The troops replied to the Arab fire sparingly at first, and more generously as the day lengthened and their patience diminished. Eventually the heavy armament of the cars was brought into play and their two-pounder shells had a very salutary effect. During the engagements several of the armoured cars and scout cars were hit but not damaged. In the middle of the morning there was a call for air support on Tel el Qadi, where the Arabs were in a strong position. In response to this request a number of Spitfires arrived soon after and carried out dummy attacks on the target area. The moral effect even of unarmed fighters was for some time enough to disperse Arabs on occasions such as this. Later in the day troops of 1st Parachute Battalion joined in the battle with 3-in. mortars. The combined effect of the British counter-measures eventually persuaded the Arabs to call off their attacks and retire over the frontier.

While the main engagements at Dan and Kafr Szold had been in progress, elsewhere skirmishing and ambushing had taken place. The Arabs tried to prevent the troops from getting to the scene of each operation by erecting road-blocks, which fortunately were hastily constructed and therefore soon removed. During the day the Jews suffered 9 killed and wounded; the Arab casualties were not known, but were probably much the same, and the troops had none. The very successful outcome of the operation was largely due to the manner in which the situation was handled throughout by Lieutenant-Colonel H. C. Blackden, Officer Commanding The Mechanized Regiment, T.J.F.F. He was responsible for the whole of the northern frontier and all British troops operating in the area came under his command. For his conduct on this and many other occasions, he was later awarded the Distinguished Service Order.

Following this operation and another very similar one four days later in the same area, representations to Syria were made through diplomatic channels requesting that she should take steps to prevent any further cases of frontier violation by her irregulars. With the possibility of relations becoming strained it was very important that there should be no more cases of British troops inadvertently crossing into Syria. There had been a number of instances of this in the past and they were quite rightly frowned on. They were usually caused by errors in map reading, and the parties concerned would find themselves taken prisoner at a frontier post inside Syria. There they would be treated with great courtesy and hospitality and later returned to the British authorities. The last recorded occasion was not without its humorous side, although perhaps this is more apparent in retrospect.

A certain unit was about to be visited and inspected by the Brigadier. Just as he was due to arrive a subaltern found in his lines a truck loaded with old tentage and salvage due to leave the same day for Sarafand. The driver was in fatigue order and his mate likewise, and neither in the opinion of the subaltern, was in a proper state to be seen by a Brigadier at any time, far less during an inspection. "Take that —— truck out of the camp at once and don't come back for half an hour" he ordered sharply and with a trace of panic in his voice. The two soldiers and their truck disappeared in a cloud of dust. Neither of them had ever been to the other side of the Lake (Sea of Galilee), and here was the ideal opportunity for a nice spin round the far shore and back to lunch, by which time the Brigadier would certainly be gone. Unfortunately, neither of them realized that the Syrian frontier followed the north-east shore of the Lake and the inevitable happened. The ensuing correspondence still remains to this day a testimony to the difficulties which ultimately confronted two private soldiers, a subaltern and many more senior officers.

CHAPTER XV

THE BIRTH OF "CRAFORCE"

THE new areas of responsibility in the North Sector had hardly come into force in December, 1947, before news was received of the forthcoming disbandment of the T.J.F.F. The Force was due to leave Palestine in mid-January ostensibly for training in Trans-jordan, but in fact, subsequently for disbandment. It was important for several reasons that this should not become generally known until nearer the time. In the place of its Cavalry and Mechanized Regiments, 1st Battalion Irish Guards were to be placed under command of the Division. The "Micks" had already been under command on two previous occasions and the prospect of having them again was welcomed. But equally the departure of the T.J.F.F. was regretted. Their keen and hardy troops had done sterling service on the frontier, and, like the Arab Legion, were liked and respected by the British units which worked with them.

In order to maintain control of the frontier areas it was necessary to raise a force and provide it with a commander and headquarters to relieve the T.J.F.F. The 17th/21st Lancers and 1st Parachute Battalion were already deployed on the frontier, and to these was added 1st Battalion Irish Guards. Here was the equivalent to a first-class brigade and the Commander of the Divisional Royal Artillery, Brigadier C. H. Colquhoun, O.B.E., was appointed to command it. His headquarters, consisting mainly of Gunners, but including representatives from many other arms and services, was established in Tiberias in the same camp as the Regimental Headquarters of 17th/21st Lancers. The force was known as "Craforce."

The new layout came into being on 16th January, 1948. By this time 3rd Parachute Brigade and its headquarters had been disbanded, and Brigadier Rome had taken over command of 1st Parachute Brigade in Haifa from Brigadier O'Brien Twohig. 1st Brigade had already assumed command of the Acre Sub-district, and in order to compensate for this additional commitment and the loss of 1st Parachute Battalion, other units were placed under its command. In addition to 2nd Battalion The Middlesex Regiment, to which reference has already been made, 1st Regiment Royal Horse Artillery and 52nd Observation Regiment, Royal Artillery, were put under command for operations. The two last-named units already had certain other commitments, but they could each provide one battery in emergency. 66th Airborne Anti-Tank Regiment had also been removed to the eastern outskirts of Haifa in order to look after that side of the town and the "oil area." 3rd Hussars were now in sole command of the Nazareth Sub-district, so this left the remainder of Galilee, that is, the Sub-districts of Safad, Tiberias and Beisan, as the responsibility of "Craforce." This area was known as the Eastern Frontier Sub-sector and together with the other Sub-sectors remained as now constituted until the start of the final evacuation.

When "Craforce" took over the frontier from the T.J.F.F., the recent Arab attacks were still uppermost in the minds of the two communities. The Arab authorities were taking great care to point out to their local inhabitants that the attacks did not mark the opening of the Arab offensive; they were merely reprisals. Their problem during the next few months was to prevent a premature uprising, which, though directed against the Jews, would have to reckon with the British. If that should happen it would fail, and when the time came at the end of the Mandate for an all-out attack, the Arabs would have shot their bolt. At the same time, they had to maintain morale among their irregulars and the local inhabitants which could only be done by some sort of offensive action against the Jews. The irregulars, which were an advanced element of the much-vaunted A.L.A. (Arab Liberation Army) were billeted in Arab towns and villages throughout Northern and Eastern Palestine. Moreover, they were there at the expense of the inhabitants, and if they had nothing to show for their board and lodging the necessity for their presence would naturally be questioned. As it was, they were by no means welcomed by the moderate Arabs, who were not so keen on fighting the Jews as was generally imagined.

The Arab plan, at this stage, therefore, was to carry out a series

M

of small-scale actions directed principally at the Jewish lines of communication. These attacks served several purposes. They were easy to mount and never costly, which made them popular and therefore good for Arab morale. They had a definite training value, and at the same time fitted in with the long-term strategic policy by cutting off supplies to the outlying Jewish settlements. The longer a settlement could be cut off the more easily it would fall when the time came for its destruction. Apart from periodical harassing attacks on the settlements themselves, therefore, the Arabs concentrated on road ambushes, which at first had only a limited success, but as more trained experts, arms and equipment became available, grew in number and scope. They were bloody affairs and no quarter was given on either side. No prisoners were taken unless for a specific purpose, and very rarely were they returned alive. Both sides resorted on occasions to methods of torture in order to extract information or simply from deep hatred. In this respect the Jews probably used more scientific though just as unpleasant methods. The Arabs on the other hand used to mutilate the corpses of their victims beyond recognition, which resulted in some unpleasant work for the troops who had to remove them.

The role of the Army during these engagements was quite clear; it was to break them up as quickly and effectively as possible. As often as not this involved getting shot at first and then replying in order to drive off the offenders, which in this case were usually Arabs. To the units of "Craforce" this became almost a daily task, and it was necessary for their small columns to have all the firepower which would be necessary to establish their superiority. To intervene with too small a force at one time was a justifiable risk, as both the opposing communities were anxious to avoid antagonizing the British. Later the Arabs would attack troops if the latter were about to intervene; they rarely attacked a British column as such. Single vehicles or even pairs were always liable to be held up by Palestinian Arab banditti in isolated spots for the purposes of seizing arms from the drivers and passengers. If the latter resisted they would probably be shot, as on these occasions they were invariably outnumbered; otherwise, having been disarmed, they were allowed to proceed. This was possibly the worst decision which many dutiful British officers and other ranks had to make—whether

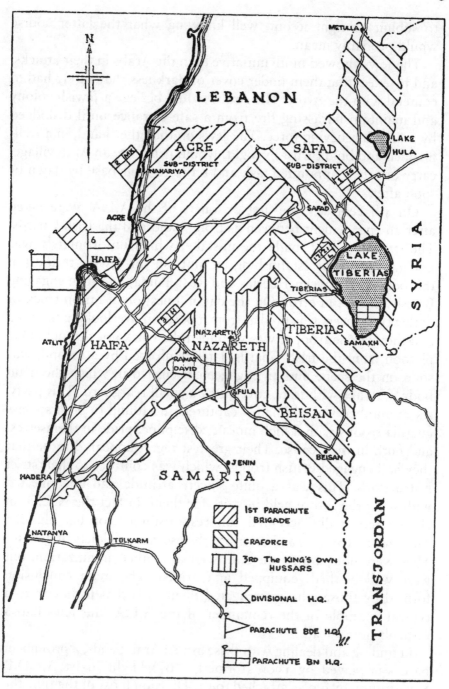

DIVISIONAL LAYOUT IN NORTHERN PALESTINE, 1948.

to submit or fight it out, well knowing what the latter course would probably mean.

The Jews showed more initiative than the Arabs in their attacks, and by executing them under cover of darkness they rarely had to contend with the Army. The Arabs would besiege a Jewish colony and maintain harassing fire from a safe distance until dislodged by a British relieving force. The Jews on the other hand, in a well-planned and bold thrust by night, would penetrate an Arab village, carry out their appointed task and retire to their base by dawn or soon after.

On 4th February the first prisoners of the A.L.A. were taken after an engagement between a strong band and the Irish Guards. The irregulars had made the mistake, which unfortunately was not infrequent, of establishing an ambush for Jewish traffic (on this occasion between Tiberias and Rosh Pinna) and then engaging British vehicles in error. On the day in question, a ration truck of 17th/21st Lancers was fired at from a position overlooking the road and though one trooper was wounded the truck got through. One platoon from the Irish Guards, later reinforced by a second, was soon on the scene and an engagement ensued in which the main body of Arabs withdrew, covered by a small rearguard. This party, six in number, was ultimately captured and found to be first-class guerilla troops with a high morale, discipline, pride in themselves, and faith in their cause. Their greatest regret appeared to be that they had engaged British troops, which was contrary to their strict instructions. This was a quite sincere attitude and unconnected with what the future held in store for them; in fact the N.C.O. in charge repeatedly accepted full responsibility for his blunder. They were all Syrians and described themselves as soldiers of honour. They were not paid by the A.L.A. or any other organization, but were well clothed, equipped and armed. The main conclusion formed by those who interrogated them, was that if they were a typical example of the remainder of the A.L.A. the Jews had a difficult time ahead.

In finding and dealing with these armed Arab bands, a prominent part was played by 1909 (formerly "B") Flight, 651st Air O.P. Squadron, which was attached to the Division most of the time the latter spent in Palestine. In their slow-moving and manoeuvrable aircraft, these gunners did some extraordinary things and sent back reports of incredible accuracy. On one occasion a pilot who had been flying over a hilly Arab area spotted a military truck which he was surprised to see by itself in that locality. He came low enough to take its registration number, and on reporting it the vehicle turned out to be one recently stolen from a unit in Haifa. On another occasion a pilot reported the strength of a party of Arabs who were dug in on a hillside to be "approximately twelve Syrians." They were eventually all captured and the T.J.F.F. sent back an immediate report giving their strength as eleven. As a result of this discrepancy in numbers, a strongly worded signal was sent to the Air O.P. Flight stating that " . . . the repercussions of such wild guesses cannot be over-emphasized . . . such lapses cannot be accepted, and it is requested that the attention of the pilot be drawn to this complaint." The laugh was with them in the end, however, as soon after a message was received from the T.J.F.F. amending their original figure from eleven to twelve. And twelve there were. The time came when the riggers were reported to be sickening of patching all the bullet holes in the wings and fuselages of the air O.Ps. and from then on, the pilots were not allowed below 3,000 feet when flying in an area of operations.

FIGHTING IN HAIFA

Until the announcement of Partition in November, 1947, Haifa had been remarkably free from communal strife. From the beginning of December until the final Battle of Haifa in April, 1948, the town was the scene of an ever-increasing struggle for mastery between its Jewish and Arab inhabitants. The British Security Forces were thus faced with the responsibility of maintaining law and order, a task which became more difficult with every day that passed.

Within the town the tactical advantages lay mainly with the Jews. From the main Jewish quarter of Hadar hak Carmel, which is the upper and modern part of the town, the Jews occupied a commanding position overlooking the Old Town, the main Arab quarter. Outside these areas the two communities in the remainder of the town were so intermixed that it would have been impossible for either side to lead an independent existence. Four roads lead into Haifa. The main coast road from the south, a second-class road which follows the line of the Carmel Ridge south-eastwards; the main road which runs under the eastern slopes of Mount Carmel and leads either to Nazareth or through the Plain of Esdraelon; and finally the road to Acre and the north. Neither the Arabs nor the Jews were in a position to command any one of these roads, all of which in their last few miles before entering the town passed through areas dominated by both communities. As a result either side was in a position to use its superiority within its own areas, and attack vehicles of the other as they passed through. Keeping these roads open therefore became a major military problem, as not only were they essential for the use of the Army, but on them depended the economic structure of the country. The Port of Haifa is the Port of Palestine, and not only was there a considerable volume of imports passing through it, but it was vital to the plan for the British withdrawal. The latter operation started months before the end of the Mandate, with the evacuation of all manner of stores by road, rail and sea. It is obvious, therefore, that it was of paramount importance to keep the port working. Nor could this be achieved unless there was some measure of law and order within the town. Without public confidence there would be no labour to run the port and the working of it would come to a virtual standstill. Nor was the labour only required in the port itself, but also in the depots whose stocks had to be moved, and on the railways which had to move them. There were also other associated problems such as the protection of the oil industry.

During the final six months as these problems began to show themselves, it became obvious that the Army was in for a difficult time. The communications and the oil installations stretched out into the open country, and even if these could be kept in a healthy condition, there remained the fundamental problem of Jew versus Arab within the town and its surrounds. To meet all these demands, 6th Airborne Division had at its disposal an ever-decreasing force with which to stand between the two communities who were daily becoming stronger. 3rd Parachute Brigade was in the process of disbanding, the T.J.F.F. was about to be withdrawn, as were a little later the Arab Legion. To replace these units, the equivalent of half the losses was all that could be spared. After all, the Army had to start thinning out some time, and to delay this process would only make the programme unworkable at the other end. So those troops which were available settled down to the task with determination, and what is more, enthusiasm. The brunt was taken by 2nd/3rd and 8th/9th Parachute Battalions commanded at this time by Lieutenant-Colonel T. H. Birbeck, D.S.O., and Lieutenant-Colonel J. H. M. Hackett, D.S.O., respectively. While one controlled the town, the other carried out escort duties, found the necessary reserves with which to back up the first, and took over a number of other tasks. There was little rest for either of them, and at approximately monthly intervals they changed over.

As in the case of other troubles which had gone before, Haifa flared up in spasms. Following the announcement on Partition, there was a short period of mob violence, in which the Arabs indulged in a campaign of arson and stoning attacks. The Jews reacted just as sharply, and from then onwards the situation deteriorated steadily. In mid-December there was a difficult period lasting for a few days in which reinforcements in the shape of the 3rd Hussars and part of the Divisional Royal Artillery had to be brought into the town to help restore confidence. Christmas saw a recrudescence, this time more pronounced, and again heavy calls were made on the troops to restore order. By this time certain bad spots in the town were becoming apparent. In these places the armed elements of either side were concentrated and carrying on their own little private war. Neither side was by any means ready for a large-scale offensive, and, as has already been mentioned, the Arabs in particular were very frightened of committing themselves prematurely. But they had their hotheads as had the Jews, and it took very few of them from either side to start a proper battle. At first it had been a matter of sniping. This soon developed into small-arms battles, backed with a few light automatics, and these rapidly increased in numbers as time passed. Later mortars and heavy machine guns were brought into play and, added to these, went on the battle of the bombs. Both sides were fascinated by the use of explosives; bombing and counter-bombing became more frequent and effective as more experts and material became available. From time to time there would be a truce, and indeed, for some days or even a week there would be no trouble apart from the sniping at night. While these uneasy truces lasted both sides were building up for the next onslaught; and when it broke it was usually bigger and better than the one before.

And what were the Security Forces doing all this time? It might be thought that only a little firm action was required in order to stop all the nonsense. Several factors, however, must be taken into account. Firstly, trouble of this description was taking place all over the country; not perhaps to the same extent, although in Jerusalem it was probably worse than in Haifa. It was not merely a matter of drafting an overwhelming weight of reinforcements into Haifa; they were not available, being committed elsewhere. Secondly, the British were on their way out of the country, and were no longer regarded by the rival communities in the same light as they had been formerly. What the authorities said now had to be backed with more power than hitherto and they were no longer the only party which was organized and ready to use force. To the Jews and Arabs only one thing mattered seriously now, and that was the balance of power between themselves. If the British got in the way they were prepared if necessary to oppose them, though both sides were anxious to avoid doing so for as long as possible. To oppose the British would be bad strategy, and would play into the hands of their enemies. For this reason the Security Forces were never faced with the organized and determined opposition of either side. This was most fortunate, though had it come about, the Army still had much up its sleeve.

In spite of all the fighting that went on in Haifa, the situation was never out of hand. The initiative was never lost. Most of the fighting was at night and the damage, which was heavy in places, was confined in main to the strips of no-man's-land. For a time, the Army took a hand in these proceedings at night, but this only added to the noise and general confusion, and threatened to risk British lives without gaining anything. So it was decided early on that no real harm could be done by night whether the troops intervened or not, provided that the movement of the contestants was restricted as much as possible by the imposition of curfews. By day it was essential that the Army took a very active part in the maintenance of order, and to this end it spared no efforts. The key to controlling

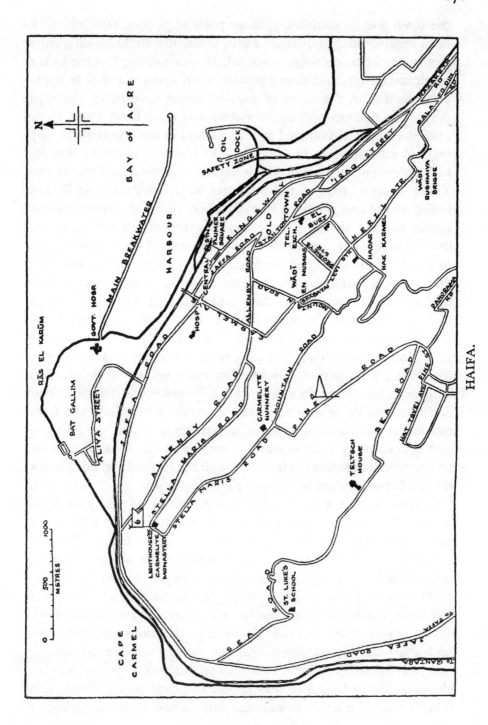

HAIFA.

the town was to establish military posts of platoon strength in the most commanding positions. From these, fire could be directed at any sniper or machine-gun nest which was causing trouble in that particular sector, and strong patrols could operate and take appropriate action in the event of trouble, being covered by the static posts. The best example of this system was Wadi Rushmiya. There, until the Army was obliged to take a hand in the proceedings, sniping and machine-gun fire used to take place regularly by day and night between the Jews on the west side and the Arabs on the east. This was soon brought under control when 1st Parachute Brigade took over the best positions on each side of the Wadi and established strong posts in them. It by no means stopped all the firing, but from then onwards any Arab or Jew who started shooting was liable to get more than he had bargained for. There were many other similar posts, where, by selecting the right buildings, it was possible to dominate all the surrounding area. Having done this, thought had to be given to the many other problems which emerged from the adoption of these positions. Their security was a matter of prime importance. They had to be of such a strength as to look after themselves for a period of a week or more without their garrisons becoming too weary from guards, O.P. duties and patrols. They had to be secure against all forms of attack, particularly the forms concerned with large quantities of explosives which could be presented in such a variety of ways. There had to be a sound administrative plan for feeding; in fact nearly all the tactical and administrative problems applied as for street-fighting in war.

At times when there was a battle in progress both Jews and Arabs used to keep within their own areas, but during the lulls it was necessary for traffic to move freely throughout the town. Naturally each side restricted its own movements into no-man's-land as much as possible because of the ever-present danger of sniping, but the movement of Arab traffic through Jewish-dominated areas, and vice versa, had to be maintained in order to avoid an economic breakdown. It was under cover of this necessity that both sides used their explosive vehicles and other means of causing widespread damage and casualties. The obvious counter to this was a system of roadblocks on all roads leading into Jewish and Arab areas, where every vehicle would be liable to examination. These began to spring up like mushrooms, quite unauthorized by the British authorities, and often manned by illegally armed Jews and Arabs. A small number of them were eventually given permission to remain and were provided with at least one policeman to represent the law. If they had confined their attentions to the vehicles of the other community they would have caused less trouble, but the Jews soon started to disguise their members as British troops and put them into British vehicles in order to escape examination by the Arabs. As a result, the Arabs tried to extend their assumed authority over army and police vehicles. This in itself might not have been a particularly serious matter, because the road-blocks were established by the Arab National Guard, a defence organization which was moderately disciplined and reasonable in outlook. The danger lay in the ambushes which were set up by the lawless elements in the guise of road-blocks. These forced military vehicles to stop, whereupon the miscreants would steal the arms of the passengers. They were always of sufficient strength to discourage resistance by single or even pairs of unarmoured vehicles, and as soon as an armoured patrol came into sight they were dissolved as quickly as they were established.

On the occasions when a party of Jews dressed as British troops and travelling in military vehicles succeeded in making a successful attack against an Arab objective a wave of anti-British feeling was liable to be directed against the nearest troops. Any soldiers who fell into Arab hands at such times were in great peril, and it was a matter of extreme urgency to circulate the true account of these attacks as soon as possible. On 22nd March there was an incident which very nearly ended disastrously for the three members of the Division concerned. Late in the afternoon, a jeep containing four Jews dressed as Airborne soldiers, and a three-ton truck containing two others similarly disguised, drove into Iraq Street. At the appointed place the Jews abandoned the truck which contained some 1,000 lb. of explosives with a time fuse attached and drove off in the jeep. The truck exploded soon after, killing four Arabs and wounding nineteen. As the story circulated through the Arab quarter the inhabitants became frenzied, and while they were in this state a jeep containing two British officers and their driver, belonging to Headquarters 1st Parachute Brigade, arrived on the scene to investigate the cause of the explosion. They were immediately seized by the enraged Arabs who were about to kill them, when some of the more responsible ones succeeded in moving them into the Suq in an ambulance. The ambulance itself, however, was boarded by about eight of the unruly ones and during the journey a heated council of war took place between them and the Arab escort as to whether the soldiers should not be killed without further ado. The moderates just managed to prevent this and the prisoners were handed over to the Headquarters. of the Arab Liberation Army in the Suq. There they were interrogated closely for some hours, and it was only after the Police had confirmed that they were *bona fide* British soldiers, and had nothing to do with the outrage, that they were released. In the end, the Arabs' apologies were profuse and genuine, but it had been a near thing.

The Jewish equivalent to the Arab National Guard was Mishmar Ha'am, their Civil Defence Organization. From these two bodies and various others in addition there came a never-ending series of requests to carry arms. This was only understandable, as unarmed men were in no position to stop fully armed gangsters from doing very much as they pleased. But an overriding principle which the Security Forces had to observe was to reduce the number of arms in circulation and not increase them. Any Jew or Arab who was found by a military patrol to be armed was immediately arrested and his weapon confiscated. The road-blocks which were ostensibly guarded by unarmed men were covered from unseen machine-gun positions. It was difficult for the Army to know just when to search for arms and when not to. Towards the end when both sides were so heavily armed there was little to be gained by arms searches unless there was some particular object. By so doing both sides would become antagonistic towards the British and many lives would be lost as a result. It was very doubtful, too, whether it would have had any appreciable effect on the volume of firing which was carried out during the periods of fighting. So from January onwards, searches were reserved for those parts of the town from which opposition was directed towards our troops or in which after due warnings, the inhabitants continued to make a nuisance of themselves. Then a number of vehicles containing troops and possibly police would converge on the selected area, establish a cordon and carry out a

FIGHTING IN HAIFA BY NIGHT.

THE FOLLOWING DAY.

PATROLLING WADI RUSHMIYA, HAIFA.

EXPLOSION BETWEEN HADAR HAK CARMEL AND
THE SUQ, HAIFA.

thorough arms search. The Jews had been collecting arms and ammunition for years and much of their war stores had been imported into the country, while the Arabs were bringing their supplies into the town daily from their own sources. Some came by road and some were smuggled in by night across country. It was impossible for the Security Forces to examine all traffic, as the vehicles carrying arms and ammunition were invariably loaded with some innocent load on top, such as oranges or cement. Unless there was any particular reason for suspecting a vehicle, the time factor alone ruled out the possibility of finding arms by searching at road-blocks. Even the effect of identity checks was enough to produce traffic blocks for hundreds of yards on the busy roads leading into Haifa.

A factor of tremendous importance to all sides was good intelligence. The Jews were experts at this, and not only did their own community co-operate freely in passing on to the Hagana anything of interest that they found out, but the latter organization also had working for them a number of Arab traitors whose greed for money exceeded their loyalty to their race. Once having accepted a bribe for information they were thereafter liable to blackmail by the Jews who were in a position to hand them back to their own side. The penalty for this crime, if discovered by their own side, was a very painful death. This gave the Jews a great advantage over the Arabs, as a Jewish agent working for the Arabs was unheard of. An example of how the Jews were able to make use of their intelligence service was the destruction of a small convoy of Arab vehicles on their way to Haifa from a neighbouring country. They were loaded with arms and explosives and carried the Commander-designate for the Arab forces in Haifa. They were attacked at a place several miles outside Haifa and a lucky shot detonated the explosives estimated at two tons, in one of the vehicles, and the convoy was destroyed and all the Arabs killed. There was no fluke about this, as one ambush had failed to stop the convoy some twenty miles away and the second one was established at very short notice. Against this standard of intelligence the Arabs were unable to compete, and in the end it contributed in no small measure to their downfall in Haifa.

To the British, intelligence was of equal importance. But just as much depended on good liaison with the Jewish and Arab leaders on all levels. Often it was difficult to establish who in fact were the leaders of the Jews and Arabs in the various areas; this was only natural because the latter did not want to be liable for the consequences of their actions or those of their subordinates. Thus, at times, negotiations and instructions had to be passed through mediums who were known to the authorities. Even so, as much trouble was avoided by this means as by the direct threat of force on the ground.

In March it became apparent that perhaps after all it might not be the Arabs who would open the offensive for the mastery of Haifa. The Jews were very conscious of the fact that time was on the side of the Arabs, and by waiting until the British had withdrawn, they might lose their opportunity of defeating the Arabs. In the meantime the latter had received considerable reinforcements of Syrian and Iraqi irregulars, some hundreds of whom were reported to be in the Suq and adjacent areas. At this stage, more than at any other, it was vitally important to "show the flag" in Haifa. For this purpose a mixed troop of tanks and self-propelled guns from Chestnut Troop of 1st Regiment Royal Horse Artillery was moved into the town. A squadron of 3rd Hussars had been under command of the Haifa Brigade for some months and together with the Chestnuts, much use was made of this armour in maintaining order. At varying intervals by day and night, mixed columns of tanks, armoured cars and infantry would patrol the streets. They had a very marked effect on the conduct of the opposing communities and if there was any cause to open fire on a Jewish or Arab post, there was a weight of firepower available which could take charge of all situations. Normally, machine-gun fire from the opposition was replied to in kind, but in the event of a sniper or post not "taking the hint," a round or two of 77 mm. or 25 pr. would be fired. On one occasion this treatment had to be applied to a particularly troublesome Arab post, and, in order to obtain the best results and endanger none of the surrounding property, the gun was fired at a range of 20 yards. The post was never occupied again !

Throughout these operations the troops concerned maintained an admirable impartiality. When they went into action it was normally against those who had first fired at them, and in these circumstances it was easy to fight. In the last few months which the

Division spent in Palestine, much of the sympathy which its members had felt inwardly towards the Arabs declined. The lawless elements had shown in this short period that they could carry out attacks very similar to those of the Jews, and many casualties were suffered at their hands. Their reason was almost invariably the stealing of arms, or the result of mistaken identity. But these excuses were little compensation to the troops. One important difference, however, was noticeable; there was rarely any lack of co-operation on the part of the responsible Arab leaders following a deliberate attack on troops. These they disliked as much as the British authorities, and made genuine and helpful efforts to prevent their taking place, to bring the perpetrators to justice and restore stolen arms and property.

CHAPTER XVI

THE DIVISION STARTS TO WITHDRAW

IT was in the middle of 1946 that the first serious rumours began to circulate about the move of the Division to Germany. At intervals thereafter, followed a series of reports which foretold how and when the move would happen. Indeed, their frequency was such that it became a standing joke among all ranks, and eventually there were many who would never believe another report until they found themselves on board ship. As a certain Brigadier announced one day: "For years Germany has been dangled before the Division like a carrot to a donkey. I should say we are no more likely to go there than West Africa." It was appropriate, therefore, that when at last by virtue of the Mandate nearing its end, the Division received executive instructions on its forthcoming move, the operation was given the code word "Carrot."

The plan provided for the return of the whole of the Division, less the Brigade Group already in Germany, to England in March and April where it would rest, refit and receive reinforcements before moving to join the British Army of the Rhine. In a matter of weeks, hopes of a brighter future crashed when it became known that it had been decided to disband the Division. News reached the Divisional Commander from the War Office at the end of January. In a signal to General Cassels who had recently been appointed to the Directorate which dealt with Airborne matters, the G.O.C. began "Personal for Cassels from poor old Stockwell." As might have been expected, the cipher branch at the War Office took this to be a corruption, and the signal was delivered without this characteristic touch. After conferences had been held in London and Palestine at which it was decided how and when the disbandment should be effected, the unwelcome news was released to all ranks on 18th February. Beside this sad announcement, all other setbacks which the Division had suffered appeared of little importance.

A VANTAGE POINT IN HAIFA OCCUPIED BY TROOPS OF
1st PARACHUTE BRIGADE.

ROYAL MARINE COMMANDOS IN DEFENCE OF HAIFA PORT,
APRIL, 1948.

The forthcoming disbandment made little difference to the plan for the withdrawal from Palestine. In any case, the broad outline plan had already been made, and the Division was scheduled to leave during March and April. In the end, because it was not going to Germany, several of its units and part of its Headquarters were retained in Palestine until after the end of the Mandate. The remainder, starting at the beginning of March with the Divisional Royal Artillery, moved as originally planned.

The British evacuation as a whole was to be carried out as a normal military operation. The withdrawal would take place in phases when the Mandate terminated, and for a period not exceeding two and a half months a British enclave would be established round Haifa from which the final evacuation would be carried out. It was thought at one time that there might be a security force of the United Nations to take over the country, or at least Jerusalem, and the U.N.O. Commission for Palestine which had been appointed to supervise the implementation of partition pressed strongly for such a force. It was not forthcoming, however, and as Britain had at last convinced the world of her resolution to quit, her forces prepared to withdraw leaving a vacuum behind them. Not that anyone expected it would remain a vacuum for long, as in all areas that were not wholly occupied by Jews or Arabs, there would obviously be a trial of strength sooner or later. In many cases it took place before the British had left, because the farther the withdrawal progressed, the fewer the troops available for the maintenance of law and order, and those which were available were largely committed on tasks of major importance such as the guarding of communications. A problem with which commanders were increasingly faced was how to adopt the best course in dealing with the two communities. On the one hand, there were the obligations until 15th May, when the Mandate ended, to uphold the administration and preserve the peace; on the other was the necessity of saving British lives and avoiding the antagonism of either side which might develop in the event of undue force being used in holding the ring. In the latter event, the successful completion of the British withdrawal itself might be jeopardized. The course to be taken called for a nice judgment.

In the last week of January there had arrived in Haifa, 40th

N

Commando Royal Marines who were based on Malta. This unit was placed under operational command of the Division and was given as its main task the responsibility of protecting the Port of Haifa and thus ensuring that the evacuation by sea might proceed with the minimum interference. This they did with an enthusiasm and efficiency similar to that of the Parachute Battalions who were their neighbours employed on similar duties outside the Port. For a short time after their arrival some wondered how red and green berets would mix, but they need not have worried, as each recognized the worth of the other and a firm friendship was soon established. At the same time, the Division was thankful to hand over to the Royal Navy the entire commitment for the transhipment of the Jewish illegal immigrants who were still arriving at Haifa. 40th Commando Royal Marines also played a prominent part in these operations.

The first troops of the Division to leave Palestine were those of the advance parties who sailed in H.T. *Franconia* from Haifa, on 6th March. From then onwards, troopships visited Haifa almost weekly and on occasions several in quick succession. Others in which the Division travelled were *Samaria, Durban Castle, Otranto, Georgic, Empress of Australia, Empress of Scotland,* and *Strathnaver.*

At noon on 3rd April, Divisional Headquarters closed down. For two and a half years the Operations Room had been manned day and night, and to those who had worked there it was strange to realize that at last it was all at an end. The telephone stopped ringing and the wireless crackling, and the last of countless thousands of log sheets was finished. In those sheets was written the hour-to-hour story of 6th Airborne Division in Palestine.

On the closing down of Divisional Headquarters, control of the North Sector passed to a small Tactical Headquarters headed by the Divisional Commander, who attached himself to Headquarters North Palestine District which was situated a mile farther back along the Carmel Ridge close to Headquarters 1st Parachute Brigade. The new headquarters, which was to command the late Divisional area until the end of the Mandate, was known as Headquarters G.O.C. North Sector.

On 6th April, 1st Parachute Brigade handed over control of Haifa to 1st Guards Brigade, which, until 15th May came under command of G.O.G. North Sector, and thereafter under Head-quarters Palestine which moved from Jerusalem to Haifa as the Mandate ended, 1st Parachute Brigade, less 1st Parachute Battalion, embarked on 16th and 23rd April for England. There remained in Palestine a Divisional rearguard consisting of the G.O.C. with his Tactical Headquarters, 3rd Hussars, 1st Airborne Squadron Royal Engineers, 1st Parachute Battalion and 317th Airborne Field Security Section. Of all these and the parts they played there will be more to say later.

THE ARAB LIBERATION ARMY

It was not easy to follow, even in a general sense, the developments in the formation and growth of the Arab Liberation Army, since those who affected it most deeply chose to make few announcements. The British authorities, therefore, could only await events and piece together reports which came in from all quarters. The Arab tends to place his belief in what he likes to believe and not in what established facts should lead him to believe. He is given to unbounded optimism, for which too often there is no justification. Moreover, having convinced himself of something he proceeds to pass it on to others in a slightly exaggerated form. Thus, before the story has passed through many mouths, it becomes quite unrecognizable from the original. Largely because of this characteristic, accurate information on such a red-hot topic as their own Liberation Army became almost impossible to gather. Following the original grandiloquent announcements broadcast from the neighbouring Arab states on the composition of the Arab League Army which was preparing to invade Palestine, a series of wild rumours followed each other round the country. Reports were received of vast concentrations of fully armed Arabs supported by a formidable array of tanks, artillery and aircraft. These stories, however, were gradually broken down, and by February, 1948, it was possible to gain some sort of picture of what in fact the A.L.A. then in Palestine, consisted.

The strength of the "Army" by the end of February had perhaps reached 10,000, but even this figure might have been on the high side. Reinforcements were thought to be arriving from the neighbouring Arab states at the rate of 1,000 a month, so it was going to be some time before the force was likely to achieve spectacular results. All its members were trained up to a reasonable level and carried a firearm of some description, although there was no standardization in that respect. The heavy equipment was thought to include a small number of pieces of varying calibre, a few armoured cars, perhaps a few tracked vehicles (carriers or light tanks) and no aircraft. The "Army" was organized into several "Divisions" which were named after past Arab successes in the field, or notable Arab leaders. The field commander at the time was one Fawzi Kawukji, a colourful guerilla leader during the Arab Rebellion, whom the British had placed in exile. He established his headquarters in that part of the country known by the Arabs during their Rebellion as "The Dangerous (or 'Terror') Triangle" (Nablus–Jenin–Tulkarm), which he hoped to restore to its legendary fame in the forthcoming campaign against the Jews. How firmly Fawzi was established as army commander was uncertain, as many others were known to be in the running, and behind the scenes was the ex-Mufti trying to place his own nominees in as many important posts as he was able. The post of C.-in-C. to the A.L.A. which at that time appeared not to entail its command in the field, but the policy behind its growth and administration, was held by an Egyptian.

In the "Army" was reported to be a number of skilled Europeans who occupied posts as instructors and commanders, but it was difficult to estimate how many they were. In recruiting their troops, the Arabs were reported to be having difficulties in avoiding those whose enthusiasm was inspired by hopes of banditry and looting; they were likely to be more of a hindrance than a help to the "cause" and were not encouraged. The standard of discipline was commendable, and penalties were severe. Bad cases of stealing were punishable by death and that sentence was on occasions carried out.

The Arab commanders by no means confined their attentions to their troops, but assumed authority over the whole of the Arab population in their areas. They issued edicts from time to time announcing their policy, and it took a strong and possibly foolhardy man to disagree with a "Liberation Army Officer." A communiqué issued in the Old City of Jerusalem by the local Arab commander after two British constables had been murdered on 17th February, read as follows:—

1. It is forbidden for the inhabitants of the Old City to be out after 10 p.m. or to use firearms except by military (Arab) order until further notice.
2. Every person who kills a Britisher or opposes any member of the Palestine Police or Army will be tried before the military commander responsible for the safety of the inhabitants.
3. Any person who has any knowledge of the killing of the two British constables must give a statement before the military commander of the Old City, and if it is proved that the criminal is the killer and does not give himself up, he will be sentenced to death by shooting and his family expelled to another town.
4. Any person who attempts to steal arms from any member of the Palestine Force or from civilians will be punished most violently and sentenced to imprisonment for an unlimited period at the expense of his family.
5. Thieves or persons forging Palestine currency will be sentenced to life imprisonment at the expense of their families until the cessation of the National Struggle.
6. Persons who oppose the National Guard in his duties which he has been ordered to carry out by the Military Commander will be punished by an emergency field court martial.
7. Any person whom it is proved to us has disobeyed any of these orders will be considered a traitor to his fellow men and will be tried by a court-martial in a secret committee.

In other parts of the country, Arab underground courts adopted a less stringent attitude as reflected in the following statement issued one day in Gaza:—

Last Friday thieves broke into the store of the Public Works Department in Gaza and carried away all the contents. Arab Defence Personnel and National Guardsmen apprehended the thieves in less than twelve hours and returned the goods. The thieves were tried. Sentence is expected on Monday, as the court arose early for the week-end to shoot quail in the Negeb.

The first major engagement fought by the A.L.A. took place during the night, 15th/16th February, when a force of some 500 irregulars attacked a Jewish settlement in the Jordan Valley called Tirat Tsevi, which lies a few miles south of Beisan. The operation was under the command of a Syrian whose instructions were to cut the roads leading to the settlement in order to prevent Jewish reinforcements or British relief from interfering. This done, he was to deploy his force and invest the settlement; under no circumstances was he to engage British troops.

Fortunately for the Jews, the plan miscarried. The demolition parties, whose task it was to blow certain culverts on the roads leading north from the settlement, made a poor job of it, and later, a small force from 1st Parachute Battalion was able to bypass the craters. But it was probably the sound of these demolitions that gave the Jews the alarm, and when eventually the attack came, they were completely prepared for it, and from their settlement defences they made havoc with the Arab assault. The attackers advanced with great gallantry though little skill, and never reached their objective. Insufficient training resulted in a frontal attack at dawn, supported by inadequate covering fire, being broken up with heavy casualties. While the Arabs were reorganizing and a further assault was threatened, the Mukhtar signalled by lamp (their telephone wires had been cut) to a neighbouring settlement for police and military assistance. The message was passed on to Beisan, and at 0730 hours a platoon with 3-in. mortars and machine-guns under command was on its way from the company of 1st Parachute Battalion stationed at Beisan, together with a party of Police.

At the Arab village of As Samariya, three miles west of the besieged settlement, the small British column met the Arab Headquarters and echelon. The situation which was tense to start with was soon brought under control when the British and Arab commanders went into conference. The Arab was instructed to withdraw immediately with the whole of his force, an order which would have been difficult to enforce had the Arabs chosen to ignore it. Fortunately, however, the Arab commander was under clear instructions from his own superior officer to avoid such an impasse, and he agreed to withdraw on one condition; in order not to lose face with the Jews he requested that the British column should simulate a battle by putting down a concentration of mortar and machine-gun fire to a flank. This being a harmless request and not worth disputing, the British Commander (Major R. Steele) agreed, and at the appointed time the barrage was produced and the Arabs started to withdraw.

At 1300 hours the platoon group made its way to Tirat Tsevi where it found the Jews engaged in mopping-up operations. There was still firing in progress, and it appeared that either the orders for withdrawal had not reached some of the Arabs, or they were engaged in a protracted rearguard action. An area to the south-west of the settlement was still proving troublesome and the troops put down a concentration of mortar and machine-gun fire to speed the Arabs on their way. When the casualties were reckoned for each side the weight of the Jewish victory became obvious. The Arabs suffered some eighty casualties of which about half were killed, while the Jews lost one killed and two wounded.

As can well be imagined, this reverse lowered morale somewhat in the "Dangerous Triangle" and a period of some six weeks was spent in reorganizing and recovering from the defeat. The Syrian commander was relieved of his post the following day. Farther afield, news of the attack spread through Arab towns and villages with customary speed, but the account became so distorted in the telling that soon the Arabs were convinced that the operation had been a resounding success rather than the miserable failure that it was. This habit of falsification and exaggeration, which was prac-tised to such an extent by the Arabs, rarely affected the British troops one way or the other; when it did the effect could be either amusing or exasperating. A typical example occurred ten days after the Tirat Tsevi operation.

On 26th February, a reconnaissance patrol of two armoured cars of the 3rd Hussars was ordered to try and find out whether it was possible for armoured vehicles to cross the Plain of Esdraelon from Ramat David to Lajun. The route took the patrol close to the Arab village of Kafr Lidd. When about 200 yards distant from the village, the two cars were engaged with intense small-arms fire by the inhabitants, some thirty of whom advanced from the village towards the patrol, firing as they came. The officer in com-

mand and two others of the patrol had been in the process of recon-
noitring on foot the River (Brook) Qishon and were a short
distance from their cars. Nevertheless, hastened somewhat by the
Arabs, and covered with fire from the patrol, they succeeded in
regaining their turrets without mishap. In order to avoid inflicting
unnecessary casualties on the Arabs the patrol then withdrew.

The following day the same officer with a small escort returned
to Kafr Lidd, this time by the normal track leading to the village
which they reached without incident. Once they were identified
as British the Arabs became very friendly. The officer then asked
for an account of the shooting which had occurred the previous
day. Thereupon he was treated by the Mukhtar to a dramatic
account of how the village had been attacked by 300 fully armed
Jews supported by four armoured vehicles. After a bloody engagement in which 100 of the Jews had been killed, the attack had been
broken up and the Jews put to flight. Arab casualties had been
"very few." The officer then explained that he had been the object
of the Arabs' attacks and he wanted to know the reason why. The
Arabs showed a suitable degree of astonishment and were definitely
impressed by the harangue which followed, and explained that they
must have mistaken the British patrol for Jews; they were most
apologetic and the visit ended on a very cordial note with the
customary coffee party.

MEDIATION AT MISHMAR HA EMEQ

While the withdrawal of the major part of the Division from
Palestine was in full swing, a difficult situation arose on the main
road between Haifa and Jenin. This road was obviously vital to
the Arabs, not only as a military line of communication, but also
for commercial purposes. It appeared from reports that the Jews
had been conducting harassing attacks and sniping on Arab transport and some sort of counter-action was expected.

The first indication of abnormal activity was at 1700 hours,
on 4th April, when small-arms and mortar fire was observed in the
area of the Jewish settlement of Mishmar ha Emeq which lies
midway between Haifa and Jenin overlooking the disputed road.
The nearest British unit was the 3rd Hussars, stationed at Ramat

OPERATIONAL ROUTINE.

David on the other side of the Plain of Esdraelon. They were unable to intervene on the opening night owing to the approach of darkness, but on the following morning three troops went to investigate, and found a large Arab force surrounding the settlement. Firing had temporarily stopped and after the Arab commander had been found, talks were opened in rather a strained atmosphere as the British commander made it quite clear that the Arabs would have to withdraw without any further fighting. The Arab commander, however, was only a deputy and was unable to accede to such an order without permission from his superior, who was not available. The conference became more cordial after a while and the local Arab District Officer undertook to see that no more fighting occurred, so the British force withdrew and returned to its base. In any case it would have been unable to impose its will on the Arabs even with the use of all the force at its disposal, had the latter chosen to be difficult. From reports and evidence available it appeared that the Arab force numbered about 1,000 armed irregulars of the A.L.A. supported by a few armoured cars and some artillery. There were in addition a large number of local Palestinian Arabs, inadequately armed, totally undisciplined, and thoroughly despised by the irregulars of the A.L.A.

The night passed without incident and on the following day all was quiet until the late afternoon when firing broke out again in the same area; this time the Arab artillery was heard in action and shells were seen to be bursting in and around the settlement. Once more it was too late to intervene until the following morning when three troops of armoured cars set out again for the settlement, this time with the Commanding Officer, Lieutenant-Colonel C. A. Peel. The settlement appeared to be peaceful, but the Arabs were still very much in evidence, and this time the Arab Commander of the operation together with his higher commander was present. On being told that the fighting must stop he replied that he had come to Palestine to fight and not to eat. He went on to say that he was quite prepared to delay his operations until after 15th May, but he had to protect the Arabs in his area. According to him the Jews had started the fighting, and had completely demolished the village of Tahta close by; if they would undertake not to carry out any further attacks on this area, and to stop their sniping of Arab traffic, he would withdraw his troops. Colonel Peel then visited the Jews in the settlement and spoke to one who was acting as Mukhtar. He explained the Arabs' terms for a truce which he backed as perfectly fair; would the Jews accept them and make the necessary undertaking? The answer was that neither he (the Jew) nor anyone else present had the necessary authority to do so, but he would get into touch with his superiors; in the meantime he would support a truce for twenty-four hours. This being agreed, all the women and children in the settlement were evacuated by the 3rd Hussars to another colony outside the area of operations. The local Arabs hailed the truce as a great victory for some reason known only to themselves, and to show their approval they started firing their weapons wildly into the air. This only infuriated the irregulars who set upon them with sticks and anything else which came to hand. Fortunately the fusillade was not taken as a violation of the truce.

The next day the negotiations were continued, but the Jews had been unable to obtain the necessary authority to give their undertaking, so the truce was extended for a further twenty-four hours. The Jews remarked, as the troops prepared to leave, that the additional time would enable them to bring up reinforcements during the night. Colonel Peel instructed that under no circumstances should they do this as it would be breaking the truce. However, that is exactly what did happen, and during the night the Hagana not only brought up a great number of reinforcements from Afula and the neighbouring settlements, but carried out an attack on the adjoining Arab village of Abu Shusha which they partially destroyed. In the morning, when negotiations were due to start again, the Jews failed to turn up, and after the events of the night the Arabs were in no mood to agree to any further truces. In such a position it was difficult to remain impartial, but Colonel Peel instructed them firmly to disengage, and he prepared to visit the settlement once more. He appreciated that with such a concentration of excited Arabs and Jews in the area, to try and reach the colony with a show of force would take more than the two or three troops which he had available, so he set out in his jeep with a British policeman. 1,000 yards from the settlement they came under small-arms fire and were forced to withdraw.

The truce having thus broken down completely, there was little for the British to do unless it was intervene with a very superior force; that, however, was not available in the necessary strength. The main road had been cratered and was impassable to wheeled vehicles without the necessary repairs and without the occupation of the high ground by picquets. The Arabs had in the early stages of the negotiations stated that even if the British were compelled to fire on them in the execution of their duty they would not return the fire. This sentiment was genuine and therefore touching, but although their attitude towards the troops was no less friendly later, it was doubtful whether in view of the violation of the truce, they could easily be removed. Very reluctantly it was decided that there was nothing further to be done without risking many British lives and incurring the antagonism of certainly one and possibly both sides. The troops were therefore withdrawn.

What happened ultimately was not accurately known as the road remained closed for a period, and it was impossible to observe the results of the fighting. It seemed, however, that stalemate was reached, and the Arabs eventually withdrew after both sides had suffered a number of casualties.

CHAPTER XVII

THE BATTLE FOR HAIFA

DURING April, the A.L.A. in Haifa had received very considerable reinforcements composed mainly of Iraqi, Syrians, ex-T.J.F.F. and a few Europeans. For a variety of reasons the Arab force had been getting the worst of the fighting with the Jews. Most significant was the lack of unity in the Arab command; unlike the Jews the Arabs had no uniform policy, added to which was the poor standard of their leadership and an inferior tactical position. The reinforcements, however, enabled the Arabs to take a more offensive line, and for a short time they were threatening to drive a wedge into the centre of Hadar hak Carmel. The Jews replied vigorously to the threat and themselves called up reinforcements. The result was an intensification of the fighting between Jews and Arabs throughout all the contested areas of the town. Firing of small arms and mortars and demolition of strong-points went on continuously at night, with the British troops (now 1st Guards Brigade) joining in only when they became the object of aggression. Even so, they became involved in a number of engagements mostly by night in which the use of 37-mm. guns of the 3rd Hussars and P.I.A.Ts. (Projectors, Infantry, Anti-Tank) were accompanied by a great weight of machine-gun fire. By 17th April these alarms and excursions had developed into a battle for fire superiority and judging by both sounds and results was comparable to a street-fighting battle of modern war.

The troops were having a particularly trying time of it; 1st Battalion Coldstream Guards in the town based on Peninsula Barracks, 1st Battalion Grenadier Guards on the eastern side and outskirts of the town, and 40th Commando Royal Marines in the port were all fully committed. They got little rest by night owing to the noise of the battle and the necessity for guarding their own positions against attack, while during the day from first light onwards they were patrolling, picqueting, escorting and dealing with the infiltrations and sniping of both sides. Equally stretched and playing a vital part in supporting the Infantry and Royal Marines were the armoured cars of the 3rd Hussars (now reduced to one sabre squadron—"C" Squadron) and a troop of the 1st Regiment, Royal Horse Artillery consisting, of one Comet tank and two self-propelled guns. As the situation deteriorated and "minimum force" in local troop and platoon engagements had to give way to something approaching maximum force, the roles of the armour became more vital. The effect of their guns on snipers' posts resulted in their being called upon more and more, and at times they were the only vehicles which could travel with impunity in areas under small-arms fire.

The Jewish-Arab struggle for domination of the town continued to intensify, and by 19th April it was obvious that an open battle was about to develop in which the British, by virtue of their relative weakness in numbers and their dispersion of troops would be unable to play a decisive part. An assault by Jews or Arabs would no longer respect British lives, as the major issue would be the domination of the town through the defeat of their opponents. In order to achieve this object, whichever side launched the offensive would require a number of the tactical positions then held by British troops. There would be heavy fighting and loss of life.

The Divisional Commander (now G.O.C. North Sector) was faced with a particularly difficult decision. There were no reinforcements available from outside the sector, as elsewhere British troops, now steadily withdrawing from the country, were no less occupied. Within the Sector, "Craforce" constituted the only possible reserve, but not only was it doubtful whether the whole or part of it could be redeployed in time, but the British authorities were still responsible for the security of Galilee, and in that district "Craforce" was already having its own troubles. To have reduced it would have endangered the balance of the force left behind; to have moved the whole of it would have been the signal for open warfare to develop behind it. It was therefore impossible to strengthen the British positions in Haifa. The decision to be taken was whether to leave the troops in their widely dispersed positions throughout the town or concentrate them in the areas which were vital to the successful completion of the British withdrawal. In the former case, heavy casualties were to be expected, one or both of the contestants were likely to be estranged with a resultant threat to the British withdrawal, and even then the effort might fail in its object. It was most questionable whether, with less than a month to go until the end of the Mandate, the possible retention of control over a non-vital area was worth the British lives at stake. The second course would enable the areas vital to the British, such as the port and the main roads leading to it, to be held firmly and the evacuation of troops and stores to proceed unopposed. Furthermore, it was less likely to involve the British in bloody fighting against either the Jews or the Arabs over an issue of no great material importance. On balance the evidence pointed towards this being the wiser course and it was therefore adopted.

No sooner was this decision made and put into effect than the final battle for Haifa took place. The Jews, who had been gradually gaining the upper hand, lost no time in mounting a well-planned attack which took place during the night 21st/22nd April. For several reasons it met with success so quick and complete that even the Jews themselves were confounded. Both Jews and Arabs had been informed of the British plan by the G.O.C. within an hour of each other on the morning of the redeployment (21st April), so there was no question of one side being in a position to plan an offensive through prior knowledge. Unfortunately, the Arabs seized on this distorted theory in order to lessen the blow of defeat and avoid recriminations for their own shortcomings. In fact, all their responsible leaders fled from Haifa immediately before or in course of the battle, and their troops who were completely demoralized by this example cracked under the weight of the Jewish attack. Early on 22nd April when complete Jewish victory was assured, members of the Arab National Committee approached the G.O.C. with the request that he should forthwith open truce negotiations on their behalf with the Jews. To this he readily agreed and the Jewish leaders were approached and expressed their willingness to enter into negotiations under British chairmanship. They produced their terms, which, considering the completeness of their victory, were fair and reasonable. They provided for the disarming of all Arabs and the placing under British guard of all alien Arabs and Europeans of the A.L.A. then in Haifa. After much deliberation the Arab leaders, fearing the consequences of agreeing to such total surrender, fought shy of their self-appointed task, and, on the pretext of not being able to guarantee observance of the truce terms, they withdrew. Nevertheless, the Jews had little difficulty in establishing their authority over all parts of the town not already under British control. There developed simultaneously an Arab refugee problem of vast proportions. The majority of the population panicked and thousands surged out of the town into the port whence they were evacuated to Acre. While they were thus in full flight they were engaged by the advanced Jewish posts which inflicted a number of casualties on them. The British Police did great work in restoring some measure of order outside the Suq and minimizing the effects of the panic, and the Royal Marines were equally outstanding in the port. The latter had three officers wounded by Jewish fire as they sought to control the stream of refugees, and there were some spirited exchanges of fire in which once again the armoured cars of the 3rd Hussars were prominent, using their 37-mm. and 3-in. guns with good effect. Meanwhile, the two Guards Battalions also had their problems in trying to restore confidence among the Arabs, helping to evacuate their wounded, and preventing looting. In all these tasks they were handicapped by Jewish snipers one of whom wounded Lieutenant-Colonel J. Chandos-Pole, commanding 1st Battalion Coldstream Guards.

As the situation was brought under control the firing died down and eventually stopped; the town was quiet by night for the first time for months, and the Jews set about consolidating their gains. Casualties were difficult to assess but from reports it appeared that the Jews had suffered some 20 killed and 40 wounded and the Arabs, 100 killed and 200 wounded. No sooner had the Jews consolidated their gains in Haifa than they planned to exploit their success with offensive operations farther afield using Haifa as their base. These intentions, however, were thoroughly thwarted by the Army which placed road-blocks on all exits from the town and denied passage to armed Jews. The town remained quiet until the final British evacuation, but the refugee problem increased. Tens of thousands of panic-stricken Arabs streamed out of Haifa and its surrounding villages, and made their way to the neighbouring States where they sought sanctuary. The journey was not without its perils since they were open to attack by the Jews on the way, so whenever practicable their convoys were afforded military protection as far as the frontiers. Within a week of their defeat at the hands of the Jews there were only 8-10,000 Arabs left in Haifa out of a normal population of some 50,000, and later that number was further reduced.

DIVISIONAL REARGUARD

The last of the main body of the Division left Haifa in the *Empress of Scotland* on St. George's Day, but there remained enough Red Berets in Palestine to justify this narrative being carried a stage farther. As will be seen, the Divisional Rearguard became even more widely scattered than the Division had been as a whole, and it is therefore difficult to trace simultaneously the various courses of its units through the last few eventful weeks. There remained until the end of the Mandate on 15th May, the G.O.C. with his Tactical Headquarters, Headquarters "Craforce," 3rd Hussars, 1st Parachute Battalion, 1st Airborne Squadron, Royal Engineers, and 317th Airborne Field Security Section.

The original plan for the withdrawal of the Division provided for 1st Parachute Battalion to return to the United Kingdom on or about 18th April at the same time as the remainder of 1st Parachute Brigade. In order to allow the necessary time for the closing down of its camps at Samakh and Beisan, the move to Haifa, the handing in of vehicles and stores, and the various other administrative complications, the Battalion was relieved of its operational commitments on 8th April. After the last few hectic months there was time for a little relaxation, but not for long. Early on 10th April a signal was received from Headquarters Palestine with a warning that the Battalion might be required to concentrate near Ramallah (for duties unknown). An hour or so later this was confirmed and the unit was ordered to move to Latrun "soonest," (this terrible but expressive word became very overworked). The Battalion was on the move in a matter of several hours for Haifa where it staged while detailed orders were awaited from 1st Infantry Division under whose command it had been placed. While in Haifa it drew from the Ordnance Depot a dozen assorted armoured vehicles which it manned with trained crews as though such was a matter of normal routine. The ability to do this lay with those in the Battalion who had served in the Guards Armoured Division during the war. In the following weeks this element of armour played a vital part.

Owing to the demands of demobilization and the shortage of reinforcements, the Battalion was down to a strength of less than 300 all ranks. The principal task assigned to it in the new areas was to assist in the protection of the Jerusalem–Sarafand road, via Ramallah. With Battalion Headquarters at the Latrun Police Post, which was the base, three strong detachments were deployed in important tactical positions, one of which was the pumping station at Bab el Wad at the foot of the pass leading to Jerusalem. There the Arabs carried out attacks on the heavily defended Jewish convoys on their way to Jerusalem with supplies. On 20th April the largest engagement to date between Jews and Arabs on this road took place at the same spot, and the Platoon in the pumping station was cut off completely. A small but formidable party consisting of a company commander, the Adjutant and the Regimental Sergeant-Major went out to lodge a protest with the Arab Commander and stop the fighting. Unfortunately they did not realize that there were several commanders, and after they had secured the co-operation of one who stopped the fighting in his own area, they ran into trouble on the way back at a spot where operations were still being conducted. Warning of danger was given by a host of Arabs on the roadside and the jeep was stopped at once right on top of a culvert from which a thin spiral of smoke was then seen. The jeep was evacuated in record time and the explosion happened a few seconds later. Fortunately something went wrong with the arrangements and the culvert was only cracked and the rather shaken party of umpires in the ditch was uninjured. The Arabs were unable to conceal their delight at such unexpected entertainment.

The battle continued to rage, without the British troops who were on the spot or those on the fringe, being able to influence it. The Arabs had obviously had prior warning of the arrival of the convoy and had concentrated in such numbers that the Jews suffered heavily losing some 40 lives, and 50 out of an estimated 150 vehicles. So thorough were the Arab demolitions that the road was indefinitely impassable to motor transport, and when after several days the

o

beleaguered platoon was relieved, it was by camel that they evacuated their equipment. This episode too was not lost on the Arabs.

On 24th April the Battalion was moved to Ramallah Police Station, from which it was ordered to do a battalion attack with the object of demilitarizing the Sheik Jarrah quarter of Jerusalem, which, at the time, was a battlefield for Jews and Arabs. However, with one detachment remaining at the Latrun pumping station and the one in Bab el Wad still cut off, it was decided that the Battalion was too weak to attempt the task, and 1st Battalion The Highland Light Infantry did it instead. The following day the Battalion was ordered to move into the Sheik Jarrah quarter and maintain it in a demilitarized state. The task was not an easy one, as Jews and Arabs were determined to infiltrate back into their former positions if opportunity offered, so the maximum effort had to be maintained by day and night. On 3rd May, 42nd Commando Royal Marines arrived fresh from Malta to reinforce the troops in Jerusalem; it was placed under command of 1st Parachute Battalion, which enabled most of the latter to return to Ramallah and carry out its original task of keeping the roads open. There was further fighting between Jews and Arabs on this road and the Battalion's armoured patrols in particular did much to minimize bloodshed. Here we must leave the Battalion for a while and examine how others of the Divisional rearguard were employed.

When 1st Parachute Battalion became unoperational in Galilee on 8th April in readiness for its embarkation, the only replacement which could be spared to "Craforce" was one troop from 1st R.H.A. which went to Beisan together with "B" Squadron 17th/21st Lancers. In Samakh the garrison was reduced to one platoon of the Irish Guards and one troop 17th/21st Lancers. With the numbers and intensity of Arab-Jew clashes growing daily and the reduced number of troops available to maintain control, it was no longer a proposition to try and cover the whole of Galilee. As a result, emphasis had to be placed increasingly on the control of a limited number of vital spots, and the keeping of the main roads open to traffic.

Within a few days of the withdrawal of 1st Parachute Battalion, the disturbances in Tiberias and Safad came to a head. In Tiberias there had for some time been street fighting on a smaller scale, but similar to that in Haifa, and on 14th April, while truce negotiations were in progress under the direction of Brigadier Colquhoun, the Jews launched a heavy attack which, after four days, resulted in the defeat and complete evacuation of the Arab population. Again, owing to weakness in numbers, British troops were unable to intervene materially, and their efforts were directed to prevent excesses, and whenever possible, by timely intervention, to localize the fighting. On 18th April the town was entirely in Jewish hands. Meanwhile, in Safad the tempo had also increased. With a handful of troops, the Irish Guards had controlled the town for three months and prevented any major engagement from developing, but with the British withdrawal approaching, both sides began to prepare for the onslaught. On 11th April it was estimated that Arab forces in the area totalled some 3-4,000 irregulars, with a number of pieces and armoured cars. The Hagana were perhaps 600 strong in the town and its surrounds, with strong reinforcements available from the Rosh Pinna area. British forces amounted to 55 guardsmen, one troop of 17th/21st Lancers and a small force of British Police in Safad, and a small mobile reserve at Rosh Pinna. The Arabs were quite frank about their plans for attacking the town when the time came, and they regretted that they would have to cut the road leading down to Rosh Pinna in order to prevent any Jewish reinforcements from interfering. If this happened before the withdrawal of the British force, it would be cut off in the town for an indefinite period and possibly necessitate the mounting of a major operation to effect its relief. Furthermore, if they became beleaguered in the town, they would have little freedom of movement with which to influence the situation. On 16th April, therefore, the garrison, together with the remaining British officials and Police, left the town. Before the rearguard was clear, a battle developed in which it became involved, and it was obliged to fight its way out with the use of 6-pr. anti-tank guns, 3-in. mortars and machine guns. This action was successfully concluded under the command of Lieutenant-Colonel D. M. L. Gordon-Watson, M.C., commanding 1st Battalion Irish Guards. Just previous to this withdrawal, the detachments of "Craforce" at Metulla, Khalsa and Nabi Yusha, in and overlooking the Huleh Valley, were pulled back into positions of greater security. Had they been left in their advanced positions following the evacuation of Safad, their lines of communication would have been unduly exposed. In recent months the Jewish settlements in the Huleh Valley had been concentrating on the construction of fortifications, as a result of which they were far less vulnerable to Arab attacks. They had also stocked up with some months' supplies which would enable them to withstand all but the most protracted sieges. The withdrawal of British troops at this juncture was, therefore, no more likely to assist one side than the other. On 28th April, the area of "Craforce's" responsibility was further reduced when the Headquarters and 17th/21st Lancers (less "B" Squadron which went to Haifa) moved from Tiberias to Nazareth, and the Irish Guards rejoined their own Brigade at Haifa.

While "Craforce" was closing in towards the final British enclave around Haifa, 3rd Hussars were preparing to move south to Camp 21, near Nathanya (familiar in the past to 1st and 2nd Parachute Brigades). The Regiment was due to return to the United Kingdom when the Mandate ended, and its duties in Haifa were taken over by 4th/7th Royal Dragoon Guards. In their new area 3rd Hussars were charged with the task of maintaining law and order in the civil district of Samaria for the final two weeks. Troops of the Regiment were also detached for various duties in Jerusalem, Jaffa and Sarafand.

In Haifa there remained of the Division, 1st Airborne Squadron, R.E., engaged in a variety of tasks mostly designed to speed the evacuation, and 317th Airborne Field Security Section, engaged in work which resembled some of that done in normal times by the C.I.D. branch of the Palestine Police. The Sappers in Palestine never had an idle time but during the closing stages work of every type was thrust upon them from all quarters. In the North Sector, 1st Airborne Squadron were the only Field Engineers left, and on them devolved the work formerly done by two squadrons, plus a lot extra. In addition to the various routine tasks such as mine disposal, route maintenance, and the supervision of defence works of other arms, there were many novelties. One of the greatest successes was the construction of a hard for L.S.Ts. (Landing Ships, Tank) which was built adjoining the lee breakwater of Haifa Harbour in order to speed the evacuation of vehicles. It was used extensively during the final three months, and was the evacuation point of the last troops to leave. Another task designed to assist the evacuation, was the construction of a road 800 yards long which led into the docks from the eastern outskirts of the town. The route it followed was planned to allow "soft-skinned" vehicles to move to and from the docks out of observation, and be secure against sniping from Hadar hak Carmel. There were also destructive tasks such as the destruction of obsolete armoured vehicles which were not worth evacuating, and whose subsequent use had to be denied to both Jews and Arabs. A total of 612 were destroyed between April and June. The most unpleasant, and possibly the most dangerous job of all, was the lifting of some of the British anti-personnel minefields laid during the past few years for the defence of vital points. They are so much easier to lay than to lift, and their removal is a task which is occasionally accompanied by mishaps. But as in the case of all the other work, everything went according to plan.

THE END OF THE MANDATE

With every day bringing the cessation of British rule nearer, the warring communities became bolder in their behaviour towards the British. Already much severe fighting had taken place and obviously more lay ahead. A factor of the greatest importance to both sides was the state of their equipment; with their sources of supply limited, every weapon, every box of ammunition, and above all, every armoured vehicle counted. For this reason, as British authority in their eyes began to wane, and the expedience of retaining British good will diminished, Arabs and Jews alike cast longing eyes at the equipment of the remaining units of the Security Forces and schemed for its capture. To achieve their object it was reported that both sides were prepared to stage a major operation. In consequence, the British further increased their security arrangements. As the Army reduced its areas of influence, all the operational moves which were undertaken in May were planned with this threat in mind. If in the end, nothing sensational happened, and no column had to fight its way through, that is a tribute to the alertness and efficiency of the troops, the foresight of their commanders, and the standard of staff work behind all the detailed arrangements.

When at last on 14th May the time came for the final British evacuation from Jerusalem, a responsible job fell to 1st Parachute Battalion to which was given the command of the vast column bound for the Haifa enclave. For the preceding three days the Battalion had been honoured by having with it General MacMillan, G.O.C. British Troops in Palestine, and his Tactical Headquarters. On the final day, H.E. the High Commissioner, General Sir Alan Cunningham, called at Battalion Headquarters on his way out of Jerusalem to Kolundia airport whence he flew to Haifa. Immediately after his plane had taken off, the column of over 250 vehicles under the command of Lieutenant-Colonel J. B. Nelson, D.S.O., M.C., commanding 1st Parachute Battalion, moved off towards Haifa. The column included 1st Parachute Battalion, 42nd Commando, Royal Marines, and detachments of 4th/7th Royal Dragoon Guards, 17th/21st Lancers, 4th Battalion The Royal Tank Regiment, 6th Field Regiment, R.A., 1st Airborne Squadron, R.E., R.A.S.C., R.A.M.C. and R.E.M.E. Its move went smoothly and entirely according to plan, and while it moved northwards, the 2nd Infantry Brigade left Jerusalem in the opposite direction on the first stage of their journey to Egypt.

Meanwhile in the North Sector, Headquarters "Craforce" was commanding the British withdrawal—military, police and civil— from Nazareth, the only major town in the two northern districts then remaining in Arab hands. On arrival in the enclave, "Craforce" had no further responsibilities, and, having no recognized establishment, it considered itself immediately disbanded. In the Port there had been a ceremonial parade to mark the departure of the High Commissioner, who embarked in one of His Majesty's Ships which left soon after midnight when the Mandate ended.

In Samaria, 3rd Hussars moved south to join in the general withdrawal of 1st Infantry Division to which it afforded flank and rear protection through southern Palestine and thence to Egypt. After staging the night in the Lydda District, the Regiment moved to Rafah on 15th May, passing on the way elements of the Egyptian Army which was invading the country in accordance with Arab League plans. They watched the fighters of the Egyptian Air Force in action against the Jews and passed the scene of several minor engagements which had taken place in the Negev. The Regiment (less Headquarter Squadron, still in Haifa) embarked at Port Said for the United Kingdom on 21st May.

The Mandate ended at one minute past midnight on the morning of 15th May, at which time various changes and developments took place. The Jews proclaimed the establishment of their State of Israel, the Arabs from the surrounding states began their invasion of the country, and the Haifa Enclave came into existence for the purpose of facilitating the final British withdrawal. The North Sector ceased to exist and Divisional Tactical Headquarters closed down. General Stockwell handed over operational command of the area still under British military control to Brigadier G. F. Johnson, D.S.O., Commander 1st Guards Brigade. The same day, the Divisional Commander left Palestine by air for England to return to his rapidly disbanding Division. Three days later, 1st Parachute Battalion, Headquarters "Craforce," and Divisional Tactical Headquarters embarked at Haifa and followed the remainder of the Division, leaving behind 1st Airborne Squadron, R.E., and the Divisional Field Security Section. The Haifa Enclave continued in existence for a further six weeks, but was reduced in size gradually as the evacuation neared completion, until in its final form, it comprised the Port alone. The few remaining troops of the British Army to leave Palestine embarked at Haifa on 30th June; they included "B" Troop of 1st Airborne Squadron, the last of the Red Berets.

So after nearly three years, the duties of the Division in Palestine came to an end. For those who stayed to the last to finish off the job, there was a grim satisfaction, but, like many of those who left before them, perhaps they went with mixed feelings. Their responsibility was over, and that in itself was a relief. But for those who had been there long enough to become attached to the country there were also regrets. Perhaps, also, as they sailed away from Haifa and watched Mount Carmel disappear on the horizon, some thought back over the centuries of British History, and many wondered how long it might be before they returned.

EPILOGUE

IT would be unfair in many ways to ask or try to explain what was achieved in this obscure and repugnant campaign. The British Army in Palestine with 6th Airborne Division as part of it were faced with a task with which they competed to the best of their ability. What mattered to them at the time was not so much the outcome of the fundamental problem which had caused their service in the country; with others lay the responsibility for its solution. Their concern was primarily with their own problems, and how they might best solve them within the limits allowed. Perhaps the foregoing chapters have helped to present a picture of some of their difficulties, but only to a minor extent have they described those which faced the individual. The human factor in all forms of service will always remain one of the most interesting and important, and for this reason it may be of value to describe some of the reactions towards their environment of those who served with the Division in Palestine.

It was unfortunate that the Division never saw an untroubled Palestine in which the communities went peacefully about their work, and in which the administration progressed without interference. Had it done so, Palestine as a country would have made an even deeper impression. It was only on account of the continual tension, bickering, and political manœuvring that most of those who served in this country soon wished themselves far from it. Yet how many of those in the Division who for one reason or another left the country were before long only too willing to return ? In spite of the conditions, morale was so consistently high that it deeply impressed all those who visited the country and saw the troops at work. It is important at this point to dispel a popular fallacy concerning the element of danger and its effect on the forces in Palestine. It is not the intention to minimize the loss of life—the Roll of Honour speaks for itself; but such danger as there was, appeared in no way to influence the troops. The reverse was probably the case, as without this spark of uncertainty, the effects of an otherwise monotonous existence would have become a matter of far greater consequence. Many units recorded that the effect of a forthcoming operation (in which there was usually some slight chance of opposition) had the most beneficial effect on morale.

To the private soldier, an operation, or "stunt" as he termed it, meant a break in routine, though he probably worked much harder than when he was in camp, and certainly got less sleep. But all the time things were going on around him, and, most important, he was in every sense of the word, operational. This was probably the factor which made the most important contribution to his high morale. It is otherwise hard to understand the reasons for the enthusiasm which was shown in the performance of the unattractive duties which faced the Security Forces. Another probable reason was that many of the junior ranks had just missed serving in the war. Here they found themselves for the first time on active service, and they were determined to acquit themselves well. As a result there was never any shortage of volunteers for any operational duties, and few tasks were more popular than road escorts. By day or night, near or far, men vied with each other for the job, and the farther it took them the more they liked it. This was the effect which the hazards of Palestine had on British troops.

When not operationally employed the soldier spent most of his time in camp. There the routine of fatigues, picquets, and guards took much of his time. Foremost of all his duties came the endless guards for which he paraded probably one night in three. He might be posted on the entrance to his camp, his company armoury, or a sandbagged gun-pit from which he surveyed in the beams of his spotlight the protective barbed and dannert wire fence which formed his camp perimeter. Or he might prowl between posts, often with another, and together they would wonder where it was all leading. For their hard work there were no results to show, except that each time they dismounted in the cold dawn the camp had passed another night unmolested because of their vigilance. That was the routine which had to be broken; the officers realized it and so did the men, and though the necessity of these guards could not be questioned, the effort they entailed was irksome beyond description. Without doubt guards would head the list of any soldier's blackest memories of Palestine.

When off duty there was little for him to do. During most of the time, if he wished to go out on recreation, he had to be armed and in the company of three others and this by itself imposed its restrictions. Before the situation deteriorated too far, sightseeing trips were organized to the Holy places which aroused much interest among the troops and also gave them something to write home about. Other trips to places like the Sea of Galilee, Nazareth, Bethlehem and Jericho also helped to relieve the monotony. But most of these came to an end towards the end of 1947. There was no gaiety, and much of the time the large towns were out of bounds for security reasons. Eventually there was hardly any attraction in leaving camp at the end of the day's duties, except for bathing, which in the warmer months was always popular. The general effect, then, was involuntarily to confine the individual to his unit lines. So he became dependent on his comrades for his amusement, and this dependence helped to foster a corporate spirit which had its own beneficial effect on morale. On the other hand, one of the drawbacks which arose from this state of confinement was the danger of developing a "barbed wire complex." With so much emphasis devoted to the perfection of defence there was a natural tendency to become defensively minded. To some extent this was unavoidable, but if allowed to develop too far it might have had an adverse effect on morale. Thus, all minor operations, patrols, and any other duties which took the troops outside their camps did much to counteract the effects of normal routine and so prevent staleness.

A factor which undoubtedly helped all ranks in their duties was a clear idea of the purpose for which they were in the country. Whatever the political complications, and they were many, all knew what the *object* was. It was the reverse of war; it was simply "to keep the peace." As time went on and the situation became more tense and obscure, this object grew in importance. Moreover, the simplicity of its meaning (though not always of its attainment) contrasted strongly with so many of the issues which were mainly political, and often beyond the understanding of officers and soldiers alike. It became therefore the guide to which all who had to make decisions turned, and those decisions were as much those of the lance-corporal on patrol as the senior commander in his headquarters. The degree of impartiality which was achieved was reflected in the lamentations of both Arabs and Jews that they were the victims of biased treatment. Had one side shown itself satisfied it would probably have been a true indication that the Security Forces had not been acting impartially.

Not the least of the trials and hardships which the Army had to endure was the effect of cumulative frustration. This is not the place to discuss British policy in Palestine. It could not have been longer suffering, and no matter how firm it might have been, it would always have had its critics on the spot who were possibly too close to events to hold a balanced outlook. But human nature being what it is, the troops were bound to regard the problems as they appeared to them at the time. The bloody attacks of the Jewish dissident groups and the limited action which could be taken in reply caused feelings of the greatest exasperation, and produced occasions when the bonds of discipline were strained to the utmost. Possibly the hardest task of all in this connection was that of the Platoon and Company Commanders, who, while probably sharing the views of their men, had to try and convince them otherwise.

When considering the prevailing conditions, it would be reasonable to suppose that the atmosphere of political uncertainty and racial hatred would overshadow all the natural virtues of the land, and so narrow the outlook of those who were there for the sole purpose of maintaining peace. To some extent this was undoubtedly so, as the job was an unpleasant one, dealing much of the time with unpleasant people. It is only natural therefore that Palestine for some should have become synonymous with discomfort, uncertainty, frustration and, occasionally, danger. But there were many who would not allow themselves to be dominated by events and conditions, and they, determining to gain from their experiences, learned much of the country and its inhabitants. For them the memories which will be most enduring may not be of the day-to-day events, but of the scenery, the places of historical interest, the simple domestic scenes of Biblical times, the fascinating way of life and hospitality of the Arabs, and the forceful drive of the Jews for progress and development. All these and countless other impressions were bound to leave their mark on those for whom, every now and again, the charm of the land rose supreme above the prevailing atmosphere of suspicion and strife.

6TH AIRBORNE DIVISION ROLL OF HONOUR—PALESTINE
1945-8

PART I—KILLED IN ACTION AND DIED FROM WOUNDS

RANK AND NAME	UNIT	DATE
	6th Airborne Division	
Capt. S. Adamson	9th Airborne Squadron, R.E.	18.11.46
Lieut. J. F. Bailey	1st Airborne Squadron, R.E.	4.3.48
Lieut. G. Dwyer	2nd/3rd Battalion The Parachute Regiment	6.1.48
Lieut. G. J. Graham	147th Airborne Park Squadron, R.E.	15.5.47
Lieut. M. H. H. Holdway	H.Q. Royal Engineers 6th Airborne Division	15.5.47
Lieut. D. M. Kennedy	9th Airborne Squadron, R.E.	22.3.46
Capt. M. C. Kissane	9th Battalion The Parachute Regiment	29.6.47
Capt. J. M. Newton	1st Airborne Squadron, R.E.	17.11.46
L./Bdr. P. Axtell	33rd Airborne Light Regiment, R.A.	29.2.48
Gnr. K. W. Baker	2nd Forward Observer Unit (Airborne) R.A.	2.12.46
L./Cpl. R. Barton	6th Airborne Division Provost Company	9.12.47
L./Cpl. F. H. J. Bond	6th Airborne Division Provost Company	2.3.47
Sergt. J. P. Buckley	6th Airborne Division Signals Regiment	29.2.48
Pte. K. Carroll	2nd/3rd Battalion The Parachute Regiment	18.3.48
Gnr. P. Christoffersen	87th Airborne Field Regiment, R.A.	10.11.47
Gnr. R. Crampton	334th Forward Observer Battery (Airborne), R.A.	15.2.48
Pte. J. B. Eyre	195th Parachute Field Ambulance	31.10.46
Pte. J. A. Gilliard	5th Battalion The Parachute Regiment	25.4.46
Spr. Hancock	9th Airborne Squadron, R.E.	29.2.48
L./Cpl. J. Hand	H.Q. R.A.S.C. 6th Airborne Division	27.1.48
Pte. K. J. Hewitt	2nd/3rd Battalion The Parachute Regiment	26.3.48
Pte. J. Hope	5th Battalion The Parachute Regiment	25.4.46
Pte. N. E. Knight	5th Battalion The Parachute Regiment	25.4.46
Sergt. E. N. Lambert	7th Battalion The Parachute Regiment	10.9.46
Q.M.S.I. L. A. Lemon	A.P.T.C. attached H.Q., 1st Parachute Brigade	1.10.46
Pte. H. Lewis	5th Battalion The Parachute Regiment	25.4.46
Cpl. T. McInnes	224th Parachute Field Ambulance	22.9.46
Pte. H. S. McKay	5th Battalion The Parachute Regiment	25.4.46
Pte. A. Morrison	5th Battalion The Parachute Regiment	25.4.46

RANK AND NAME	UNIT	DATE
Pte. C. Murray	5th Battalion The Parachute Regiment	30.7.46
Cpl. R. O'Dwyer	147th Airborne Park Squadron, R.E.	9.3.48
L./Cpl. R. G. Ogilvie	6th Airborne Division Provost Company	1.3.47
Pte. J. H. Park	5th Battalion The Parachute Regiment	26.4.46
Gnr. C. R. Pearson	2nd Forward Observer Unit (Airborne) R.A.	2.12.46
Gnr. N. Prossen	33rd Airborne Light Regiment, R.A.	29.2.48
Sgmn. J. W. Rich	6th Airborne Division Signals Regiment	27.3.48
Sergt. J. Sturtevant	8th/9th Battalion The Parachute Regiment	12.2.48
L./Cpl. G. W. Voce	195th Parachute Field Ambulance	31.10.46
Gnr. N. Wilkins	33rd Airborne Light Regiment, R.A.	29.2.48
Sergt. J. Woozley	317th Field Security Section (Airborne)	5.1.48

Units under Command of 6th Airborne Division

Capt. J. L. Ashley	R.A.M.C. attached 23rd Battalion, The King's African Rifles	6.2.46
Gdsmn. J. Balmer	1st Battalion Irish Guards	12.2.48
Gnr. J. P. Clarke	1st Regiment Royal Horse Artillery	18.3.48
Gnr R. L. Cheek	1st Regiment Royal Horse Artillery	18.3.48
Pte. Jinibi Timbwa	23rd Battalion The King's African Rifles	6.2.46
L./Cpl. T. E. Jones	1st Battalion Irish Guards	4.2.48
Sergt. J. Matthew	2nd Battalion The Middlesex Regiment	28.12.47
Tpr. J. F. O'Brien	17th/21st Lancers	21.7.47
Gnr. R. M. Pythian	1st Regiment Royal Horse Artillery	18.3.48
Cpl. F. Shakespeare	17th/21st Lancers	19.2.48
Gdsmn. H. Sheldrake	1st Battalion Irish Guards	17.1.48
Gnr. G. Taylor	1st Regiment Royal Horse Artillery	13.12.47
Gnr. J. Tierney	1st Regiment Royal Horse Artillery	18.3.48
Gnr. H. Yates	2nd Field Regiment, R.A.	1.11.45

PART II—DIED ON ACTIVE SERVICE

6th Airborne Division

Capt. T. K. Burridge	2nd Forward Observer Unit (Airborne) R.A.	24.1.46
Lieut. A. McK. Elliot	R.A.M.C. attached 3rd Battalion The Parachute Regiment	7.10.47
Capt. F. T. T. Field	17th Battalion The Parachute Regiment	8.5.46
Capt. J. P. Hattrell	3rd Battalion The Parachute Regiment	24.3.47
Capt. B. C. Jeffrey	R.A.M.C. attached 6th Battalion, The Parachute Regiment	3.3.46
Lieut. T. S. Parish	53rd (W.Y.) Airlanding Light Regiment, R.A.	9.4.46
Lieut. D. Younger	Headquarters 6th Airborne Division	10.7.47
Pte. E. W. Alexander	2nd Battalion The Parachute Regiment	25.10.47

RANK AND NAME	UNIT	DATE
Pte. C. H. Ayliffe	R.A.M.C. attached 9th Battalion The Parachute Regiment	6.5.46
Pte. D. J. Baker	2nd Battalion The Parachute Regiment	18.8.46
Sgmn. J. R. Benson	6th Airborne Division Signals Regiment	23.12.46
Gdsmn. E. J. Bevan	1st Battalion The Parachute Regiment	19.9.47
Gnr. L. C. Blackmore	2nd Forward Observer Unit (Airborne), R.A.	24.3.47
Dvr. F. R. Brown	1st Airborne Squadron, R.E.	18.8.46
Pte. W. R. Brown	2nd Battalion The Parachute Regiment	27.6.47
Pte. F. C. Butcher	4th Battalion The Parachute Regiment	31.8.46
Sergt. B. E. B. Caravias	2nd Battalion The Parachute Regiment	18.8.46
Pte. L. Carter	3rd Battalion The Parachute Regiment	17.12.46
Pte. T. A. Carter	8th Battalion The Parachute Regiment	19.10.46
Sergt. P. Carter	R.A.E.C. attached 195th Parachute Field Ambulance	2.2.48
Fus. W. H. Cartwright	6th Battalion The Parachute Regiment	9.11.45
Sergt. A. J. Chadd	No. 1 Wing, The Glider Pilot Regiment	17.5.47
Pte. L. Charnley	2nd Battalion The Parachute Regiment	26.7.47
Dvr. H. Clarkson	63rd Composite Company (Airborne), R.A.S.C.	3.4.46
Pte. R. B. Clements	8th Battalion The Parachute Regiment	5.4.47
Pte. A. F. Cooke	21st Independent Parachute Company	25.5.46
Pte. J. Cosgrove	3rd Battalion The Parachute Regiment	11.10.46
Bdr. L. Cousins	2nd Forward Observer Unit (Airborne) R.A.	14.7.46
L./Cpl. D. Coutts	6th Airborne Division Provost Company	31.10.47
Pte. P. Darbyshire	2nd Battalion The Parachute Regiment	25.10.47
L./Cpl. N. R. Davies	2nd Battalion The Parachute Regiment	25.10.47
Pte. T. S. Dix	8th Battalion The Parachute Regiment	27.5.47
L./Cpl. A. C. Dixon	6th Airborne Division Provost Company	30.10.47
Pte. J. Duncan	2nd Battalion The Parachute Regiment	26.10.47
Cpl. J. H. Dunsby	317th Field Security Section (Airborne)	24.10.46
Gnr. R. Dutton	2nd Airlanding Anti-Tank Regiment, R.A.	24.1.46
Pte. E. Fletcher	6th Battalion The Parachute Regiment	14.10.46
L./Cpl. H. A. J. Goddard	6th Airborne Division Signals Regiment	30.5.46
Gdsmn. W. Grey	1st Battalion The Parachute Regiment	26.3.48
L./Sergt. W. Grundy	2nd Airlanding Anti-Tank Regiment, R.A.	24.1.46
Pte. B. G. Hall	195th Parachute Field Ambulance	17.10.45
Pte. R. Hallisay	4th Battalion The Parachute Regiment	7.10.46
Dvr. F. L. Hammond	398th Airborne Company R.A.S.C.	17.3.46
Cpl. K. F. Harris	6th Airborne Armoured Reconnaissance Regiment	12.2.46
Cpl. D. A. Hart	2nd Battalion The Parachute Regiment	21.9.46
Pte. C. T. Hodson	R.A.O.C. attached 6th Airborne Division Workshops, R.E.M.E.	30.12.45

RANK AND NAME	UNIT	DATE
Tpr. J. E. Hughes	3rd The King's Own Hussars	Feb.1946
L./Cpl. D. Inwood	2nd Battalion The Parachute Regiment	25.10.47
Spr. A. Jarman	249th Airborne Park Squadron, R.E.	7.2.47
Dvr. J. Jenkins	716th Airborne Light Company, R.A.S.C.	13.10.46
Pte. P. D. Jones	4th Battalion The Parachute Regiment	6.1.46
Spr. J. C. Jordon	147th Airborne Park Squadron, R.E.	5.4.47
Dvr. D. Kelvey	716th Airborne Light Company, R.A.S.C.	10.3.46
Sergt. A. Kirkpatrick	4th Battalion The Parachute Regiment	5.12.46
Pte. E. A. Knox	9th Battalion The Parachute Regiment	3.3.47
Gnr. S. O. Korup	87th Airborne Light Regiment, R.A.	12.8.47
Pte. J. Lang	4th Battalion The Parachute Regiment	29.12.45
Pte. J. T. Leech	Parachute Regiment attached 9th Airborne Squadron, R.E.	16.6.47
Pte. G. W. Leatherland	2nd Battalion The Parachute Regiment	25.10.47
Pte. N. Leonard	2nd Battalion The Parachute Regiment	29.5.46
L./Cpl. R. Matthews	2nd Battalion The Parachute Regiment	25.10.47
Pte. A. McBride	1st Battalion The Parachute Regiment	23.5.46
Spr. T. H. McLean	1st Airborne Squadron, R.E.	4.12.45
Pte. F. T. Millard	2nd Battalion The Parachute Regiment	26.10.47
Pte. A. Milton	2nd Battalion The Parachute Regiment	25.10.47
Spr. S. A. Minshull	286th Airborne Park Squadron, R.E.	5.1.46
Gnr. E. E. Nielson	159th Parachute Light Regiment, R.A.	29.4.47
Pte. W. D. O'Dey	2nd Battalion The Parachute Regiment	25.10.47
Pte. J. O'Donnell	9th Battalion The Parachute Regiment	10.3.47
Cpl. C. Penfold	1st Battalion The Royal Ulster Rifles	25.10.45
Cpl. J. Phillips	6th Airborne Armoured Reconnaissance Regiment	10.11.45
Gnr. R. W. Pike	2nd Airlanding Anti-Tank Regiment, R.A.	24.1.46
Tpr. R. A. Preece	3rd The King's Own Hussars	31.8.47
Pte. A. L. Price	A.C.C. attached 2nd Forward Observer Unit (Airborne), R.A.	24.3.47
Gnr. J. M. Price	66th Airborne Anti-Tank Regiment, R.A.	11.11.47
L./Cpl. D. Preston	2nd Battalion The Parachute Regiment	25.10.47
Bdr. J. T. Renshaw	33rd Airborne Light Regiment, R.A.	18.10.47
Pte. A. Richardson	9th Battalion The Parachute Regiment	2.6.46
Pte. N. Stanford	2nd Battalion The Parachute Regiment	25.10.47
Pte. S. G. Stedman	1st Battalion The Parachute Regiment	19.7.47
Gnr. A. R. Stent	2nd Airlanding Anti-Tank Regiment, R.A.	23.9.46
L./Cpl. E. E. Smale	6th Airborne Division Workshops, R.E.M.E.	28.5.47
Pte. F. A. Smith	1st Battalion The Argyll and Sutherland Highlanders	22.1.46

RANK AND NAME	UNIT	DATE
Pte. H. O. Swales	3rd Battalion The Parachute Regiment	5.9.47
L./Cpl. S. Sykes	6th Airborne Armoured Reconnaissance Regiment	18.11.45
L./Cpl. H. Taylor	224th Parachute Field Ambulance	27.1.48
Pte. W. B. Tromans	8th Battalion The Parachute Regiment	21.10.47
Pte. F. Vickers	2nd Battalion The Parachute Regiment	1.8.47
Gnr. G. Wain	2nd Airlanding Anti-Tank Regiment, R.A.	24.1.46
Dvr. G. Wallace	6th Airborne Division Royal Engineers	24.3.47
Dvr. A. Warrior	63rd Composite Company (Airborne), R.A.S.C.	29.8.46
L./Cpl. G. Wheatley	6th Airborne Division Provost Company	21.8.47
Dvr. B. Wilde	Headquarters, R.A.S.C., 6th Airborne Division	2.7.47
Pte. A. E. Williams	3rd Battalion The Parachute Regiment	8.6.46
Sergt. G. Williams	6th Airborne Armoured Reconnaissance Regiment	12.2.46
Pte. F. R. Wood	2nd Battalion The Parachute Regiment	25.10.47
Cfn. W. M. Wood	6th Airborne Division Workshops, R.E.M.E.	20.12.46
Pte. A. S. J. Woodward	2nd Battalion The Parachute Regiment	25.10.47
Gnr. E. Young	53rd (W.Y.) Airlanding Light Regiment, R.A.	26.8.46

Units under Command of 6th Airborne Division

Lieut. J. N. Boardman	Lancashire Fusiliers attached 23rd Battalion The King's African Rifles	8.11.45
Major L. Deacon	1st Battalion The Hertfordshire Regiment	31.3.46
Lieut. T. Hill	1st Battalion Irish Guards	5.2.48
Capt. E. T. G. Meade-Waldo	R.A.M.C. attached 12th Royal Lancers	30.5.46
Lieut. D. J. E. Shaw	17th/21st Lancers	9.4.47
Capt. S. E. Whitfield	Cavalry Regiment Transjordan Frontier Force	29.3.47
Pte. P. Connelly	2nd Battalion The Middlesex Regiment	15.3.48
Tpr. W. Fisher	17th/21st Lancers	Feb. 1948
Gdsmn. A. Kinnealy	1st Battalion Irish Guards	3.2.48
L./Cpl. Levi Nguliwe	5th Battalion The Northern Rhodesia Regiment	17.4.46
Pte. Maingi Mutucho	23rd Battalion The King's African Rifles	8.3.46
L./Cpl. A. E. Paget	1st Battalion The Hertfordshire Regiment	8.8.46
C.S.M. Joseph Sifuwe	5th Battalion The Northern Rhodesia Regiment	17.4.46
Sergt. W. G. Slater	6th Battalion The Gordon Highlanders	6.8.46
Trooper R. J. Sullivan	12th Royal Lancers	6.12.46

P

APPENDIX B

6TH AIRBORNE DIVISION ORDER OF BATTLE IN JANUARY, 1946

Headquarters 6th Airborne Division

2ND PARACHUTE BRIGADE
4th Battalion The Parachute Regiment.
5th Battalion The Parachute Regiment.
6th Battalion The Parachute Regiment.

3RD PARACHUTE BRIGADE
3rd Battalion The Parachute Regiment.
8th Battalion The Parachute Regiment.
9th Battalion The Parachute Regiment.

6TH AIRLANDING BRIGADE
2nd Battalion The Oxfordshire and Buckinghamshire Light Infantry.
1st Battalion The Royal Ulster Rifles.
1st Battalion The Argyll and Sutherland Highlanders.

ROYAL ARMOURED CORPS
6th Airborne Armoured Reconnaissance Regiment.

ROYAL ARTILLERY
53rd (Worcestershire Yeomanry) Airlanding Light Regiment.
2nd Airlanding Anti-Tank Regiment.
2nd Forward Observer Unit.

ROYAL ENGINEERS
1st Airborne Squadron.
9th Airborne Squadron.
286th Airborne Park Squadron.

ROYAL CORPS OF SIGNALS
6th Airborne Divisional Signals.
21st Independent Parachute Company.

ROYAL ARMY SERVICE CORPS
63rd Composite Company (Airborne).
398th Composite Company (Airborne).
716th Company (Airborne Light).

ROYAL ARMY MEDICAL CORPS
>127th Parachute Field Ambulance.
>224th Parachute Field Ambulance.
>195th Airlanding Field Ambulance.
>74th Field Hygiene Section.

ROYAL ARMY ORDNANCE CORPS
>6th Airborne Division Ordnance Field Park.

ROYAL ELECTRICAL AND MECHANICAL ENGINEERS
>6th Airborne Division Workshops.
>Airlanding Light Aid Detachments (Seven).

6th Airborne Division Battle School.

6th Airborne Division Training School.

6th Airborne Division Provost Company.

317th Field Security Section.

16th Field Cash Office (Light).

6th Airborne Division Air Photographic Interpretation Section.

2nd Mobile Photographic Enlargement Section.

6th Airborne Division Postal Unit.

6TH AIRBORNE DIVISION ORDER OF BATTLE IN JANUARY, 1947

Headquarters 6th Airborne Division

1ST PARACHUTE BRIGADE
>1st Battalion The Parachute Regiment.
>2nd Battalion The Parachute Regiment.
>7th Battalion The Parachute Regiment.

2ND PARACHUTE BRIGADE
>4th Battalion The Parachute Regiment.
>5th Battalion The Parachute Regiment.
>6th Battalion The Parachute Regiment.

3RD PARACHUTE BRIGADE
>3rd Battalion The Parachute Regiment.
>8th Battalion The Parachute Regiment.
>9th Battalion The Parachute Regiment.

ROYAL ARMOURED CORPS
>3rd The King's Own Hussars.

ROYAL ARTILLERY
>53rd (Worcestershire Yeomanry) Airlanding Light Regiment.
>2nd Airlanding Anti-Tank Regiment.
>2nd Forward Observer Unit.

ROYAL ENGINEERS
>1st Airborne Squadron.
>3rd Airborne Squadron.
>9th Airborne Squadron.
>249th Airborne Park Squadron (changed from 286th).

ROYAL CORPS OF SIGNALS
>6th Airborne Division Signals Regiment.
>Number 1 Wing Glider Pilot Regiment.

ROYAL ARMY SERVICE CORPS
>63rd Composite Company (Airborne).
>398th Composite Company (Airborne).
>716th Company (Airborne Light).

ROYAL ARMY MEDICAL CORPS
>127th Parachute Field Ambulance.
>224th Parachute Field Ambulance.
>195th Airlanding Field Ambulance.
>74th Field Hygiene Section.

ROYAL ARMY ORDNANCE CORPS
6th Airborne Division Ordnance Field Park.

ROYAL ELECTRICAL AND MECHANICAL ENGINEERS
6th Airborne Division Workshops.
Airlanding Light Aid Detachments (Seven).

6th Airborne Division Battle School.

6th Airborne Division Training School.

6th Airborne Division Provost Company.

317th Field Security Section.

16 Field Cash Office (Light).

6th Airborne Division Air Photographic Interpretation Section.

2nd Mobile Photographic Enlargement Section.

6th Airborne Division Postal Unit.

2nd Parachute Brigade Group composed of the following units, sailed for the United Kingdom on 24th January, 1947, from Haifa:—

4th Battalion The Parachute Regiment.
5th Battalion The Parachute Regiment.
6th Battalion The Parachute Regiment.
"B" Squadron, The King's Own Hussars (did not leave Palestine to join 2nd Parachute Brigade until 14th June, 1947).
211th Battery, 53rd (Worcestershire Yeomanry) Airlanding Light Regiment, Royal Artillery.
300th Battery, 2nd Airlanding Anti-Tank Regiment Royal Artillery.
Number 1 Section, 2nd Forward Observer Unit, Royal Artillery.
3rd Airborne Squadron, Royal Engineers.
"K" Troop, 6th Airborne Division Signals Regiment.
Detachment, 249th Airborne Park Squadron, Royal Engineers.
63rd Composite Company (Airborne), Royal Army Service Corps.
127th Parachute Field Ambulance, Royal Army Medical Corps.
One Section, 6th Airborne Division Ordnance Field Park.
One Section, 6th Airborne Division Workshops, Royal Electrical and Mechanical Engineers.
One Airlanding Light Aid Detachment, Royal Electrical and Mechanical Engineers.
One Section, 6th Airborne Division Provost Company.

This Brigade Group eventually left for B.A.O.R. in February, 1948.

6TH AIRBORNE DIVISION ORDER OF BATTLE IN JANUARY, 1948

Headquarters 6th Airborne Division

1ST PARACHUTE BRIGADE
    1st Battalion The Parachute Regiment.
    2nd/3rd Battalion The Parachute Regiment.
    8th/9th Battalion The Parachute Regiment.

2ND PARACHUTE BRIGADE (In United Kingdom)
    4th/6th Battalion The Parachute Regiment.
    5th Battalion The Parachute Regiment.
    7th Battalion The Parachute Regiment.

ROYAL ARMOURED CORPS
    3rd The King's Own Hussars.

ROYAL ARTILLERY
    33rd Airborne Light Regiment.
    66th Airborne Anti-Tank Regiment.
    87th Airborne Field Regiment.
    334th Forward Observer Battery.

ROYAL ENGINEERS
    1st Airborne Squadron.
    *3rd Airborne Squadron.
    9th Airborne Squadron.
    147th Airborne Park Squadron (changed from 249th).

ROYAL CORPS OF SIGNALS
    6th Airborne Division Signals Regiment.

ROYAL ARMY SERVICE CORPS
    *63rd Company (Parachute Brigade).
    398th Company (Parachute Brigade).
    716th Company (Parachute Brigade).

ROYAL ARMY MEDICAL CORPS
    *23rd Parachute Field Ambulance (changed from 127th).
    195th Parachute Field Ambulance.

---

  * In United Kingdom with 2nd Parachute Brigade.

224th Parachute Field Ambulance.
74th Field Hygiene Section.
16th Field Hygiene Section.
17th Field Hygiene Section.

ROYAL ARMY ORDNANCE CORPS
6th Airborne Division Ordnance Field Park.

ROYAL ELECTRICAL AND MECHANICAL ENGINEERS
1st Airborne Workshops.
*2nd Airborne Workshops.
3rd Airborne Workshops.
Light Aid Detachments (eight including the one with 2nd Parachute Brigade).

6th Airborne Division Battle School.

6th Airborne Division Training School.

6th Airborne Division Provost Company.

317th Field Security Section.

16th Field Cash Office (Light).

6th Airborne Division Air Photographic Interpretation Section.

2nd Mobile Photographic Enlargement Section.

6th Airborne Division Postal Unit.

* In United Kingdom with 2nd Parachute Brigade.

UNITS UNDER COMMAND

UNITS of many Arms and Services were placed under command of 6th Airborne Division for varying periods between October, 1945, and April, 1948. To them belongs a very full share of any credit to which the Division may be entitled for its work in Palestine.

ROYAL ARMOURED CORPS
     1st King's Dragoon Guards.
     12th Royal Lancers.
     17th/21st Lancers.
     8th Battalion The Royal Tank Regiment.

ROYAL ARTILLERY
     1st Regiment Royal Horse Artillery.
     2nd Field Regiment.
     6th Field Regiment.
     33rd Field Regiment.
     12th Anti-Tank Regiment.
     52nd Observation Regiment (late 2nd Survey Regiment).
     1909th (late "B") Flight 651st Air Observation Post Squadron.
     339th Movement Light Battery (late 591st Searchlight Battery).
     204th Coastal Battery.

ROYAL CORPS OF SIGNALS
     2nd Air Support Signals Unit (Detachment).

FOOT GUARDS
     1st Battalion Irish Guards.

INFANTRY OF THE LINE AND ROYAL MARINES
     1st/6th Battalion The Queen's Royal Regiment.
     2nd Battalion The East Surrey Regiment.
     40th Commando, Royal Marines.
     2nd Battalion The Middlesex Regiment.
     2nd Battalion The King's Royal Rifle Corps.
     6th Battalion The Gordon Highlanders.
     2nd Battalion The Royal Ulster Rifles.
     1st Battalion The Hertfordshire Regiment.

ROYAL ARMY ORDNANCE CORPS
    2nd Air Maintenance Company.

ROYAL ELECTRICAL AND MECHANICAL ENGINEERS
    123rd Corps Troops Workshop.

INDIAN ARMY
    482nd (Royal Bombay) Indian Field Company, R.I.E.

KING'S AFRICAN RIFLES
    23rd Battalion.

NORTHERN RHODESIA REGIMENT
    5th Battalion.

TRANSJORDAN FRONTIER FORCE
    Cavalry Regiment.
    Mechanized Regiment.

ARAB LEGION
    1st Mechanized Regiment.
    3rd Mechanized Regiment.

6TH AIRBORNE DIVISION STAFF LIST FOR 1945

HEADQUARTERS 6TH AIRBORNE DIVISION

Major-General E. L. Bols, C.B., D.S.O.

Lieutenant-Colonel G. E. Pike, D.S.O., M.B.E. (General Staff Officer, Grade 1—Operations).

Lieutenant-Colonel C. R. W. Brewis, M.C. (General Staff Officer, Grade 1 —Air).

Lieutenant-Colonel T. N. S. Wheeler (Assistant Adjutant and Quartermaster-General).

2ND PARACHUTE BRIGADE

Brigadier C. H. V. Pritchard, D.S.O.

Lieutenant-Colonel J. L. de V. Martin (4th Battalion The Parachute Regiment).

Lieutenant-Colonel J. N. H. Christie (5th Battalion The Parachute Regiment).

Lieutenant-Colonel A. Tilly (6th Battalion The Parachute Regiment).

3RD PARACHUTE BRIGADE

Brigadier G. W. Lathbury, D.S.O., M.B.E.

Lieutenant-Colonel W. B. P. Bradish (3rd Battalion The Parachute Regiment).

Lieutenant-Colonel G. Hewetson, D.S.O., O.B.E. (8th Battalion The Parachute Regiment).

Lieutenant-Colonel N. Crookenden, D.S.O. (9th Battalion The Parachute Regiment).

6TH AIRLANDING BRIGADE

Brigadier R. H. Bellamy, D.S.O.

Lieutenant-Colonel M. Darell-Brown, D.S.O. (2nd Battalion The Oxfordshire and Buckinghamshire Light Infantry).

Lieutenant-Colonel G. P. Rickcord, D.S.O. (1st Battalion The Royal Ulster Rifles).

Lieutenant-Colonel R. H. L. Webb, M.C. (1st Battalion The Argyll and Sutherland Highlanders).

6TH AIRBORNE ARMOURED RECONNAISSANCE REGIMENT

Lieutenant-Colonel C. P. D. Legard.

ROYAL ARTILLERY

    Brigadier W. McT. T. Faithfull, D.S.O.

    Lieutenant-Colonel R. A. Eden, D.S.O. (53rd Airlanding Light Regiment).

    Lieutenant-Colonel R. A. Gorle, M.C. (2nd Airlanding Anti-Tank Regiment).

ROYAL ENGINEERS

    Lieutenant-Colonel J. R. C. Hamilton, D.S.O.

ROYAL CORPS OF SIGNALS

    Lieutenant-Colonel P. E. M. Bradley, D.S.O.

GLIDER PILOT REGIMENT

    Lieutenant-Colonel R. Q. Gaitley.

ROYAL ARMY SERVICE CORPS

    Lieutenant-Colonel A. K. Woods, O.B.E.

ROYAL ARMY MEDICAL CORPS

    Colonel M. MacEwen, D.S.O., O.B.E., D.F.C., T.D.

    Lieutenant-Colonel F. Murray (127th Parachute Field Ambulance).

    Lieutenant-Colonel A. D. Young, D.S.O. (224th Parachute Field Ambulance).

    Lieutenant-Colonel S. Smith (195th Airlanding Field Ambulance).

ROYAL ARMY ORDNANCE CORPS

    Lieutenant-Colonel R. J. Meech, M.B.E.

ROYAL ELECTRICAL AND MECHANICAL ENGINEERS

    Lieutenant-Colonel J. M. Neilson.

6TH AIRBORNE DIVISION BATTLE SCHOOL

    Colonel M. Crawford, D.S.O.

N.B.—In each staff list the officer shown as holding each appointment is the one who held the appointment during most of the year.

6TH AIRBORNE DIVISION STAFF LIST FOR 1946

HEADQUARTERS 6TH AIRBORNE DIVISION

Major-General A. J. H. Cassels, C.B.E., D.S.O.

Lieutenant-Colonel H. H. van Straubenzee, D.S.O. (General Staff Officer, Grade 1—Operations).

Lieutenant-Colonel W. P. B. Bradish (General Staff Officer, Grade 1—Air).

Lieutenant-Colonel H. E. N. Bredin, D.S.O., M.C. (Assistant Adjutant and Quartermaster-General).

1ST PARACHUTE BRIGADE

Brigadier R. H. Bellamy, D.S.O.

Lieutenant-Colonel T. C. H. Pearson, D.S.O. (1st Battalion The Parachute Regiment).

Lieutenant-Colonel J. D. Frost, D.S.O., M.C. (2nd Battalion The Parachute Regiment).

Lieutenant-Colonel W. D. H. McCardie (17th Battalion The Parachute Regiment).

2ND PARACHUTE BRIGADE

Brigadier J. P. O'Brien Twohig, C.B.E., D.S.O.

Lieutenant-Colonel J. L. de V. Martin (4th Battalion The Parachute Regiment).

Lieutenant-Colonel J. N. H. Christie (5th Battalion The Parachute Regiment).

Lieutenant-Colonel A. Tilly (6th Battalion The Parachute Regiment).

3RD PARACHUTE BRIGADE

Brigadier G. W. Lathbury, D.S.O., M.B.E.

Lieutenant-Colonel G. P. Rickcord, D.S.O. (3rd Battalion The Parachute Regiment).

Lieutenant-Colonel G. Hewetson, D.S.O., O.B.E. (8th Battalion The Parachute Regiment).

Lieutenant-Colonel M. A. H. Butler, D.S.O., M.C. (9th Battalion The Parachute Regiment).

3RD THE KING'S OWN HUSSARS

Lieutenant-Colonel P. H. Labouchere, O.B.E.

ROYAL ARTILLERY
>Brigadier W. McT. T. Faithfull, D.S.O.
>Lieutenant-Colonel K. Scott-Foster, O.B.E. (53rd Airlanding Light Regiment).
>Lieutenant-Colonel R. A. Gorle, M.C. (2nd Airlanding Anti-Tank Regiment).

ROYAL ENGINEERS
>Lieutenant-Colonel P. H. M. Moore, D.S.O., M.C.

ROYAL CORPS OF SIGNALS
>Lieutenant-Colonel P. E. M. Bradley, D.S.O.

GLIDER PILOT REGIMENT
>Lieutenant-Colonel R. Q. Gaitley.

ROYAL ARMY SERVICE CORPS
>Lieutenant-Colonel A. K. Woods, O.B.E.

ROYAL ARMY MEDICAL CORPS
>Colonel M. J. Kohane, M.C.
>Lieutenant-Colonel F. Murray (127th Parachute Field Ambulance).
>Major G. W. H. Patterson (224th Parachute Field Ambulance).
>Lieutenant-Colonel S. Smith (195th Parachute Field Ambulance).

ROYAL ARMY ORDNANCE CORPS
>Lieutenant-Colonel R. J. Meech, M.B.E.

ROYAL ELECTRICAL AND MECHANICAL ENGINEERS
>Lieutenant-Colonel J. M. Neilson.

6TH AIRBORNE DIVISION BATTLE SCHOOL
>Lieutenant-Colonel F. M. Bucher, D.S.O.

6TH AIRBORNE DIVISION STAFF LIST FOR 1947

HEADQUARTERS 6TH AIRBORNE DIVISION

Major-General E. L. Bols, C.B., D.S.O.

Lieutenant-Colonel H. C. B. Cook (General Staff Officer, Grade 1—Operations).

Lieutenant-Colonel P. H. M. May, D.S.O., M.C. (General Staff Officer, Grade 1—Air).

Lieutenant-Colonel P. G. F. Young (Assistant Adjutant and Quartermaster-General).

1ST PARACHUTE BRIGADE

Brigadier J. P. O Brien Twohig, C.B.E., D.S.O.

Lieutenant-Colonel E. J. B. Nelson, D.S.O., M.C. (1st Battalion The Parachute Regiment).

Lieutenant-Colonel D. R. W. Webber (2nd Battalion The Parachute Regiment).

Lieutenant-Colonel T. C. H. Pearson, D.S.O. (7th Battalion The Parachute Regiment).

2ND PARACHUTE BRIGADE (In United Kingdom).

Brigadier R. H. Bellamy, D.S.O.

Lieutenant-Colonel H. B. Coxen, D.S.O., M.C. (4th Battalion The Parachute Regiment).

Lieutenant-Colonel A. G. F. Monro (5th Battalion The Parachute Regiment).

Lieutenant-Colonel J. H. Cubbon, O.B.E. (6th Battalion The Parachute Regiment).

3RD PARACHUTE BRIGADE

Brigadier F. D. Rome, D.S.O.

Lieutenant-Colonel G. P. Rickcord, D.S.O. (3rd Battalion The Parachute Regiment).

Lieutenant-Colonel J. H. M. Hackett, D.S.O. (8th Battalion The Parachute Regiment).

Lieutenant-Colonel P. C. Hinde, D.S.O. (9th Battalion The Parachute Regiment).

3RD THE KING'S OWN HUSSARS

Lieutenant-Colonel C. A. Peel.

ROYAL ARTILLERY

Brigadier C. H. Colquhoun, O.B.E.

Lieutenant-Colonel A. F. D. Colson (33rd Airborne Light Regiment).

Lieutenant-Colonel R. A. Gorle, M.C. (66th Airborne Anti-Tank Regiment).

Lieutenant-Colonel M. I. Gregson, M.B.E.(87th Airborne Field Regiment).

ROYAL ENGINEERS

Lieutenant-Colonel A. D. Hunter, D.S.O.

ROYAL CORPS OF SIGNALS

Lieutenant-Colonel D. A. Pringle.

GLIDER PILOT REGIMENT

Lieutenant-Colonel F. A. S. Murray, M.C.

ROYAL ARMY SERVICE CORPS

Lieutenant-Colonel A. W. Salmon.

ROYAL ARMY MEDICAL CORPS

Colonel M. J. Kohane, M.C.

Major D. C. J. B. Nixon (127th Parachute Field Ambulance).

Lieutenant-Colonel J. C. Watts, M.C. (195th Parachute Field Ambulance).

Lieutenant-Colonel A. T. Marrable, D.S.O. (224th Parachute Field Ambulance).

ROYAL ARMY ORDNANCE CORPS

Lieutenant-Colonel R. J. Meech, M.B.E.

ROYAL ELECTRICAL AND MECHANICAL ENGINEERS

Lieutenant-Colonel J. M. Neilson.

6TH AIRBORNE DIVISION BATTLE SCHOOL

Lieutenant-Colonel J. H. Marriott, M.C.

6TH AIRBORNE DIVISION STAFF LIST FOR 1948

HEADQUARTERS 6TH AIRBORNE DIVISION

Major-General H. C. Stockwell, C.B., C.B.E., D.S.O.

Lieutenant-Colonel M. P. D. Dewar, M.B.E. (General Staff Officer, Grade 1—Operations).

Lieutenant-Colonel P. H. M. May, D.S.O., M.C. (General Staff Officer, Grade 1—Air).

Lieutenant-Colonel P. G. F. Young (Assistant Adjutant and Quarter-master-General).

1ST PARACHUTE BRIGADE

Brigadier F. D. Rome, D.S.O.

Lieutenant-Colonel E. J. B. Nelson, D.S.O., M.C. (1st Battalion The Parachute Regiment).

Lieutenant-Colonel T. H. Birbeck, D.S.O. (2nd/3rd Battalion The Parachute Regiment).

Lieutenant-Colonel J. H. M. Hackett, D.S.O. (8th/9th Battalion The Parachute Regiment).

2ND PARACHUTE BRIGADE (With British Army of the Rhine).

Brigadier R. H. Bellamy, D.S.O.

Lieutenant-Colonel J. H. Cubbon, O.B.E. (4th/6th Battalion The Parachute Regiment).

Lieutenant-Colonel P. S. Sandilands (5th Battalion The Parachute Regiment).

Lieutenant-Colonel P. D. Maud, M.B.E. (7th Battalion The Parachute Regiment).

3RD THE KING'S OWN HUSSARS

Lieutenant-Colonel C. A. Peel.

ROYAL ARTILLERY

Brigadier C. H. Colquhoun, O.B.E.

Lieutenant-Colonel A. G. Stuart (33rd Airborne Light Regiment).

Lieutenant-Colonel R. A. Gorle, M.C. (66th Airborne Anti-Tank Regiment).

Lieutenant-Colonel D. G. Cannal, D.S.O. (87th Airborne Field Regiment).

ROYAL ENGINEERS

Lieutenant-Colonel A. D. Hunter, D.S.O.

ROYAL CORPS OF SIGNALS

Lieutenant-Colonel D. A. Pringle.

GLIDER PILOT REGIMENT

Lieutenant-Colonel F. A. S. Murray, M.C.

ROYAL ARMY SERVICE CORPS

Lieutenant-Colonel A. W. Salmon.

ROYAL ARMY MEDICAL CORPS

Colonel P. J. Richards, D.S.O., O.B.E.

Lieutenant-Colonel A. T. Marrable, D.S.O. (16th Parachute Field Ambulance).

Lieutenant-Colonel D. G. C. Whyte, D.S.O. (23rd Parachute Field Ambulance).

ROYAL ARMY ORDNANCE CORPS

Lieutenant-Colonel R. J. Meech, M.B.E.

ROYAL ELECTRICAL AND MECHANICAL ENGINEERS

Lieutenant-Colonel M. F. Scott.

6TH AIRBORNE DIVISION BATTLE SCHOOL

Lieutenant-Colonel J. H. Marriott, M.C.

Q

BATTLE CASUALTIES, OCTOBER, 1945, TO APRIL, 1948

MONTH	KILLED	WOUNDED	TOTAL
1945			
October	—	—	—
November	1	13	14
December	—	2	2
Total	1	15	16
1946			
January	—	8	8
February	2	1	3
March	1	2	3
April	7	16	23
May	—	2	2
June	—	3	3
July	1	2	3
August	—	—	—
September	2	12	14
October	3	12	15
November	2	15	17
December	2	11	13
Total	20	84	104
1947			
January	—	12	12
February	—	1	1
March	2	4	6
April	—	6	6
May	2	3	5
June	1	2	3
July	1	10	11
August	—	2	2
September	—	—	—
October	—	11	11
November	1	3	4
December	3	17	20
Total	10	71	81
1948			
January	4	20	24
February	10	22	32
March	7	12	19
April	6	12	18
Total	27	66	93
Total 1945-48	58	236	294

Appendix J 2.

GRAPH OF BATTLE CASUALTIES SUSTAINED BY 6TH AIRBORNE DIVISION, NOVEMBER 1945, TO APRIL, 1948.

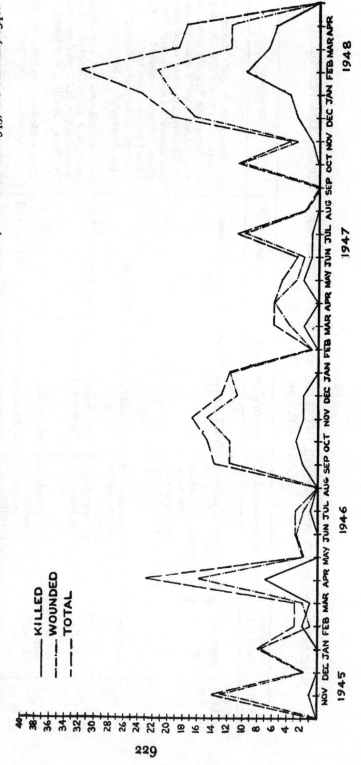

SUMMARY OF MAJOR AND MINOR INTERNAL SECURITY OPERATIONS DURING THE PERIOD OCTOBER, 1945, TO APRIL, 1948

DATE	NAME OF OPERATION	TYPE OF OPERATION	TROOPS INVOLVED	PLACE	REMARKS
1945 21 Oct. to 8 Nov.	"Benzine"	Deployment of units of 6th Airborne Division preparatory to taking action to maintain order, with particular reference to Tel Aviv.	6th Airborne Division	Lydda and Samaria Districts	3rd Parachute Brigade moved to Lydda District. On 28th October, 6th Airlanding Brigade moved to area of Lydda and Ras al Ein, and on 8th November started to move into Samaria District. 2nd Parachute Brigade remained in the Gaza District. (See text.)
14 ,,	"Bellicose"	Restoration of law and order, and a subsequent curfew.	3rd Parachute Brigade	Tel Aviv	Followed large-scale rioting on 14th November. (See text.)
23 ,,	—	Cordon and search in support of police.	One company 8th Parachute Battalion	Area North of Tel Aviv	Area searched as a result of illegal immigrant ship *Demetrius* being intercepted by R.N. off shore near Tel Aviv. Nothing was found.
25 ,,	"Guy Fawkes"	Cordon and search in support of police	3rd Parachute Brigade	Shefayim and Rishpon	First settlement searches by the Division. (See text.)
25 & 26 Nov.	—	Cordon and search in support of police	6th Airlanding Brigade	Givat Haiyim and Hogla	First settlement searches by the Division. (See text.)
28 Dec.	—	Imposition of house curfew	3rd Parachute Brigade ; 4th Parachute Battalion; one squadron 3rd Hussars	Tel Aviv	Imposed as punitive measure to prevent reoccurrence of dissident activity.
29 ,,	"Pintail"	Cordon and search	3rd Parachute Brigade with 4th Para-	Ramat Gan	This search was carried out as a result of disturbances in Tel Aviv

Date	Code name	Operation	Troops under command	Locality	Remarks
			chute Battalion under command		on 27th December. 59 persons were detained for further interrogation. (See text.)
1946 8 Jan.	"Heron"	Cordon and imposition of house curfew	3rd Parachute Brigade; 4th Parachute Battalion; one squadron 3rd Hussars	Rishon le Zion	The troops cordoned the town and enforced the curfew while police searched for suspects. 55 persons were detained, one of whom was a known wanted man. The cordon was withdrawn at 1300 hours.
16 ,,	—	Countrywide search of buses and parcel offices in support of police.	3rd Parachute Brigade; 6th Airlanding Brigade	Countrywide	Police made a number of arrests and some explosives were found.
22 to 28 Jan.	—	Nightly patrols of airfields	3rd and 9th Parachute Battalions	Lydda District	To counteract likelihood of Jewish attacks on aircraft and airfield installations.
24 & 25 Jan.	—	Patrols to Police Stations	5th and 6th Parachute Battalions	Majdal and Iraq Suweidan	To maintain contact with isolated Police Stations. No result.
24 Jan.	—	Small-scale search in support of police	8th Parachute Battalion	Tel Aviv	
30 ,,	"Pigeon"	Cordon and search	3rd Parachute Brigade (less 9th Parachute Battalion)	Shapiro quarter of Tel Aviv	Carried out in support of police. A number of civilian suspects were arrested.
18 Feb.	—	Snap search	One platoon 8th Parachute Battalion	Hashomer Street, Tel Aviv	With detachment of Police Mobile Force, the platoon raided house thought to contain Stern radio transmitter. Transmitter was captured, 20 persons were arrested and some arms were found.
25 & 26 Feb.	—	Imposition of house curfew	3rd Parachute Brigade	Petah Tiqva and Rehovoth	Punitive measure resulting from Jewish raids on airfields at Qastina, Petah Tiqva and Lydda on 25th February. The estimated damage to aircraft was £750,000. The house curfew on Petah Tiqva and Rehovoth was lifted on 26th February and was replaced by a
26 ,,	—	Imposition of road restriction order in Divisional area	3rd Parachute Brigade; 6th Airlanding Brigade	Lydda District and part of Samaria	

DATE	NAME OF OPERATION	TYPE OF OPERATION	TROOPS INVOLVED	PLACE	REMARKS
6 Mar.	—	Searches	3rd Parachute Brigade with 4th Battalion under command	Area surrounding Sarafand	road restriction order. Road blocks were established throughout the affected area. Kefar Menahem was also searched during the course of the day. Searches were carried out in an effort to apprehend gangsters and recapture ammunition which was stolen from 3rd Hussars in Sarafand. Operations successful.
25 "	—	Restoration of law and order in support of police	Mobile Column 8th Parachute Battalion; one Squadron 3rd Hussars	Tel Aviv	This force was sent into Tel Aviv to quell communal disturbances which had broken out, possibly as a cover for illegal immigration. 1 Jew was killed.
3 Apr.	—	Cordon and search in support of police	One Company 4th Parachute Battalion	Kefar Marmorek and Ezra Bitsaron	The police detained a number of suspected persons thought to have been implicated in the attacks on the railways at Yibna and Isdud. A rifle and ammunition were found in Kefar Marmorek.
23 "	—	Road-blocks established	5th Parachute Battalion; 6th Battalion The Gordon Highlanders	Ramat Gan area	Established to apprehend Jews who had attacked the Ramat Gan police station, killing 1 British constable and stealing arms. No one was arrested by the road-block personnel.
25 "	—	Imposition of house curfew and cordon	2nd Parachute Brigade Group	Tel Aviv	Curfew was imposed at 2300 hours, after murder of 7 Airborne soldiers at the car park by Jews. The Karton quarter of the town was also cordoned and later searched by the police on 26th

Date	Operation	Action	Unit	Location	Remarks
					April. 79 persons were detained. (See text.)
23 May	—	Patrols	1st Parachute Battalion	Nathanya	The town was patrolled after two loud explosions had been heard. Nothing found.
19 June	—	Imposition of house curfew	2nd Parachute Brigade	Tel Aviv	Imposed from 0500 hours as a result of kidnapping of 5 British officers from the Officers' Club in Tel Aviv on 18th June. (See text.) Approximately 200 curfew breakers were arrested before the curfew was revoked at midnight. No results.
19 „	"Chestnut"	Cordon and Search	3rd and 8th Parachute Battalions	Becrot Yits-haq	Anti-dissident patrols to prevent illegal training and curtail movement by day.
21 to 26 June	"Harry"	Patrols	2nd Parachute Brigade	Lydda District	Search for kidnapped officers. No results.
22 „	"Exercise"	Cordon and search	6th Battalion The Gordon Highlanders	Gat Rimmon	No trace of kidnapped officers, but small number of arms and ammunition found. 7 Jews detained.
24 „	"Window"	Cordon and search	6th Battalion The Gordon Highlanders	South-east quarter of Rehovoth	4 Jews were arrested and a quantity of arms and ammunition was located. No trace of missing officers.
25 „	"Blind"	Search	One Company 6th Battalion The Gordon Highlanders	Orange groves, S.E. of Rehovoth	No results.
26 „	—	Search	5th Parachute Battalion	Area, S.E. of Rehovoth	
29 „	"Agatha"	Settlement searches to apprehend all possible members of Palmach, and certain Hagana leaders	6th Airborne Division	Divisional area	One of the largest operations in which the Division was involved. (See text.)
30 „	—	Imposition of house curfew	3rd Parachute Brigade	Rehovoth	Punitive curfew imposed until 1800 hours due to bad behaviour of Jews in town during operation "Agatha" the previous day.

DATE	NAME OF OPERATION	TYPE OF OPERATION	TROOPS INVOLVED	PLACE	REMARKS
23 July	—	Searches	8th and 9th Parachute Battalions	Jerusalem (Jewish quarter of Old City, Moshe Yemen and area north of Italian Hospital)	Searches carried out after attack on King David Hotel on 22nd July by I.Z.L. 46 Jews detained, 1 dead and 1 wounded Jew found in Old City, who had taken part in the attack. A nightly house curfew imposed on Jerusalem from 24th July. (See text.)
30 July to 2 Aug.	"Shark"	Cordon of the town and search of every house and building with the object of screening all inhabitants and detaining any suspects.	6th Airborne Division with troops of 1st Infantry Division under command	Tel Aviv and part of Jaffa	The largest operation of its type in Palestine. (Full account in text.)
28 Aug. to 2 Sep.	"Bream"	Cordon and search for illegal arms	8th Parachute Battalion	Dorot	Very thorough searches of settlements for arms. (See text.)
	"Eel"	Cordon and search for illegal arms	3rd Parachute Battalion	Ruhama	
29 Aug.	"Weed Out"	Search	2nd Parachute Brigade Group	Latrun detention Camp	Objects of the search were: to identify all detainees; transfer 9 important detainees to Jerusalem and search for weapons and tools hidden for purposes of escaping. The operation achieved all its objects.
10 Sep.	—	Cordon and search for suspects	3rd Parachute Brigade Group	Ramat Gan	1,931 persons screened, of whom 47 were detained for further interrogation. No illegal arms found.
10 ,,	"Hazard"	Imposition of house curfew to prevent further acts of violence taking place	2nd Parachute Brigade Group	Tel Aviv	During the curfew, Voolvolski Street on Jaffa/Tel Aviv border was searched and 54 persons detained.
13 ,,	"Windfall"	Cordon and search	2nd Parachute Brigade Group	Jaffa and Tel Aviv	To prevent escape of dissidents after they had attacked three

Date	Code	Task	Unit	Place	Result
23 „	—	Cordon and search for illegal arms	2nd Parachute Brigade	Orange grove near Petah Tiqva	banks almost simultaneously. During small searches 27 persons were detained. Small quantity of arms found.
1 Oct.	—	Imposition of house curfew	2nd Parachute Brigade Group	Petah Tiqva	Lasted two nights and was imposed to curtail night movement.
3 „	—	Road restriction imposed during hours of darkness	2nd Parachute Brigade	Petah Tiqva, Benei Beraq, Ramat Gan, Givat Haiyim, Rishon le Zion, Rehovoth	This was imposed following numerous recent minor attacks carried out on troops in these areas.
3 „	—	Cordon and search for illegal arms	3rd Parachute Battalion	Orange grove at Kefar Beilu	C.R.M.P. mine-detecting dogs were used during search, but nothing was found.
9 „	—	Cordon and search for illegal arms	1st Parachute Battalion	Part of Nathanya	4 Jews were arrested for illegal possession of arms and a small quantity of arms was located.
23 „	—	Cordon and search for suspects	4th Parachute Battalion	Area of Tel Aviv near shore	1 suspect gangster arrested.
23 „	—	Cordon and search for suspects	One Company 8th Parachute Battalion	Yemenite quarter of Rehovoth	4 males detained for further interrogation.
31 „	—	Search of two buildings for suspected I.Z.L. headquarters at night	Four platoons, 1st Parachute Battalion	Tel Aviv	Some military equipment and I.Z.L. membership cards found.
31 „	—	Search of school for arms	Two Companies 2nd Parachute Battalion	Petah Tiqva	No results.
20 Nov.	"Earwig"	Railway protection	Parachute Brigades and Divisional Royal Artillery	Divisional area (Hadera to Rafah)	A large-scale operation carried out over almost the entire main railway system of Palestine. (See text.)
30 Dec.	"Prawn"	Cordon and search for dissidents	1st Parachute Brigade; 8th Parachute Battalion; 3rd Hussars	S.E. part of Petah Tiqva	Search completed by 1035 hours on 31st December. Of the 939 persons screened, 19 males were detained. A small arms cache was also found.

235

DATE	NAME OF OPERATION	TYPE OF OPERATION	TROOPS INVOLVED	PLACE	REMARKS
30 Dec.	"Noah"	Cordon and search for dissidents	2nd Parachute Brigade; one Squadron 12th Lancers	Gevah, Ramat Tiomkin (S.E. of Nathanya)	24 males were arrested. Search finished at 1415 hours on 31st December.
31 "	"Ark"	Cordon and search for dissidents	3rd Parachute Battalion; one Company 2nd Battalion King's Royal Rifle Corps	Yemenite quarter of Rishon le Zion	Search was completed the same day and 18 males were detained.
1947 1 Jan.	"Lobster"	Cordon and search for dissidents	1st Parachute Brigade; 3rd Hussars; Composite Regiment Royal Artillery	Karton quarter of Tel Aviv	2,242 persons were screened of whom 47 males were arrested. Search was completed by 1700 hours.
2 "	"Mackerel"	Cordon and search for dissidents	3rd Parachute Brigade; one Squadron 3rd Hussars; "A" Company 2nd Battalion King's Royal Rifle Corps.	Yemenite quarter of Rehovoth	Search was completed the same day. 19 persons were detained. Some arms and 3 mines also found.
3 "	"Cautious"	Cordon and search for dissidents	1st Parachute Brigade Group	Sht Hat Tiqva and Sht Ezra	The search was finished by 1800 hours and of the 3,985 persons screened, 34 were arrested.
3 "	"Lonesome"	Cordon and search for dissidents	2nd Parachute Brigade Group	Montefiore	A small quantity of war stores was captured. The search was completed at 1530 hours and 30 persons were detained.
7 to 17 Jan.	"Octopus"	A series of small operations designed to keep the dissidents on the move by subjecting them to snap searches and road checks	6th Airborne Division	Divisional area	This was a series of operations conducted over a period of 10 days during which numerous suspects were arrested in snap searches. Much use was made of mobile road-blocks which achieved a great measure of surprise.
27 "	—	Imposition of house curfew by night	3rd Parachute Brigade; 2nd Battalion The East Surrey	Hadar hak Carmel, Haifa	The curfew was imposed for two nights during which 241 curfew breakers were arrested. The oper-

Date	Code name	Operation	Regiment under command	Location	Remarks
2 Feb.	"Polly"	The evacuation of non-essential British civilians from Palestine	6th Airborne Division	Divisional area	ation followed I.Z.L. kidnapping of Judge Windham and another British subject. Operation continued until 7th February by which time 1,500 women and children were evacuated from Haifa to the United Kingdom and Egypt. (See text.) The operation took 10 days to complete. (See text.)
2 ,,	"Cantonment"	The collection of all remaining British civilians and various minor units and service detachments into military cantonments	6th Airborne Division	Divisional area	
6 ,,	—	Rapid screening of spectators of soccer match for wanted men	9th Parachute Battalion	Haifa	8,000 people were screened by police and 55 were detained.
31 Mar.	—	Imposition of house curfew	3rd Parachute Brigade	Bat Galim and Hadar hak Carmel, Haifa	Curfews were imposed at 0500 hours as a result of attack on Shell Oil tanks, and lasted for six hours.
3 Apr.	—	Imposition of house curfew	3rd Parachute Brigade	Herzliya quarter of Haifa	After mining incident had taken place on Mountain Road, this curfew was enforced for 8 hours while investigations were carried out.
16 ,,	"Harp"	Escort and burial of 4 Jewish criminals after their execution at Acre Gaol	1st Parachute Brigade	Acre and Safad	The bodies were escorted from Acre to Safad where burial took place without incident.
16 ,,	—	Imposition of house curfew	3rd Parachute Brigade; 1st Battalion Irish Guards	Bat Galim and Hadar hak Carmel	Imposed from 0500 hours to coincide with the execution of 4 Jewish criminals at Acre Gaol. The curfew was revoked at 0800 hours on 17th April.
4 & 5 May	—	Cordon and search for escaped prisoners	1st Parachute Brigade	Acre, Jiddin, Ein Ham Mifrats, Mishmer Hay Yam	On 4th May, after the attack by the Jews on Acre Gaol, during which over 200 prisoners escaped,

DATE	NAME OF OPERATION	TYPE OF OPERATION	TROOPS INVOLVED	PLACE	REMARKS
					a cordon was thrown round the town. The police searched Acre at first light and at the same time the Army cordoned and searched three Jewish colonies. No prisoners were recaptured.
11 June	"Camel"	Cordon and search of Arab tented camps for illegal arms and escaped convicts	One Company 1st Parachute Battalion; one troop 17th/21st Lancers; Mounted troops Cavalry Regiment, T.J.F.F.; detachment 1st Mechanized Regiment Arab Legion	South of Beisan	The search was undertaken by the police and began at first light. The troops were used on road-block, patrol and mobile reserve duties. One rifle was found and a number of suspects were detained.
20 & 30 July	—	Imposition of nightly house curfew	3rd Parachute Brigade Group	Hadar hak Carmel and Ahuzzat areas of Haifa	This curfew was enforced for 11 nights following the decision that Jewish immigrants on the *President Warfield* were to be taken back to Europe. During the first 5 days, numerous road mining and sniping incidents occurred. Throughout the curfew, numerous Jews were arrested for being out of doors.
10 Sep.	—	Cordon and Search	One Company 3rd Parachute Battalion	Oil Refineries, Haifa	The C.R.L. installations were searched after an attempt to sabotage four oil tanks had been carried out. No arrests were made.
29 „	—	Establishment of road-blocks	1st Parachute Brigade	Roads leading into Haifa	All vehicles leaving town were checked as a result of major attack on the Police Headquarters building in Kingsway, Haifa.
7 Oct.	—	Cordon and search for wanted persons	1st Battalion Irish Guards	Hadera	260 persons were screened, 12 of whom were detained. 2 of them

21 ,,	— •	Capture of Syrian military outpost situated inside Palestine	One Squadron Mechanized Regiment, T.J.F.F.; two troops 17th/21st Lancers	Tel El Qadi	were I.Z.L. members. The Syrian outpost consisting of 1 Warrant Officer and 11 Other Ranks was captured during the morning and placed in the custody of the police. They were returned to the Syrian authorities later in the day.
15 to 20 Nov.	—	Imposition of a nightly road restriction order	1st Parachute Brigade	Hadar hak Carmel, Haifa	This order was imposed as a result of the renewal of dissident activity in the town. A number of Jewish vehicles were impounded by military patrols each night.
30 ,,	—	Restoration of law and order	One platoon 9th Parachute Battalion	Acre Gaol	Troops were used to quell a riot which broke out in the prison between Arab and Jewish prisoners after the U.N.O. announcement on the Partition of Palestine.
5 Dec.	—	Restoration of law and order	One Company from each of 1st and 7th Parachute Battalions, detachments of Royal Artillery and 3rd Hussars	Haifa	Troops were deployed in a show of force throughout the town, in order to prevent mob violence.
8 to 10 Dec.	—	Imposition of house curfew	7th Parachute Battalion; one Company 2nd Parachute Battalion	Arab quarter of Haifa, less the Suq	The curfew was enforced rigidly in order to restore order following recent outbreaks of violence in this area. During the curfew there was little trouble.
11 to 18 Dec.	—	Restoration of law and order	66th Airborne Anti-Tank Regiment, Royal Artillery; one Squadron 3rd Hussars; one Squadron 17th/21st Lancers	Haifa	Semi-static posts and armoured patrols were organized during this period in the town. They achieved good results in helping to limit the numerous minor outbreaks which had characterized the past week.
13 to 15 Dec.	—	Imposition of house curfew	1st Parachute Brigade	Hadar hak Carmel, Haifa	This was enforced to prevent the reoccurrence of recent attacks on

DATE	NAME OF OPERATION	TYPE OF OPERATION	TROOPS INVOLVED	PLACE	REMARKS
					British personnel, and also as a punitive measure against the Jews.
13 to 17 Dec.	—	Imposition of house curfew	One Company 8th Parachute Battalion; detachments of Mechanized Regiment, T.J.F.F.	Safad	As a result of communal disturbances, a curfew was enforced to restore law and order. The volume of sniping between the Arab and Jewish quarters as a result was considerably reduced.
19 to 20 Dec.	—	Imposition of road restriction.	One Squadron Mechanized Regiment, T.J.F.F.; two troops of 17th/21st Lancers	Huleh area	Tension in this district had been high since the Jews attacked Khissas on 18th December. The road restriction was enforced to prevent further trouble.
19 ,,	—	Restoration of law and order	One Company 2nd/3rd Parachute Battalion	Haifa	Deployment of small static and semi-static posts was made to restore public confidence. This measure was continued until the Division left Palestine.
21 to 23 Dec.	—	Imposition of house curfew	One Company 8th Parachute Battalion; one Squadron Cavalry Regiment, T.J.F.F.	Safad	Further outbreaks of violence resulted in the house curfew being reimposed. The situation was greatly improved. During the curfew a British N.C.O. was wounded by a sniper.
21 to 24 Dec.	—	Imposition of road restrictions	Mechanized Regiment, T.J.F.F.; two troops 17th/21st Lancers	Huleh area	The order was imposed to prevent the occurrence of further Arab-Jewish clashes.
30 ,,	—	Restoration of law and order and evacuation of civilian workers	One Company 2nd/3rd Parachute Battalion; one troop 3rd Hussars	Consolidated Refineries Ltd. Plant, Haifa	A serious riot developed between Jewish and Arab employees during which 6 Arabs and 41 Jews were killed and 42 Arabs and 11 Jews were injured. Troops and Police restored order and the Jewish

Date	Operation		Locality	Troops employed	Remarks
1948 1 Jan.	Cordon and search for illegal Jewish Immigrants	—	Nahariya	2nd Bn. The Middlesex Regiment; one Company 9th Parachute Battalion; one Battery, 1st Royal Horse Artillery; one composite Battery Airborne Royal Artillery; two platoons 8th Parachute Battalion	workers, who were greatly outnumbered by the Arabs, were later escorted to their homes by armoured cars. After evading the naval patrols, the Archimede beached near Nahariya and landed approximately 500 Jews. Troops cordoned the beaching area and the town of Nahariya, and at first light on 2nd January began the search for the immigrants. The operation was completed by 1400 hours and 131 Jews were arrested.
9 ,,	Skirmishes with Arabs during attacks on Jewish colonies	—	Kefar Szold and Dan	One Squadron 17th/21st Lancers; one platoon 1st Parachute Battalion	Arab bands from Syria engaged the two Jewish settlements during the early morning. Armoured cars were sent to investigate and were also fired on by the Arabs. Fired was returned at intervals throughout the day until the troops withdrew at dusk. Arabs failed to penetrate colonies.
11 ,,	Jeep patrols	—	Haifa	2nd/3rd Parachute Battalion; 8th/9th Parachute Battalion	To restore confidence where mixed labour was employed. This measure was continued until the Division left Palestine.
13 ,,	Skirmishes with Arabs during attacks on Jewish colonies	—	Lehoveth	Two troops 17th/21st Lancers	A small force of Syrians, having crossed the frontier to engage the Jews, were fired on by our armoured cars and driven back across the frontier.
16 ,,	Flag march through selected Arab areas	—	Tantura, Ein Ghazal, Fureidis and Umm Az Zinat	87th Airborne Field Regiment Royal Artillery	The column was fired on in error by the villagers of Umm Az Zinat, but no casualties were caused. Otherwise the troops were well received.

DATE	NAME OF OPERATION	TYPE OF OPERATION	TROOPS INVOLVED	PLACE	REMARKS
20 & 21 Jan.	—	Relief of Jewish Colony during Arab attack	One Company 2nd Battalion The Middlesex Regiment	Jiddin	On both days the settlement was heavily attacked by superior Arab forces which withdrew only on the approach of British troops. The column completed the march without incident.
24 ,,	—	Flag march through selected Arab areas	Detachments from: 3rd Hussars; 17th/21st Lancers; 1st Battalion Irish Guards; 2nd Battalion The Middlesex Regiment	Tarshiha, Hurfeish, Fassuta, Jish and Ein Az Zeitun	
28 ,,	—	Cordon and search for illegal arms	Two Companies 2nd/3rd Parachute Battalion	Jaba	Continued sniping from this village resulted in it being searched. A small quantity of arms and ammunition was confiscated.
31 ,,	—	Demolition of unauthorized Jewish road-blocks	One troop 3rd Hussars	Afula and Kefar Tavor	Two road-blocks were destroyed with explosives. One had also been demolished the previous day.
2 Feb.	—	Relief of Jewish Colony	Two troops 17th/21st Lancers; two platoons 1st Battalion Irish Guards	Ein Zeitim	The Arabs engaged in attacking the Jewish settlement were dispersed by mortar and 2-pounder fire from the troops.
4 ,,	—	Skirmish with troops of Arab Irregular Army	Two platoons 1st Battalion Irish Guards	Jubb Yusef	During an attack with automatic fire by an Arab band on a British military vehicle, one trooper of 17th/21st Lancers was wounded. Troops of the Irish Guards closed with the Arab force and engaged them with mortar and small-arms fire. The Arab position was assaulted and 6 Syrians were captured. No casualties were suffered by our assaulting troops.
5 & 6	—	Imposition of house	17th/21st Lancers	Tiberias	The curfew was enforced for twenty

Date		Operation	Force	Location	Remarks
Feb.	—	curfew			four hours as a result of communal disturbances.
6 Feb.	—	Relief of Jewish colony	One company 1st Battalion Irish Guards; one troop 17th/21st Lancers	Ein Zeitim	A force of Arabs which had been attacking the Jewish settlement, withdrew when engaged by mortar fire from British troops. The column completed its route without incident.
6 "	—	Flag march through Arab areas	Detachment of 2nd Battalion The Middlesex Regiment; one troop 3rd Hussars	Al Bassa, Sasa, Meirun, Ar Rama and Al Buqeia	
12 "	—	Skirmish with Arabs	Two platoons 1st Battalion Irish Guards	Tuba and Mishmar Hay Yarden	This force was sent to intercept Arabs seen crossing the River Jordan into Palestine. One platoon was pinned at dusk by superior Arab forces and was only extricated by reinforcements after 1 guardsman had been killed and 2 wounded. 3 Arabs were captured earlier in the day.
12 "	—	Skirmish with Arabs	One platoon 1st Battalion Irish Guards	4 miles north of Rosh Pinna	A party of 15 Arabs who had formed a road-block engaged British troops in error for Jews; they were eventually dispersed by troops with small-arms and mortar fire. One Arab was captured.
13 "	—	Cordon and search for illegal arms	8th/9th Parachute Battalion	Selected quarters in Haifa	A quantity of arms was located in Jewish houses which had been evacuated by their occupants. One Jew was arrested in possession of grenades.
14 "	—	Arrest of Jewish looters	One platoon, 2nd Battalion The Middlesex Regiment	142 Maintenance Unit, R.A.F.	Acting on information given by an Arab ghaffir, 11 Jews were arrested for looting.
15 "	—	Cordon and search for illegal arms	8th/9th Parachute Battalion	Houses at junction of Allenby Road and Bank Street, Haifa	5 Jews were arrested and a quantity of arms and ammunition was confiscated.

DATE	NAME OF OPERATION	TYPE OF OPERATION	TROOPS INVOLVED	PLACE	REMARKS
16 Feb.	—	Relief of Jewish colony	Platoon group 1st Parachute Battalion	Tirat Tsevi	A strong force of the Arab Liberation Army numbering about 500, put in a determined but unsuccessful and very costly attack on this colony. On the arrival of British troops the Arabs began to withdraw, although small engagements were still in progress at 1300 hours. The remaining small groups of Arabs were forced to disperse by small-arms and mortar fire, and the area was quiet by 1715 hours.
20 ,,	—	Relief of Jewish colony	Patrol 1st Battalion Irish Guards; one troop 17th/21st Lancers	North of Nubi Yusha	During the evening of 19th February, 7 Jewish vehicles were ambushed by an Arab guerilla force and the occupants were compelled to abandon them. At first light on 20th February, British Infantry and armoured cars approached the scene of the incident and engaged the Arabs, causing them to withdraw. Wounded Jews were evacuated to nearby colonies and escorts for vehicle recovery parties were supplied.
21 ,,	—	Cordon and search for illegal arms	8th/9th Parachute Battalion	Small part of Jewish area of Haifa	A three-hour search brought to light a small number of weapons and ammunition.
22 ,,	—	Relief of Jewish convoy on road to Ramat Naphthali	One Company 1st Battalion Irish Guards; one troop 17th/21st Lancers	Nubi Yusha	The Arabs were dispersed by fire from British troops and withdrew into hills overlooking Ramat Naphthali. Sniping at this colony was eventually stopped by use of

					2-pounder fire by 17th/21st Lancers.
22 ,,	—	Search of building	Detachment of 8th/9th Parachute Battalion	Agar Street, Haifa	An armoured car patrol saw two armed Arabs in a building which was later searched by Infantry. The two Arabs were arrested and a quantity of explosives was found.
24 ,,	—	Dispersal of Arab forces	One troop 17th/21st Lancers	Lubiya	Using maching-gun fire, the armoured cars attacked a party of 100 Arabs who were engaging Jewish vehicles on the main Nazareth–Tiberias Road. Casualties were inflicted on the Arabs who were compelled to withdraw.
25 ,,	—	Search of houses from which sniping had been located	8th/9th Parachute Battalion	Haifa	Houses were searched in five separate quarters of the town and a substantial number of arms, explosives and ammunition were found. 1 Arab was arrested.
27 ,,	—	Search of sniper's post	Platoon of 8th/9th Parachute Battalion	Wadi Rushmiya	Large quantity of arms found and 3 Arabs detained.
28 ,,	—	Relief of Jewish Settlement	87th Airborne Field Regiment Royal Artillery; 12th Anti-Tank Regiment Royal Artillery	Ma'anit Narbata	British troops and police were called out after an Arab attack had been launched on the Jewish settlement. On arrival of the troops the Arabs withdrew, but opened fire soon after on the troops. The Arabs were soon dispersed by small-arms and gun-fire.
29 ,,	—	Search for illegal arms	One platoon 2nd/3rd Parachute Battalion	Haifa Suq	Arms, ammunition and grenades were found.
8 Mar.	—	Search of Arab and Jewish houses for illegal arms	2nd/3rd Parachute Battalion; No. 40 Commando Royal Marines	Qiryat Eliyahu and Atiqa quarter of Haifa	A small quantity of grenades and sten magazines was discovered.

DATE	NAME OF OPERATION	TYPE OF OPERATION	TROOPS INVOLVED	PLACE	REMARKS
11 to 12 Mar.	—	Imposition of house curfew and search of house	17th/21st Lancers	Tiberias	Due to continued firing between the two communities on 10th March, a curfew was imposed on 11th March. A group of officers was fired on from a house which was later searched. A large number of arms were confiscated.
13 "	—	Restoration of law and order	17th/21st Lancers	Tiberias	Sniping broke out again and was silenced when 2-pounder fire was used.
16 "	—	Skirmish with Arab forces	Two troops 3rd Hussars	Near Beit Qeshet	While proceeding to the aid of Jews who had been ambushed by Arabs, the armoured cars were heavily engaged with automatic fire. The fire was returned with mortars and 37-mm. until dusk when the troops withdrew.
19 "	—	Assistance of Jews attacked by Arabs	One platoon 1st Parachute Battalion	Ein Harod	The Arabs engaged our troops who returned the fire with mortars and machine guns; the Arabs then withdrew.
26 "	—	Relief of Jewish convoy	One troop 17th/21st Lancers	Ramat Naphthali	The armoured cars restored the situation following an Arab attack on a Jewish convoy and then supervised the recovery of abandoned vehicles. One Jew was killed and 7 wounded by Arabs.
1 Apr.	—	Relief of Jewish colony	One platoon 1st Parachute Battalion	Beit Alfa	Arabs who attacked the colony with light mortar fire withdrew on the approach of British troops.
2 "	—	Restoration of law and order	One Company 1st Battalion Irish Guards; one troop 17th/21st Lancers	Safad	Communal disturbances were quelled by 2-pounder fire and a demonstration of force by the Infantry.

SUMMARY OF ILLEGAL IMMIGRATION TRANSHIPMENT OPERATIONS DURING THE PERIOD 22ND JANUARY, 1947, TO 31ST JANUARY, 1948

DATE	NAME OF SHIP	NUMBER OF IMMIGRANTS	REMARKS
1947 9 Feb.	Merica 800 tons	656	Stiff resistance was offered to the Royal Navy boarding party and 1 Petty Officer was wounded. During the boarding, 1 Jew was killed and 3 injured. The Merica was towed into Haifa and the transhipment operation began at 2105 hours. Most of the immigrants came from Eastern Europe.
17 ,,	San Miguel 472 tons	807	The Royal Navy boarding party met some opposition and had to use tear gas. The ship was towed into Haifa and transhipment of immigrants were completed peacefully.
28 ,,	Ulua 808 tons	1,398	On the morning of 28th February, the immigrants prevented a boarding party from gaining control of the ship and successfully beached the Ulua opposite Bat Gallim just west of Haifa port after evading the Royal Navy. The ship was an ex-corvette which the Royal Navy succeeded in boarding after it crossed the three-mile limit, but the boarding party was unable to bring it under control before it reached the beach. During the fighting on board the Ulua, casualties were suffered by both sides. Namely : Royal Navy, 4 ratings seriously hurt and 8 slightly injured; Jews, 3 serious and 27 minor injuries. None of the Jewish casualties suffered from gun-shot wounds. Jews were taken by "Z" craft to Haifa port for transhipment after troops of 9th Battalion The Parachute Regiment had cordoned the beaching site and prevented any of the immigrants from escaping into the nearby Jewish houses.
9 Mar.	Abril 753 tons	599	No opposition was encountered and the immigrants were transhipped without incident. The crew of the Abril, numbering 23, were all arrested.
13 & 14 Mar.	Susannah 400 tons	841	Although this ship beached in 3rd Infantry Division's area, the immigrants, after they had been rounded up, were transported to Haifa in military vehicles for transhipment to Cyprus.

DATE	NAME OF SHIP	NUMBER OF IMMIGRANTS	REMARKS
31 Mar.	San Filipo	1,577	700 immigrants had to be taken off the San Filipo at sea by the Royal Navy in order to avoid capsizing. Troops conducting the transhipment operation were compelled to use tear gas in order to evict the remainder.
14 Apr.	Guardian 1,786 tons	2,552	The Royal Navy boarding party met considerable opposition and were forced to open fire, killing 3 Jews and wounding 5 others. There were no naval casualties. Transhipment was carried out without incident.
22 "	Galata 500 tons	769	Resistance was offered to the boarding party who suffered 3 casualties, and tear gas had to be used before control of the ship was gained. She was towed into Haifa where transhipment was completed without further incident. The immigrants hailed chiefly from Central and Eastern Europe and it is thought that they sailed from Genoa.
17 May	Trade Winds 1,200 tons	1,422	The ship was brought peacefully into Haifa at 2000 hours. Slight opposition was offered by the immigrants during transhipment. The Jews came from Eastern Europe and had sailed from Genoa.
24 "	Orietta alias Agha 400 tons	1,457	The immigrant ship was boarded and transhipment completed without the occurrence of any untoward incident. She sailed from Venice carrying Jews from Central and Eastern Europe.
31 "	Anal 253 tons	399	Slight resistance was met by the boarding party, but no casualties were caused. Most of the Jews were of Sephardic origin and had sailed from Marseilles.
18 July	President Warfield	4,493	3 Jews were killed and several injured when the Royal Navy boarded the ship, which was eventually brought to Haifa at 1630 hours. The Jews, most of whom came from Eastern and North-West Europe, were transhipped to British transports on which they were taken to Hamburg where they disembarked on 9th September, 1947. During the transhipment operation, Judge Sandstrom, President of U.N.S.C.O.P., visited the docks.
28 "	Bruna	683	A very peaceful transhipment operation. The immigrants were chiefly from Central and Eastern Europe.
28 "	Luciano 100 tons	398	The immigrants were Sephardic Jews of low intelligence and filthy appearance. Savage resistance was met in isolated cases by troops conducting the transhipment.
27 Sep.	Farida	446	1 Jew was killed and 9 injured during initial opposition met by the Royal Navy boarding party. The transhipment to British transports progressed peacefully. This party of immigrants are believed to have embarked from an open beach near Naples. Most of the Jews were from Eastern Europe.

Date	Ship	Number	Remarks
2 Oct.	*Paducah*	1,385	Both ships were towed into Haifa after slight resistance had been offered to the British boarding parties. 1 Naval rating was slightly injured and the Jews sustained 3 casualties.
	Northlands 1,273 tons	2,664	Due to the large numbers of immigrants, the transhipment operation which began on 2nd October, did not finish until the afternoon of the 6th. Both ships had sailed from Balkan ports.
16 Nov.	*Rafaelluccia*	794	A peaceful transhipment operation.
23 Dec.	*Lo Takhiduno* or *Unafraid*	882	The immigrants were chiefly from Balkan countries. They had been embarked by lighter onto the *Unafraid* at Civitta Vecchie. Transhipment was completed peacefully at Haifa at 1245 hours.
29 ,,	*Maria Giovanni*	688	The immigrants were transhipped without incident during the early hours of the 29th December. Some Jews gave mild demonstrations but were not too troublesome.
1948 1 Jan.	*Pan York* 5,000 tons	7,557	Transhipment of illegal immigrants began in Famagusta Harbour, Cyprus, and progressed smoothly until 4th January when it was completed. The transhipment was carried out as usual by the Division, and this entailed the troops (mostly from Divisional R.A.) and their specialist equipment used in these operations, being sent to Cyprus at short notice.
	Pan Cresent 5,000 tons	7,612	
Totals	22 ships	40,079	

NOTES: 1. The *Aliyah* and *Achimede*, the two illegal immigrant ships which evaded the Royal Navy and beached at Nahariya on 16th November and 31st December respectively, have not been included in this Appendix. In both cases, all the Jews on board these ships landed and sought sanctuary in nearby colonies, although 131 immigrants from the latter ship were captured during a search of Nahariya.

2. The Royal Navy assumed responsibility for transhipment of I.J.Is. from the Army on 1st February, 1948.

CAPTURE OF ARMS AND WAR STORES FROM JEWS

MORTARS	MEDIUM MACHINE GUNS	LIGHT MACHINE GUNS	MACHINE CARBINES	RIFLES	PISTOLS	MINES	GRENADES	SMALL-ARMS AMMUNITION
	3	20	132	278	362	95	2,371	289,400

50 (2-inch)
30 (3-inch)
2 (81-mm.)
2 (50-mm.)
———
84

MORTAR BOMBS
3,370

CAPTURE OF ARMS AND WAR STORES FROM THE ARABS

MORTARS	MEDIUM MACHINE GUNS	LIGHT MACHINE GUNS	MACHINE CARBINES	RIFLES	PISTOLS	MINES	GRENADES	SMALL-ARMS AMMUNITION
	3	8	42	97	29	2	211	13,130

6 (2-inch)
2 (3-inch)
———
8

COMBINED TOTALS

MORTARS	MEDIUM MACHINE GUNS	LIGHT MACHINE GUNS	MACHINE CARBINES	RIFLES	PISTOLS	MINES	GRENADES	SMALL-ARMS AMMUNITION
92	6	28	174	375	391	97	2,582	302,530

DIARY OF EVENTS, SEPTEMBER, 1945, TO MAY, 1948

DATE	EVENT
1945	
3 Sep.	2nd Parachute Brigade Group came under command 6th Airborne Division.
7 ,,	1st Airborne Squadron, R.E., came under command 6th Airborne Division.
15 ,,	Divisional H.Q. Main Body and various advance parties embarked in U.K. for Palestine.
16 ,,	3rd Parachute Brigade Group sailed from U.K. for Palestine.
	Troops of Divisional Royal Engineers arrived in Palestine.
24 ,,	Main Divisional H.Q. closed at Bulford, Wilts.
	Major-General E. L. Bols and Tactical Divisional H.Q. arrived in Cairo and opened temporary H.Q. at G.H.Q. Middle East Forces.
27 ,,	Tactical Divisional H.Q. moved to Nuseirat Hospital Camp near Gaza.
29 ,,	6th Airlanding Brigade Group and 53rd (W.Y.) Airlanding Light Regiment, R.A., with the advance party of 2nd Parachute Brigade entrained in U.K. for Palestine.
30 ,,	2nd Battalion The Gordon Highlanders left the Division and were replaced by 1st Battalion The Argyll and Sutherland Highlanders.
2 Oct.	6th Airlanding Brigade Group sailed for Palestine.
3 ,,	3rd Parachute Brigade Group disembarked at Haifa.
6 ,,	3rd Parachute Brigade Group completed concentration in Al Bureij Camp near Gaza.
10 ,,	6th Airlanding Brigade Group disembarked at Haifa.
11 ,,	6th Airlanding Brigade Group concentrated in Mughasi Camp near Gaza.
12 ,,	2nd Parachute Brigade Group and 6th Airborne Armoured Reconnaissance Regiment, sailed for Palestine from U.K.
20 ,,	Tactical Divisional H.Q. moved from Gaza to Sarafand.
21 ,,	Operation "Benzine" began, in which units of the Division moved to prepared battle stations in the Lydda district, and several additional units were placed under command. (See text.)
22 ,,	Main Divisional H.Q. moved to Bir Salim and Tactical H.Q. closed at Sarafand.
	2nd Parachute Brigade Group disembarked at Haifa.
26 ,,	2nd Parachute Brigade Group completed concentration in Nuseirat Ridge Camp near Gaza.

DATE	EVENT

1945 (*contd.*)

27 Oct. 1st Battalion The Argyll and Sutherland Highlanders, units of Divisional Troops, and rear parties embarked for Palestine in U.K.

28 ,, 6th Airlanding Brigade began the move to area of Lydda Airfield and Ras al Ein.

31 ,, Widespread railway sabotage in Divisional area took place during the night. (See text.)

1 Nov. A nightly road curfew was imposed in the Divisional area as a result of Jewish attacks on railway installations.

6 ,, 1st Battalion The Argyll and Sutherland Highlanders, units of Divisional troops and rear parties disembarked at Haifa.

8 ,, 6th Airlanding Brigade began to move from the Lydda district to Camp 21 near Nathanya.

14 ,, Large-scale riots in Tel Aviv. 3rd Parachute Brigade deployed to restore order. Tel Aviv under military occupation for six days. Known as Operation "Bellicose." (See text.)

19 ,, Operation "Bellicose" concluded at 0530 hours.

21 ,, Brigadier R. H. Bower, C.B.E., assumed command of 6th Airlanding Brigade *vice* Brigadier R. H. Bellamy, D.S.O.

23 ,, A small-scale search by 8th Parachute Battalion of areas north of Tel Aviv for I.J.Is. who had succeeded in landing during night from Greek schooner *Demetrius*.

25 ,, Coastguard stations at Givat Olga and Sidna Ali blown up during night by Palmach as reprisal for arrest of I.J.Is. and the *Demetrius*. Day of great military activity in Plain of Sharon. (See text.)

26 ,, Settlements of Shefayim, Rishpon, Holga and Givat Haiyim searched by 3rd Parachute Brigade and 6th Airlanding Brigade. 174 Jews detained and a number of others killed and wounded as a result of resistance offered. (See text.)

8 Dec. Airborne Training Wing formed at Aqir.

14 ,, Formation of Divisional Training Centre which consisted of a Battle School, Vocational Training Wing and Airborne Training Wing.

18 ,, Divisional Ski School opened in the Lebanon.

28 ,, A house curfew was imposed on Tel Aviv by 3rd Parachute Brigade as from 0530 hours as a result of widespread attacks by Jews on 27th December.

29 ,, Operation "Pintail." As a further measure against dissident activity, Ramat Gan was cordoned and searched by 3rd Parachute Brigade. 59 persons detained. (See text.)

1946

8 Jan. Operation "Heron." Search of Rishon-le-Zion for wanted persons by 3rd Parachute Brigade. 55 suspects arrested.

16 ,, Troops of 3rd Parachute Brigade and 6th Airlanding Brigade supported police in a countryside search of public buses and parcel offices for explosives. Number of arrests made.

DATE	EVENT

1946 (*contd.*)

24 Jan.   Small-scale search carried out in Tel Aviv by 8th Parachute Battalion in support of the police.

29 ,,   The Adjutant-General, Lieutenant-General Sir Ronald Adam, addressed all officers at Sarafand.

30 ,,   Operation "Pigeon." 3rd Parachute Brigade Group less one battalion, cordoned and searched the Shapiro quarter of Tel Aviv. Number of arrests were made.

1 Feb.   Divisional H.Q. moved to Beit Daras twenty miles north of Gaza.

2 ,,   3rd The King's Own Hussars joined the Division to replace 6th Airborne Armoured Reconnaissance Regiment which was disbanded in February. In view of Arab one-day strike in protest against the British Government's decision on illegal immigration, Gaza was placed out of bounds to our troops.

18 ,,   A Stern Gang radio transmitter captured in a house in Hashomer Street, Tel Aviv, by search party of 8th Parachute Battalion and police. 20 persons arrested and a number of arms seized.

24 ,,   3rd Parachute Brigade established road-blocks through Lydda District.

25 ,,   Jews attacked Royal Air Force airfields at Lydda, Petah Tiqva and Qastina causing damage estimated at £750,000. One of the attackers was killed. As a result of this action, curfews were imposed on Rehovoth and Petah Tiqva by 3rd Parachute Brigade.

26 ,,   Curfews on Rehovoth and Petah Tiqva revoked and replaced by a road restriction. Kefar Menahem searched.

5 Mar.   Major-General A. J. H. Cassels, C.B.E., D.S.O., assumed command of the Division from Major-General E. L. Bols, C.B., D.S.O. (See text.)

6 ,,   3rd The King's Own Hussars' armoury at Sarafand raided by I.Z.L. Small quantity of ammunition stolen, but later recovered. (See text.)

10 ,,   Airborne Sergeant attacked and injured by Jews in Tel Aviv.
Airborne N.C.O. was also assaulted by Jews in Rishon.

17 ,,   Jeep of Divisional Signals attacked by mob in Tel Aviv and occupants injured.

24 ,,   1st Parachute Brigade sailed for Palestine from U.K.

25 ,,   Further disturbances by Jews occurred in Tel Aviv, Yibna and Sarona. Reinforcements from the Division were called for by the police. One Jew killed during restoration of order.

27 ,,   Sukreir railway station was attacked by Jews. No damage or casualties sustained.

29 ,,   8th Parachute Battalion won the Command Boxing Championship.

30 ,,   6th Airlanding Brigade less one battalion moved to Jerusalem and assumed command of the East Sector.

1 Apr.   Brigadier C. H. V. Pritchard, D.S.O., Commander 2nd Parachute Brigade left for U.K. to assume command of Airborne Establishments.

DATE	EVENT

1946 (*contd.*)

2 Apr. 1st Parachute Brigade disembarked at Port Said. (See text.)

Jews attacked railway installations at Yibna and Isdud, causing damage and casualties. Patrols of the Division active in counter-action.

3 " The search for the railway attackers continued, and an action took place near Rishon-le-Zion between section of 8th Parachute Battalion and 24 Jews. 14 Jews wounded. (See text.)

4th Parachute Battalion cordoned Kefar Marmorek and Ezra Bitsaron, which were searched by police. 14 persons arrested.

Main H.Q. 1st Parachute Brigade opened at Camp 21 near Nathanya.

4 " Brigadier J. P. O'Brien Twohig, C.B.E., D.S.O., arrived and assumed command of 2nd Parachute Brigade.

7 " Police posts at Yibna, Isdud and Sukhreir attacked by Jews but no casualties suffered.

A Company from each of 5th and 6th Parachute Battalions searched areas without result.

8 " 1st Parachute Brigade completed move to Camp 21, Nathanya, and assumed responsibility for Samaria District, less sub-district of Jenin.

13 " Six armed Jews in uniform raided convalescent Depot at Nathanya and stole a number of arms. During attack, a police armoured car was blown up outside the town, 2 policemen wounded. Jews responsible for explosion captured.

14 " 2nd Parachute Brigade relieved 3rd Parachute Brigade in the Lydda District. 3rd Parachute Brigade moved into Divisional reserve at Qastina.

6th Airlanding Brigade changed designation to 31st Independent Infantry Brigade.

16 " Communal disturbances between Jews and Arabs broke out in Jaffa and Tel Aviv.

18 " In nine attacks on troops by mobs of Jewish youths in Tel Aviv, 6 O.Rs. of 5th Parachute Battalion received injuries.

19 " The Army took over operation of trains to Egypt due to railway strike. 9th Parachute Battalion assumed responsibility for the protection of Gaza station and the railway line between Gaza and Isdud.

20 " 5 Airborne soldiers received superficial wounds when attacked by a crowd of Jews in Tel Aviv.

23 " A party of about 30 armed Jews in Arab dress attacked Ramat Gan police station, killing 2 policemen and stealing a quantity of arms. A number of the attackers were killed and wounded. A diversionary attack on Tel Aviv station was unsuccessful. (See text.)

24 " Railway strike ended but the Army continued to run a skeleton service until 26th April.

25 " Stern Gang attacked Divisional Car Park in Tel Aviv and killed 7 soldiers. A curfew was immediately enforced by units of the Division and Karton quarter was cordoned. (See text.)

DATE	EVENT

1946 (*contd.*)

25 Apr.   9th Parachute Battalion ceased to be responsible for protection of railways in Gaza area. The Divisional Commander paid farewell visit and inspected battalions of 6th Airlanding Brigade at Allenby Barracks in Jerusalem.

26 „   Karton quarter of Tel Aviv searched and 79 Jews detained.

27 „   All Jewish cafés in Tel Aviv ordered to close at 2000 hours and movement of traffic in the Divisional area was restricted during the hours of darkness as result of attacks on troops in Tel Aviv.

28 „   All Jewish towns and villages in the Lydda District were placed out of bounds to troops.

1 May   The report of the Anglo-American committee was published. (See text.)

4 „   Exercise "Gordon" began. (See text.)

8 „   Exercise "Gordon" concluded.

9 „   Lieutenant-General Sir Evelyn Barker, K.B.E., C.B., D.S.O., M.C., assumed command of British troops in Palestine and Transjordan from Lieutenant-General J. C. D'Arcy, C.B., C.B.E., M.C.

14 „   One Airborne soldier was shot and wounded during disturbances by gangs of youths in Tel Aviv.

20 „   Road-blocks established by units of 1st Parachute Brigade after a bank robbery had taken place in Nablus.

23 „   Tel Aviv and all other Jewish towns brought into bounds again.
Troops of 1st Parachute Battalion patrolled Nathanya after two explosions. Nothing found.

10 June   Three railway trains were attacked and burnt out by Jews at Na'an, Tel Aviv, and Ras al Ein. Attackers escaped.

11 „   Railway patrols were begun as result of attacks on 10th June.

14 „   3rd and 8th Parachute Battalions searched Beerot Yitz-haq with no results.

14 „   Field-Marshal Viscount Montgomery, C.I.G.S., arrived at Lydda Airport and inspected guard of honour provided by the Division.

15 „   C.I.G.S. addressed all officers of Palestine Command in the Garrison Cinema at Sarafand.

16 „   Railway bridges at Wadi Gaza and Rashida, and a road bridge at Wadi Gaza blown up by Jews. Road checks were continued vigorously by 1st and 2nd Parachute Brigades. Attacks on bridges, particularly in frontier areas, were widespread throughout Palestine.

17 „   Divisional R.E. were given the task of rebridging River Jordan at Allenby Bridge which had been demolished on 16th June.

18 „   5 officers including 2 from the Division were abducted by Irgun Zvai Leumi from the Officers' Club, Tel Aviv. 6th Battalion the Gordon Highlanders and 3rd Hussars investigated and cordoned certain areas.

DATE	EVENT

1946 (contd.)

21 June — Operation "Harry." Anti-dissident patrols by 2nd Parachute Brigade by day with object of stopping illegal training and hindering movement of gangsters.

22 ,, — Operation "Exercise." 6th Battalion The Gordon Highlanders cordoned and searched orange groves and buildings at Gat Rimmon for kidnapped officers. No result. 2 of kidnapped officers later released in Tel Aviv.
6th Parachute Battalion moved to Tel Litwinski.

24 ,, — Operation "Window." Search of S.E. quarter of Rehovoth by troops and police. 7 Jews arrested and arms and ammunition found.

25 ,, — Operation "Blind." Search by troops of orange groves S.E. of Rehovoth for abducted officers. 4 Jews detained and small quantity of arms, ammunition and explosives found.

26 ,, — Further searches in Rehovoth area. No results.

29 ,, — Operation "Agatha." Large-scale operation involving large forces throughout Palestine with object of arresting Palmach and certain Hagana members. Also designed to seize all pertinent documents from specified Jewish H.Qs. (See text.)

30 ,, — Punitive curfew imposed on Rehovoth by 3rd Parachute Brigade until 1800 hours as result of breaches of curfew on previous day.

4 July — Remaining 3 kidnapped officers released in Tel Aviv.

22 ,, — King David Hotel explosion in which 91 persons were killed and many more wounded. Carried out by Irgun Zvai Leumi with Stern in co-operation. 9th Airborne Squadron, R.E., moved to Jerusalem for rescue operations. (See text.)

23 ,, — 8th and 9th Parachute Battalions moved to Jerusalem to take part in search of Jewish areas. 1 dead and 1 wounded Jew found who had taken part in attack on King David Hotel. 46 Jews detained.

28 ,, — Advance party 5th Parachute Brigade arrived in Camp 22 (Nathanya) from S.E.A.C.

30 ,, — Operation "Shark"—1st day. The search of the whole of Tel Aviv carried out by the Division with eight major units under command. The largest operation of its kind ever to take place in Palestine. Operation lasted four days. (See text.)

2 Aug. — Operation "Shark" completed. 787 Jews arrested and taken to detainee camps for further investigation.

2 ,, — 5th Parachute Brigade arrived in Egypt from S.E.A.C. and moved to Camp 22 (Nathanya).

11 ,, — Owing to large number of I.J.Is. in Palestine, Government decision taken for all future arrivals to be transhipped and taken to Cyprus.

21 ,, — 7th and 17th Parachute Battalions amalgamated as 7th Parachute Battalion.

257

DATE — EVENT

1946 (contd.)

28 Aug. Operation "Bream." Cordon and arms search of Dorot by 8th Parachute Battalion. One arms cache found by mine-detecting dogs. Operation lasted six days.

Operation "Eel." Cordon and arms-search of Ruhama by 3rd Parachute Battalion. Arms cache found by mine-detecting dogs. Operation lasted six days.

Operation "Weedout." 2nd Parachute Brigade, with 3rd Hussars and detachment Divisional R.E., searched Latrun detention camp for arms and escape apparatus. All detainees identified during operation and nine important ones transferred to Jerusalem. Operation very successful.

2 Sep. Operations "Eel" and "Bream" completed.

8 „ Widespread attacks on railway with diversionary attacks carried out by Jews.

9 „ Widespread road-mining incidents at night. Casualties to troops in Divisional area: 1 killed and 3 wounded.

Area Security Officer of Jaffa (Major Doran) killed when his house was blown up by Jews.

10 „ 3rd Parachute Brigade cordoned and searched Ramat Gan for suspects. 47 Jews detained and sent to detainee camp at Rafah. Arms cache also found. 2nd Parachute Brigade searched Volovolski quarters of Tel Aviv and detained 54 Jews. Road-mining incident near Kefar Vitkin. Officer wounded.

13 „ Three bank robberies in Tel Aviv by Jewish dissidents. 7 captured. Three areas searched in Tel Aviv by 2nd Parachute Brigade. 27 Jews detained. 21st Independent Parachute Company disbanded.

23 „ 2nd Parachute Brigade searched orange groves near Petah Tiqva for Jewish illegal arms. Small quantity found.

30 „ Two military vehicles ambushed by Jews in Divisional area. Q.M.S.I. of H.Q. 1st Parachute Brigade fatally wounded by Jews near Petah Tiqva.

1 Oct. Further road ambushes by Jews in Divisional area. Curfew imposed on Petah Tiqva group of settlements by night to prevent movement of dissidents. Enforced by 2nd Parachute Brigade.

8 „ Four incidents of road mining in Divisional area.

9 „ Small-scale arms search in Nathanya by troops of 1st Parachute Brigade.

17 „ Divisional vehicle mined at Beit Lid by Jews. Three O.Rs. wounded.

18 „ Vehicle of 6th Parachute Battalion mined near Petah Tiqva. 2 wounded.

20 „ Jeep mined near Rishon-le-Zion. 1 officer seriously wounded, 1 O.R. slightly wounded.

21 „ 1st Parachute Battalion relieved 5th Parachute Battalion at Sarona.

23 „ Small-scale searches in Tel Aviv and Rehovoth. 5 Jews detained.

DATE	EVENT

1946 *(contd.)*

28 Oct.   1st and 2nd Parachute Brigades changed locations. 1st Brigade to Lydda District, 2nd Brigade to Samaria.

29 „   Jeep of 5th Parachute Battalion blown up near Ra'anana. 1 O.R. wounded.

31 „   Small-scale search for I.Z.L. members in Tel Aviv and arms search in Petah Tiqva by 1st Parachute Battalion. Vehicle of 195 Parachute Field Ambulance mined near Petah Tiqva. 2 soldiers killed and 2 wounded.

2 Nov.   Three-tonner containing patrol of 7th Parachute Battalion mined near Tel Litwinski, 10 wounded, 3 seriously. Vehicle of 9th Parachute Battalion forced off road by taut wire near Petah Tiqva. Driver injured.

3 „   Train mined by Jews near Ras al Ein. Crew of engine injured.

5 „   2 trains attacked by Jews in Divisional area.

7 „   Cairo-Haifa troop train mined by Jews near Beer Yaacov. 1 N.C.O. wounded.

8 „   Minor incident of railway sabotage near Na'an.

10 „   Ras al Ein railway station destroyed by suitcase-bomb planted by 4 Jews dressed as Palestine Police. 3 O.Rs. wounded.

11 „   Railway line sabotaged in two places near Qalqiliya.

13 „   Train mined near Sht Ha Tiqva by Jews. Fireman and 1 policeman injured.

14 „   Officer of 2nd Battalion The Royal Ulster Rifles wounded at Lydda junction while visiting sentries at night. Assailant escaped. Field-Marshal Viscount Montgomery, C.I.G.S., addressed all officers at Sarafand.

15 „   Brigadier F. D. Rome, D.S.O., assumed command of 3rd Parachute Brigade from Brigadier G. W. Lathbury, D.S.O., M.B.E.

17 „   1 officer killed and 1 N.C.O. wounded, both of 1st Airborne Squadron, Royal Engineers, while lifting railway mine fitted with anti-handling device.
Further incidents of road and railway mining. 8 casualties to Police and R.A.F. in Divisional area.

18 „   1 officer of 9th Airborne Squadron, R.E., killed and 1 officer and 1 O.R. of 1st Airborne Squadron, R.E., wounded while lifting railway mine.

19 „   Further incident of railway mining near Ras al Ein.

20 „   Operation "Earwig" began. Railway protection scheme involving large numbers of troops on patrolling and guarding duties. (See text.)

23 „   Railway sabotage near Sht Ha Tiqva. Tracks followed into settlements but no results.

25 „   2 single vehicles fired on near Beit Dajan. 1 officer wounded.

2 Dec.   Jeep of 2 F.O.B. R.A. (Airborne) mined by Jews near Jerusalem. 4 O.Rs. killed.

DATE	EVENT

1946 *(contd.)*

3 Dec. Jeep of 4th Parachute Battalion blown up near Ra'anana. 2 O.Rs. wounded.

5 „ 2 buildings of H.Q. South Palestine District at Sarafand, wrecked when vehicle full of explosives, parked alongside by a Jew, blew up. 2 killed, 28 wounded.

27 „ Instructions issued for forthcoming move of Division to North Palestine.

29 „ 1 officer and 3 S./Sergeants abducted by I.Z.L. and flogged in retaliation for sentence of eighteen strokes passed on I.Z.L. bank robber. Later in evening, party of 5 Jews, suspected of being implicated in the above incident attempted to crash road-block at Wilhelma. 1 Jew killed and 1 British O.R. wounded in exchange of fire. Remaining 4 Jews captured; later tried; ultimately hanged. (See text.)

30 „ Operation "Prawn." As result of previous days' happenings, 1st Parachute Brigade with 8th Parachute Battalion and 3rd The King's Own Hussars, under command, cordoned and began searching Petah Tiqva. Operation "Noah." 2nd Parachute Brigade with one Squadron 12th Royal Lancers under command, cordoned and began searching Gevah and Ramat Tiomkin.

31 „ Operations "Prawn" and "Noah" completed. 19 suspect Jews detained in former and 24 in latter. Operation "Ark." 3rd Parachute Battalion cordoned and searched Yemenite quarter of Rishon-le-Zion. 18 suspect Jews detained.

1947

1 Jan. Operation "Lobster." Cordon and search of Karton quarter of Tel Aviv by 1st Parachute Brigade, with 3rd The King's Own Hussars and a composite regiment, R.A., under command. Curfew imposed 0500 hours, search started 0635 hours. 2,242 persons screened, 47 detained. Operation concluded 1700 hours.

2 „ Major-General A. J. H. Cassels, C.B.E., D.S.O., relinquished command of Division.

Operation "Mackerel." Cordon and search of Yemenite quarter of Rehovoth by 3rd Parachute Brigade with "C" Squadron 12th Royal Lancers and "A" Company 2nd Battalion King's Royal Rifle Corps under command. 1 arms cache found and 3 road shrapnel mines of a new type. 1,280 Jews screened of whom 19 were detained. Operation lasted from 0635 hours until 1530 hours.

Battalion H.Q. of 1st Parachute Battalion in Citrus House, Tel Aviv, attacked with small-arms fire under cover of darkness by Jews. 1 O.R. wounded, attack repulsed.

4 vehicles of the Division blown up by Jews between Petah Tiqva and Hadera. 8 wounded.

Death sentence passed on a Jew, Dov Gruner. (During the ensuing months Dov Gruner acquired an entirely unmerited notoriety as a result of legal complications attached to numerous appeals on his

S

1947 (*contd.*)

behalf against the death sentence. He was eventually hanged at Acre Gaol, 16th April.)

3 Jan. Operation "Cautious." Cordon and search of Sht Ha Tiqva and Sht Ezra by 1st Parachute Brigade with various other units under command. 3,985 persons screened, 34 detained.

Operation "Lonesome." Cordon and search of Montefiore by 2nd Parachute Brigade with one Squadron 12th Royal Lancers under command. Small quantity of war stores discovered. 1,217 persons screened, 30 detained.

5 O.Rs. of 4th Parachute Battalion wounded when their vehicle was mined north of Petah Tiqva.

3 O.Rs. of 5th Parachute Battalion in jeep, wounded by electrically detonated shrapnel mine south of Petah Tiqva.

Sergeant D. Westley of Division R.E.M.E. Workshops commended for gallantry after entering a minefield at Qastina and rescuing a seriously injured Arab child.

5 ,, Major-General E. L. Bols, C.B., D.S.O., reassumed command of 6th Airborne Division.

7 ,, Operation "Octopus" began. This consisted of a series of snap searches and road checks with the object of keeping the dissidents on the defensive. (See text.)

18 ,, 3rd and 8th Parachute Battalions moved from Qastina to Athlit and Camp 148, Haifa, respectively.

19 ,, 9th Parachute Battalion moved to Peninsula Barracks, Haifa.
H.Q. 3rd Parachute moved to Haifa.

20 ,, 1st and 2nd Parachute Battalions moved from Sarona and Tel Litwinski to Camps 260 and 253 north of Acre.

21 ,, H.Q. 1st Parachute Brigade moved from Tel Litwinski to Nazareth.
7th Parachute Battalion moved from Lydda to Rosh Pinna.
3rd The King's Own Hussars (less 1 squadron) moved to Afula.
1 squadron moved to Ahuzzat near Haifa.

22 ,, Divisional H.Q. moved to Haifa.
Divisional Signals Regiment moved to Haifa.

24 ,, 2nd Parachute Brigade Group left Haifa for U.K. in H.T. *Alcantara.* (For composition of Brigade see "Order of Battle".)

27 ,, 3rd Parachute Brigade (now responsible for Haifa District) with 2nd Battalion The East Surrey Regt. and "B" Squadron 3rd The King's Own Hussars under command, cordoned and curfewed Hadar hak Carmel (Jewish quarter of Haifa) during night. This followed kidnapping by I.Z.L. on previous day of a British subject in Jerusalem, and of Judge Windham from his District Court in Tel Aviv.

28 ,, Curfew on Hadar hak Carmel raised at 0600 hours and reimposed at 1730 hours. 181 curfew breakers detained on first night and 60 on the second.

DATE	EVENT

1947 (*contd.*)

29 Jan. Judge Windham released near Ramat Gan.

28 ,, All existing curfews and road restrictions lifted throughout Palestine.

30 ,, Divisional R.A.S.C. moved from Gaza to Camp 80 in Hadera area.

2 Feb. Operation "Polly." The evacuation of all non-essential British civilians from Palestine. The operation was bound up with complexities, but was successfully completed by 7th February. (See text.)

Operation "Cantonment." The concentration of all remaining British civilians and outlying service detachments which were unable to provide for their own defence into organized military cantonments. The operation was completed in approximately one week. (See text.)

3 ,, The Chief Secretary of the Government of Palestine wrote to the Jewish Agency and Vaad Leumi and asked once more for their co-operation in eradicating the dissident groups.

5 ,, Jewish Agency and Vaad Leumi refused to co-operate with His Majesty's Government in combating dissidents.

6 ,, 9th Parachute Battalion assisted the police in search for a wanted member of Jewish gang at a football match in Haifa. The entire crowd of 8,000 people was screened after the match and 55 detained for further interrogation.

9 ,, Transhipment of I.J.Is. from their ship *Merica* began at 2105 hours.

12 ,, Lieutenant-General Sir Evelyn Barker, K.B.E., C.B., D.S.O., M.C., was succeeded as General Officer Commanding, Palestine, by Lieutenant-General G. H. A. MacMillan, C.B., C.B.E., D.S.O., M.C.

13 ,, Government launch, *Forerunner*, sunk in Haifa Harbour by limpet mine placed by Jews.

14 ,, The Foreign Secretary announced that His Majesty's Government had decided to take the Palestine problem to U.N.O. for advice.

17 ,, I.J.I. ship *San Miguel* arrived at Haifa, and transhipment of 807 I.J.Is. ensued.

19 ,, Vehicle from Command Signals blown up by electrically detonated mines in Haifa. No casualties.

20 ,, I.P.C. pipeline sabotaged by explosives near Indur (five miles N.E. of Afula) during night.

28 ,, I.J.I. ship *Ulua* beached opposite Bat Gallim, Haifa.

At 1445 hours, 2 Jews dressed as policemen deposited haversack containing a bomb in the Area Cash Office above Barclays Bank, Haifa. Explosion killed 2 and wounded 4.

1 Mar. R.N. car park in Harbour Street, Haifa, attacked by Hagana. 12 vehicles damaged or destroyed.

Division C.R.M.P. jeep mined on Mountain Road, Haifa, 3 N.C.Os. killed and 1 seriously wounded.

I.Z.L. blew up Goldsmith Officers' Club in Jerusalem. 13 killed and 16 wounded.

DATE	EVENT

1947 *(contd.)*

2 Mar.   Truck of Divisional Signals Regiment blown up by electrically detonated mine near Hadera. 2 O.Rs. wounded.

3 „   At 2100 hours five grenades thrown from passing taxi into Camp 182, Haifa. No casualties.
Office of the military car park, El Burj, Haifa, blown up by suitcase bomb. No casualties owing to alarm which was given in time.

8 „   Attacks by Stern Gang on various military camps and H.Qs. throughout Palestine. A number of casualties inflicted on Security Forces; 6th Airborne Division not affected.

9 „   I.J.I. ship *Abril* arrived at Haifa. 599 I.J.Is. transhipped without incident.

12 „   I.J.I. ship *Susannah* beached in South Sector. Area cordoned by troops of 3rd Infantry Division and 841 I.J.Is. eventually reached Haifa by road for embarkation for Cyprus.

16 „   Further minor road and oil pipeline attacks by Jews.

28 „   Sabotage by Jews to oil pipelines in Haifa. Damage not serious.

31 „   Transhipment of 1,577 passengers from I.J.I. ship *San Filipo* began at 0630 hours. Considerable opposition by Jews during operation. Major sabotage by Jews to Shell Company oil storage tanks in Haifa. 20,000 tons of oil destroyed. Damage estimated at £500,000. Blaze lasted four days. I.Z.L. claimed responsibility.

1 „   All Divisional R.A. units redesignated. (See "Order of Battle.")

3 „   Divisional H.Q. ration truck blown up on Mountain Road, Haifa. 3 O.Rs. wounded. Herzliya quarter of Haifa curfewed during day.

14 „   I.J.I. ship *Guardian* reached Haifa. Considerable opposition to R.N. boarding party. 3 Jews killed and 5 wounded. Total of 2,552 I.J.Is. transhipped.

16 „   4 Jewish criminals including Dov Gruner executed at Acre Gaol. Bodies escorted by 1st Parachute Brigade to Safad where they were buried. Operation "Harp." 3rd Parachute Brigade with 1st Irish Guards under command cordoned and curfewed Hadar hak Carmel and Bat Gallim areas of Haifa. Curfew raised 17th April without incident.

18 „   Two incidents in which troops were fired on in Haifa but no casualties sustained.

22 „   Cairo–Haifa train blown up by Stern Gang near Rehovoth, killing 5 O.Rs. and wounding 21.
I.J.I. ship *Galata* arrived Haifa. 769 passengers transhipped.

26 „   Assistant Superintendent of Police Conquest, chief of Haifa C.I.D., murdered by Stern Gang. Troops fired at and stopped taxi containing gangsters but were unable to prevent their escape on foot.

29 „   Several cases of clandestine street fighting between I.Z.L. and Hagana. (When the activities of the extremists became embarrassing to the Hagana, they chose to treat the matter as a domestic problem rather

DATE	EVENT

than let the Security Forces become involved. As a result, little was achieved in bringing the gangsters to justice.)

4 May — Attack on Acre Gaol by I.Z.L. and Stern. 217 prisoners escaped. (See text.)

5 „ — Widespread searches in Northern Palestine for escaped prisoners from Acre.

14 „ — Railway line in Binyamina area attacked by night in three places.

15 „ — Train carrying Arab and Jewish workers to 614 Army Ordnance Depot, Haifa, blown up near Bat Gallim, Haifa. No casualties. 2 officers killed and 2 wounded of Divisional R.E., while dismantling mine on railway line near Qiryat Motskin, Haifa.

17 „ — I.J.I. ship *Trade Winds* arrived at Haifa under R.N. escort. 1,422 I.J.Is. on board.

24 „ — I.J.I. ship *Orietta* arrived at Haifa with 1,457 immigrants on board.

28 „ — Unsuccessful attempt at sabotage by Jews to tanks in oil dock, Haifa harbour. 1 Police Sergeant wounded.

31 „ — I.J.I. ship *Anal* arrived at Haifa with 399 immigrants on board.

5 June — Athlit railway station blown up at 0225 hours, after Arab sentry was attacked. I.P.C. pipeline sabotaged with explosives at 0315 hours. Fire extinguished by 0830 hours. 800 tons of oil lost.

11 „ — One company of 1st Parachute Battalion stood by to support police in search of Arab tented camp south of Beisan for escaped convicts and illegal arms. 6 Arabs arrested.

12 „ — Parade in honour of H.M. The King's Birthday held in Haifa. Salute taken by G.O.C. Attended by Arab and Jewish notables.

16 „ — U.N.S.C.O.P. began its investigations in Palestine. The Committee was eagerly supported by Jews and almost boycotted by Arabs throughout its stay in the country.

19 „ — Minor bomb incident at entrance of Girls' High School, Haifa. No casualties and limited damage. Motive not clear.

28 „ — Members of Stern Gang attacked Astoria Restaurant in Haifa at night with automatic weapons. 1 officer of 6th Airborne Division fatally wounded, 1 seriously wounded and a third slightly wounded. Major E. A. D. Liddle, of Divisional H.Q., later decorated with M.B.E. for gallantry during attack.

2 July — 1st Parachute Battalion moved to Camp 7 near Zerka in Transjordan for training.

12 „ — Sergeants Paice and Martin of 252 Field Security Section, kidnapped by I.Z.L. in Nathanya. Held as hostages against 3 of their members under sentence of death for Acre Gaol attack.

18 „ — I.J.I. ship *Presiaent Warfield* boarded by R.N. Brought into Haifa at 1630 hours and total of 4,493 I.J.Is. transhipped for return to Europe. Judge Sandstrom, chairman of U.N.S.C.O.P. watched operation.

DATE	EVENT

1947 (*contd.*)

19 July Stern Gang murdered a British policeman and seriously wounded another in Haifa.

I.J.Is. from *President Warfield* left in transports for South of France where it was hoped they would be disembarked and returned to Germany.

20 ,, House curfew by night imposed in Haifa until further notice, with object of preventing incidents following return of I.J.Is. to Europe. Brigadier J. P. O'Brien Twohig, C.B.E., D.S.O., assumed command of 1st Parachute Brigade *vice* Brigadier R. H. Bellamy, D.S.O., who took command of 2nd Parachute Brigade in U.K.

21 ,, Day and night of incidents in Haifa area. A number of attacks carried out under cover of darkness by Jews. Included attack against radio station on Mount Carmel adjacent to H.Q. 6th Airborne Division. Attack repulsed by troops of Divisional H.Q. without damage or casualties. 1 Jew killed.

Jeep of Divisional Signals Regiment blown up by electrically detonated mine in Haifa. 1 O.R. wounded.

22 ,, 15-cwt. truck of 3rd The King's Own Hussars blown up by electrically detonated mine on Mount Carmel. 1 O.R. wounded.

23 ,, 15-cwt. truck of 2nd Squadron Palestine Command Signals blown up at Ahuzzat near Haifa. 1 O.R. killed and 3 wounded.

3 O.Rs. of 3rd Parachute Battalion wounded during night in Haifa by delayed-action mine while on curfew duty.

25 ,, Continued trouble in Haifa. Mines neutralized by R.E. and British troops sniped at by Jews.

26 ,, 21 Jews detained by police and troops of 8th Parachute Battalion during search in Sirkin Street, Haifa.

28 ,, I.J.I. ships *Luciano* and *Bruna* arrived at Haifa.

29 ,, 3 I.Z.L. gangsters executed at Acre Gaol. Sergeants Paice and Martin found hanged near Nathanya.

More incidents in Haifa. Destruction with explosives of police check post between Haifa and Acre, railway sabotage near Athlit, search by 8th Parachute Battalion.

31 ,, 5 Jews killed and 15 wounded in Tel Aviv in reprisals by members of Security Forces for murder of two British sergeants.

4 Aug. Bank robbery in Haifa. Barclays Bank, Herzl Street, robbed of £1,250. Bank clerk murdered by Jewish gangsters.

19 ,, Major-General H. C. Stockwell, C.B., C.B.E., D.S.O., assumed command of 6th Airborne Division from Major-General E. L. Bols, C.B., D.S.O.

21 ,, Bank robbery and bomb explosion by Jews in Haifa.

23 ,, Minor clash between Jews and Arabs in Safad area. Two members of I.Z.L. arrested by 17th/21st Lancers in Tiberias.

1 Sep. U.N.S.C.O.P. report published.

DATE	EVENT

1947 *(contd.)*

9 Sept.   *President Warfield* I.J.Is. disembarked at Hamburg. Countrywide Jewish protest strike.

10 ,,   C.R.L. refinery at Haifa attacked under cover of darkness. Bombs planted against tanks. Damage not extensive. One company of 3rd Parachute Battalion deployed for cordon and search of area.

27 ,,   I.J.I. ship (ex-L.C.T.) *Farida*, arrived at Haifa with 446 immigrants on board.

29 ,,   Central Police H.Q. Haifa, blown up by barrel bomb rolled against building from stolen 3-tonner driven by Jews. Ground floor wrecked and building extensively damaged. 10 police killed and 54 wounded. 4 Jews later arrested.

Cairo–Haifa passenger train blown up near Binyamina by Jews. Engine and two coaches derailed but no casualties.

1 Oct.   9th Parachute Battalion moved from Safad and Rosh Pinna to Camp 253, North of Acre.

2 ,,   I.J.I. ships *Paducah* and *Northlands* arrived in Haifa under R.N. escort. 3-ton truck of 8th Parachute Battalion blown up by electrically detonated mine. 1 officer and 6 O.Rs. wounded. 1 Jew arrested in vicinity.

3 ,,   1st Battalion Irish Guards came under Divisional Command for approximately 10 days.

Small-scale search of Baifour Forest by troops of 3rd Parachute Brigade established fact that the area was in use as Jewish training ground.

6 ,,   H.Q. T.J.F.F. assumed control of Safad sub-district from 9th Parachute Battalion.

7 ,,   Yemenite quarter of Hadera searched by 1st Battalion Irish Guards for wanted persons at first light. 60 Jews screened and 12 detained. 50,000 stolen N.A.A.F.I. cigarettes recovered.

8 ,,   Three-ton truck of 1st Parachute Battalion crashed into British minefield on Mountain Road, Haifa. 2 mines detonated and 26 soldiers wounded.

10 ,,   Redeployment of Divisional R.A.S.C.

11 ,,   Movement towards Palestine frontiers of Syrian, Lebanese and Egyptian troops.

14 ,,   Some 500 Hagana reinforcements moved to Huleh settlements in face of threats of Arab attacks on frontiers.

22 ,,   Syrian Army post established on Palestine territory captured near Dan by squadron of T.J.F.F.

Military patrol fired on in Haifa by Jews near Carmelia court. No casualties.

26 ,,   Serious road accident to vehicle of 2nd Parachute Battalion near Haifa resulting in 13 O.Rs. being killed and several wounded.

4 Nov.   Order of the Day issued giving details of forthcoming reorganization within Parachute Regiment. This involved amalgamation of 2nd and

DATE	EVENT

1947 (*contd.*)

3rd Parachute Battalions, 4th and 6th Parachute Battalions, and 8th and 9th Parachute Battalions, all of which would take place within the next three months.

12 Nov. Party of C.I.D. off duty in Haifa attacked by Stern Gang. 1 policeman killed and 2 seriously wounded. Attack was reprisal for recent sentence of 20 years' imprisonment against two Stern members.

13 ,, Four British oil employees murdered by Stern Gang in Haifa.

15 ,, Nightly road restriction imposed on Hadar hak Carmel following outbreak of dissident activity. 47 vehicles impounded by 1st Parachute Brigade.

16 ,, I.J.I. ship *Aliya* evaded R.N. patrols and beached near Nahariya under cover of darkness. About 150 I.J.Is. escaped to Jewish colonies in North Palestine.

I.J.I. ship *Rafaellucia* renamed *Kadiman* arrived Haifa. 794 passengers transhipped without incident.

29 ,, Vote for Partition of Palestine by U.N.O. carried by 33 votes to 13 with 10 abstentions.

30 ,, Day of communal rejoicings, thanksgivings, protestations, strikes, disorders and general confusion by the rival communities in Palestine.

1 Dec. States of elation by Jews and anger by Arabs maintained at high level and accompanied by clashes and bloodshed.

2 ,, Jewish-Arab clashes continued and Security Forces became involved while restoring order. In some incidents, Arabs stoned or fired on British troops.

3 ,, Large Jewish timberyard at Haifa fired and destroyed by Arabs. Military patrol fired on while investigating.

4 ,, Tip-and-run raids with bomb throwing and firing out of cars by Jews and Arabs in Haifa.

6 ,, Eight incidents involving Jews, Arabs and Security Forces in Haifa. Troops fighting with Arabs one minute and Jews the next. Highlight by patrol of 7th Parachute Battalion which became involved in battle on Wadi Rushmiya bridge, Haifa. Patrol repulsed Arab attack with fire and then arrested 6 armed Jews who had taken part in same engagement.

7 ,, 7th Parachute Battalion moved from Peninsula Barracks on first stage of journey to Port Said and ultimately U.K.

8 ,, Arabs attacked police armoured car in Stanton Street, Haifa, and killed British driver. House curfew imposed on Arab quarter of Haifa (less the Suq) nightly until 10th December.

Brigadier F. D. Rome, D.S.O., assumed command 1st Parachute Brigade from Brigadier J. P. O'Brien Twohig, C.B.E., D.S.O.

9 ,, 6th Airborne Divisional C.R.M.P. jeep patrol attacked during night by Stern Gang outside Eldorado Café in Pine Road, Haifa. One N.C.O. killed.

DATE	EVENT

1947 *(contd.)*

10 Dec. Disturbances in Haifa during last ten days resulted in 50 casualties to Arabs and Jews.

Incidents in Haifa confined mainly to Wadi Rushmiya, Stanton Street, Kingsway and Khamra Square.

Stern Gang attacked two British D.Rs. in Herzl Street, Haifa. One killed, one wounded. Attack made in broad daylight in crowded street. No evidence available from those who saw it and no arrests made. At 1340 hours, 18 Arab prisoners escaped from Acre Gaol. Escape aided from inside and outside. Troops of 2nd Battalion The Middlesex Regiment intervened and prevented mass escape.

Explosions and firing in various quarters of Haifa.

11 ,, 3rd Parachute Battalion ammunition dump in Peninsula Barracks exploded at 0550 hours. Not due to sabotage but very spectacular, and watched with interest from other units at safe distance. Four minor casualties sustained.

5 Arabs killed and 6 injured at At Tira village in attack by Jews. A day of incidents in Haifa during which 1 British N.C.O. was shot and killed on Mountain Road.

12 ,, 1 O.R. killed, 1 officer and 2 O.Rs. wounded of 1st Royal Horse Artillery in Herzl Street, Haifa, Jews escaped.

2nd and 3rd Parachute Battalions began to amalgamate in Peninsula Barracks, Haifa.

13 ,, Trouble between Jews and Arabs in Safad. Several killed and wounded. Curfew imposed by one company 8th Parachute Battalion and one troop T.J.F.F. Sniping continued during curfew but stopped next day.

Curfew also imposed on Hadar hak Carmel, Jewish quarter of Haifa. Enforced by troops of 1st Parachute Brigade.

14 ,, Owing to continued communal strife, house curfew in Safad reimposed at 1700 hours and continued by night until 17th December.

15 ,, Military 3-tonner carrying mail and stores ambushed by 20 armed Jews, three miles north of Acre. Stores and documents stolen. 2 British O.Rs. kidnapped, but later set free. Thought to be a Hagana operation.

16 ,, 9th Parachute Battalion moved from Camp 253, north of Acre, to Camp 148, south of Haifa. This period was occupied by a series of snap searches on Jewish and Arab vehicles by military patrols and roadblocks which resulted in frequent discovery of arms, ammunition and explosives.

18 ,, Strong party of Hagana attacked Arab village of Khissas in Huleh Basin. 10 Arabs killed, 5 wounded. Stated to be reprisal for murder of a Jew in the area a few days previously. Arab feeling ran high as a result.

DATE	EVENT

1947 (*contd.*)

19 Dec. Tension remained high in Huleh due to Khissas attack. Road restriction imposed by 17th/21st Lancers and T.J.F.F. to prevent further trouble. Aircraft also patrolled area.

20 „ Arabs wounded 2 J.S.Ps. near Khissas.
Amalgamation of 2nd and 3rd Parachute Battalions completed.

21 „ More communal disturbances in Safad causing casualties to civilian population. Troops restored situation. 1 N.C.O. of 8th Parachute Battalion wounded.
Soldiers fired on at 2200 hours in Carmel Avenue, Haifa. 1 wounded.

22 „ Battle lasting three and a half hours took place after dark at Wadi Rushmiya between Jews and Arabs. Military patrols intensified.

23 „ I.J.I. ship *Takhidune* (or *Unafraid*) arrived at Haifa with 882 I.J.Is. on board. Transhipment completed without difficulty.
Sniping in Haifa.

24 „ Arabs active in Wadi Rushmiya area with rifles and L.M.Gs. Engaged by troops of 2nd/3rd Parachute Battalion but results not known.

25 „ Nazareth (Christmas Day). Two O.Rs. of H.Q. 3rd Parachute Brigade attacked and wounded by Arabs. Motive: the stealing of arms.
British civilian of I.P.C. murdered in Haifa by Jews.

26 „ Bomb accidentally exploded in Jewish bus while passing Arab Legion Camp at Neve Shannan. Legionnaires opened fire on bus mistaking explosion for attack on their camp. 9 Jews wounded.
N.C.O. of 2nd/3rd Parachute Battalion wounded while on patrol in Khamra Square, Haifa.

27 „ 17th/21st Lancers less one squadron, 1st Parachute Battalion less one company, and detachments of Divisional R.A., R.E., R.A.M.C. and R.E.M.E. placed under command T.J.F.F. for use in Huleh area where tension was still rising.

28 „ Escape of Arab prisoners from Acre Gaol thwarted by troops of 2nd Middlesex, but Sergeant of that unit killed by prisoners as he attempted to reach one of his sentry posts on the prison roof.

29 „ I.J.I. ship (Hagana) *Nov. 29th*, 1947, alias *Maria Giovanni*, arrived Haifa with 688 I.J.Is. on board after interception by R.N.
Party of Arabs engaged convoy of T.J.F.F. south of Rosh Pinna and killed 1 trooper and wounded another. Convoy mistaken as Jewish. Same band later attacked Jewish colony of Jubb Yosef, but was repulsed.

30 „ Two bombs thrown from passing vehicle by I.Z.L. or Stern members at crowd of Arab employees standing outside C.R.L., Haifa. 6 Arabs killed and 42 wounded. Arabs inside and outside refinery reacted spontaneously and attacked Jewish employees who were outnumbered. 41 Jews killed and 48 injured. Arrival of troops of 2nd/3rd Parachute Battalion and police prevented loss of further Jewish lives.

DATE	EVENT

1947 (*contd.*)

30 Dec. Disembarkation of I.J.Is. from *Pan York* and *Pan Crescent* began in Famagusta, Cyprus Operation carried out by troops of 6th Airborne Division moved to Cyprus for the purpose.

31   „   4 O.Rs. from Divisional Battle School in Tel Aviv attacked, and 3 of them wounded by Jews.

1948

1 Jan. Arab village Balad Es Sheik attacked by Jews at night, as reprisal for massacre at C.R.L. 14 Arabs killed, 11 wounded. 3 Jews killed, wounded unknown.

I.J.I. ship *Achimeda* evaded R.N. patrols and military Observation Posts ashore, beached at Nahariya, and landed unknown number of I.J.Is. Cordon established round town by sub-units of 1st Royal Horse Artillery, 6th Airborne Division R.A., 2nd Middlesex, 8th and 9th Parachute Battalions, in preparation for search the following day.

8th Parachute Battalion moved to Camp 148, south of Haifa, to start amalgamation with 9th Parachute Battalion.

2   „   Search of Nathanya for I.J.Is. resulted in 130 being arrested.

Jewish-Arab fighting in Safad and Ein Zeitun resulted in nine casualties.

1 officer and 2 O.Rs. of 2nd/3rd Parachute Battalion wounded when fired at by Arab whilst on patrol in Khamra Square, Haifa.

3   „   Vehicle of Divisional Battle School attacked near Nahariya. 1 O.R. wounded.

Officer of 2nd/3rd Parachute Battalion wounded in Safad.

Raid by Jews against Arab village of Abu Shusha. Casualties sustained by both sides.

4   „   Disembarkation of *Pan York* and *Pan Crescent* completed at Famagusta, Cyprus. 15,000 I.J.Is. landed.

5   „   N.C.O. of 317 Airborne Field Security Section killed by Arabs in Stanton Street, Haifa.

Hagana blew up Semiramis Hotel in Jerusalem killing 12 Arabs and injuring 2.

6   „   Officer of 2nd/3rd Parachute Battalion killed by Arab ambush outside Acre.

3rd Hussars assumed command of Nazareth Sub-District from 3rd Parachute Brigade.

9   „   Arab band from Syria attacked Dan and Kefar Szold. Attacks repulsed by British troops. (See text.)

10   „   8th and 9th Parachute Battalions amalgamated in Camp 148.

Command assumed by Lieutenant-Colonel J. H. M. Hackett, D.S.O.

11   „   Hagana destroyed bridge across River Jordan at Jisr Banat Yacub thus cutting road communications with Syria.

1948 (*contd.*)

11 Jan. A day of sniping and minor attacks in Haifa in which 1 O.R. was wounded.

Arabs carried out further attack on Dan. No result.

12 ,, Fighting continued in north of Huleh Valley. 4 Jews wounded, 2 Arabs killed.

Several incidents in Haifa in which 2 Jews were killed and one O.R. wounded.

13 ,, Syrians investing Lahovoth driven back over frontier by troops of 17th/21st Lancers.

14 ,, Arab bomb left in Post Office van exploded at corner of Bank Street and King George V Avenue, Haifa. 1 British constable killed, 6 Jews killed, 34 wounded. In firing which broke out as a result, 5 Arabs were killed, 52 wounded and 4 Jews killed and 10 wounded. Patrols of 2nd/3rd Parachute Battalion eventually restored order.

15 ,, 3rd Parachute Brigade disbanded. (See text.)

Withdrawal of T.J.F.F. to Transjordan began. (See text.)

1 O.R. wounded in incidents in Haifa.

16 ,, Jews demolished 3 Arab houses during the night.

1 officer and 1 O.R. wounded in Haifa fighting.

"Craforce" assumed command of eastern Galilee. (See text.)

17 ,, 1 O.R. of 1st Battalion Irish Guards wounded on Northern Frontier by Arab ambush.

19 ,, Jews attacked Shafa Amr and Tamra inflicting casualties on Arabs in both places.

20 ,, 8th/9th Parachute Battalion relieved 2nd/3rd Parachute Battalion as Haifa Battalion.

Yechiam attacked by Arabs. Settlement relieved by platoon of 2nd Battalion The Middlesex Regiment. Jewish casualties approximately 25 killed and wounded.

27 ,, N.C.O. of H.Q., R.A.S.C., killed in attack by Arabs on Jewish traffic, south of Haifa.

29 ,, Band of some forty Arabs attacked train near Beisan. Surprised in act by troops of 1st Parachute Battalion who captured 13. Of the remainder, 18 were captured with their loot by a road-block manned by 3rd Hussars at Afula.

1 Feb. R.N. assumed responsibility for all future transhipment operations.

9 Jews arrested in Haifa by troops of 8th/9th Parachute Battalion for being in possession of a large quantity of arms.

2 ,, Tear gas used by troops in Haifa against crowd of Arabs threatening military vehicles.

Tension followed by Arab-Jew fighting at Ein Zeitim near Safad. Order restored by troops of 17th/21st Lancers and 1st Battalion Irish Guards. 2 O.Rs. wounded.

DATE	EVENT

1948 *(contd.)*

3 Feb.   Day of minor incidents in Haifa in which casualties were suffered on all sides.

4   ,,   Syrian section of A.L.A. captured by troops of 1st Battalion Irish Guards on Tiberias–Rosh Pinna road following brief engagement.

6   ,,   Arab attack on Eiu Zeitim near Safad broken up by troops using 3-inch mortars.

8   ,,   Troops of 8th/9th Parachute Battalion in action against armed Arabs and Jews in Haifa.

11   ,,   1 O.R. shot and killed by Arabs in Haifa.

12   ,,   Day of attacks, counter-attacks, and searches in Haifa.
Fighting between troops and armed Arab bands in Rosh Pinna area.

13   ,,   Number of Arabs and Jews detained in Haifa following searches by 8th/9th Parachute Battalion in which arms were found.

14   ,,   Barrel bomb attack by Jews against unknown objective failed when bomb rolled off lorry prematurely at eastern end of Hadar hak Carmel. Bomb destroyed *in situ* by R.E.
Hagana attacked Sasa in Northern Frontier area, destroyed 14 houses and inflicted 14 casualties on Arabs.

15   ,,   1 O.R. killed and 4 wounded in incidents in Haifa.

16   ,,   Large force of A.L.A. attacked Tirat Tsevi south of Beisan and suffered severe defeat at hands of Jewish inhabitants. (See text.)

17   ,,   Arab Legion in action against Hagana post near Ahuzzat on Mount Carmel. Jews withdrew when British troops appeared.

18   ,,   All ranks of 6th Airborne Division informed of decision to disband the Division later in the year. (See text.)

19   ,,   Jewish convoy ambushed by Arabs near Manara on Eastern Frontier. 3 Jews killed, 11 wounded. Arabs driven off by troops of 17th/21st Lancers and 1st Battalion Irish Guards.

20   ,,   Mortars used in Haifa fighting for first time by Jews and Arabs.

25   ,,   Troops of 8th/9th Parachute Battalion carried out five searches in Haifa and found arms in each case.

27   ,,   Khantara–Haifa train blown up near Rehovoth by Jews. 27 British soldiers killed and 36 wounded.
2nd/3rd Parachute Battalion relieved 8th/9th Parachute Battalion as Haifa Town Battalion.

3 Mar.   Stern Gang destroyed Salameh Buildings in Haifa with explosive vehicle. 11 Arabs killed, 27 wounded.
Advance party of U.N.O. Commission for Palestine arrived in Jerusalem.

4   ,,   Officer of 1st Airborne Squadron, R.E., shot and killed near Armon Cinema in Haifa when going to assistance of Jew shot by Arab sniper.
Post Office van containing large Arab bomb discovered by Jews at road-block outside Bat Gallim. Driver shot dead. Bomb later destroyed by Divisional R.E.

DATE	EVENT

1948 (*contd.*)

6 Mar. Divisional advance parties returning to U.K. embarked on H.T. *Franconia* at Haifa.

9 „ 87th Airborne Field Regiment, R.A., and 9th Airborne Squadron, R.E., embarked on the *Samaria* in Haifa for U.K.

11 „ Curfew imposed on Tiberias following heavy fighting during previous day between Jews and Arabs.

12 „ H.Q. R.A., 33rd Airborne Light Regiment, and 66th Airborne Anti-Tank Regiment, R.A., embarked on the *Otranto* for U.K.

18 „ Disturbances in Haifa in which 1 O.R. of 2nd/3rd Parachute Battalion was killed.
Arabs laid ambush for Jewish vehicles outside Acre and attacked a party under British escort. 5 British soldiers and 4 Jews killed.

21 „ Arab explosive vehicle caused considerable damage to Jewish property in Harbour Street, Haifa, and caused 20 Jewish casualties. This was followed by widespread sniping which stopped when guns of 1st Regiment, R.H.A., went into action against the offending positions.

22 „ Jews dressed in British Airborne uniforms carried out attack with explosive vehicle in Iraq Street, Haifa. Attack resulted in 23 Arab casualties.

27 „ Jewish convoy from Nahariya to Jiddin ambushed by Arabs. 45 Jews killed out of 90. 2nd Battalion The Middlesex Regiment intervened.

31 „ Jews blew up train near Benjamina killing 24 Arabs and injuring 61.

1 Apr. Arabs attacking Beit Alpha driven off by troops of "Craforce" using mortar fire.
Disbandment of 6th Airborne Division Battle School.

2 „ Heavy communal fighting in Safad stopped by intervention of 17th/21st Lancers and 1st Battalion Irish Guards.

2 „ H.Q. 6th Airborne Division closes down in Palestine.
Control passes to H.Q. G.O.C., North Sector.

4 „ Arab attack supported by artillery and machine guns, opens on Mishmar ha Emeq.
H.Q. R.E.; H.Q. R.A.S.C.; H.Q. R.A.O.C.; H.Q. R.E.M.E. embarked at Haifa on the *Franconia* for U.K.

5 „ Patrol of 2nd/3rd Parachute Battalion captured Jewish armoured car with a number of weapons in Haifa.

6 „ 1st Guards Brigade took over command of Haifa from 1st Parachute Brigade.

7 „ Fighting between Jews and Arabs east of River Jordan, in upper Huleh valley, 17th/21st Lancers intervened, but handicapped by blown bridges and soft going.
147th Airborne Park Squadron, R.E., 16th Parachute Field Ambulance, R.A.M.C., 1st Airborne Workshops, R.E.M.E., embarked for U.K. on the *Georgic*.

9 „ Heavy fighting in Tiberias between Jews and Arabs. Volume of firing reduced after intervention with 2-pounders by 17th/21st Lancers.

DATE	EVENT

1948 (*contd.*)

10 Apr.   Main H.Q. 6th Airborne Division embarked on the *Samaria* for U.K.

13 „   Divisional Signals Regiment, 716th Airborne Light Company, R.A.S.C., embarked in *Otranto* for U.K.

14 „   Further heavy communal fighting in Tiberias and Safad.

16 „   Battle developed in Safad as British troops withdrew from the town. H.Q. 1st Parachute Brigade and 2nd/3rd Parachute Battalion embarked in the *Empress of Australia* for U.K.

18 „   1st Battalion Grenadier Guards took over from 8th/9th Parachute Battalion in Haifa.

21 „   Battle for Haifa between Jews and Arabs began.

22 „   Battle for Haifa ended with victory for the Jews. British troops in action against Jews who were engaging Arab refugees. (See text).

23 „   Rear H.Q. 6th Airborne Division and 8th/9th Parachute Battalion embarked in *Empress of Scotland* for U.K.

14 May   The High Commissioner and last British troops, including 1st Parachute Battalion left Jerusalem.

15 „   British Mandate in Palestine ended.
Operational control of North Sector passed from G.O.C., North Sector, to 1st Guards Brigade.
G.O.C. 6th Airborne Division and North Sector of Palestine emplaned for U.K.
Haifa enclave came into being.

18 „   Tactical H.Q. 6th Airborne Division, H.Q. "Craforce" and 1st Parachute Battalion embarked in *Empress of Australia* for U.K.

21 „   3rd Hussars embarked Port Said for U.K. in *Strathnaver*.

30 June   Last British troops including troops of 1st Airborne Squadron, R.E., left Palestine.

Appendix O

NUMBER OF RECORDED INCIDENTS INVOLVING SECURITY FORCES AND DISSIDENT GROUPS IN
6TH AIRBORNE DIVISIONAL AREA, NOVEMBER, 1945—MARCH, 1948.

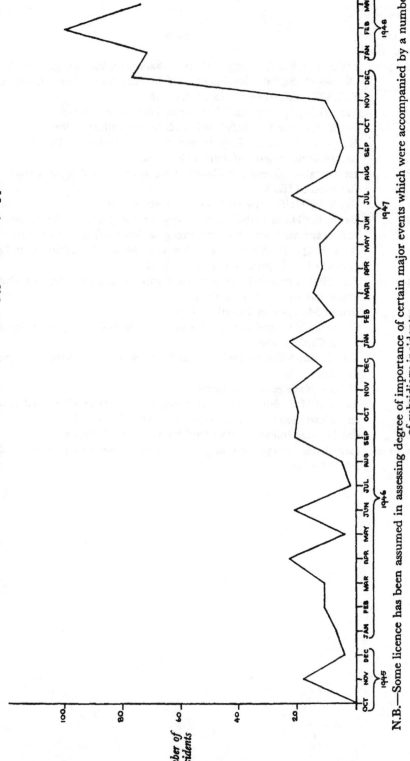

N.B.—Some licence has been assumed in assessing degree of importance of certain major events which were accompanied by a number of subsidiary incidents.

DIVISIONAL SPORTS RESULTS, 1946-8

1946

Athletics	5th Battalion The Parachute Regiment.
Boxing	8th Battalion The Parachute Regiment (Command Championship winners).
Cross-Country Running	9th Battalion The Parachute Regiment.
Cricket	6th Airborne Divisional Signals Regiment.
Hockey	1st Battalion The Hertfordshire Regiment.
Rugby	6th Battalion The Parachute Regiment.
Association Football	1st Battalion The Royal Ulster Rifles.
Swimming	8th Battalion The Parachute Regiment (Command Championship winners).
Tug of War	3rd Battalion The Parachute Regiment.

1947

Athletics	3rd Battalion The Parachute Regiment
Boxing	8th Battalion The Parachute Regiment (Command Championship winners).
Cross-Country Running	2nd Battalion The Parachute Regiment (Command Championship winners).
Cricket	17th/21st Lancers.
Hockey	3rd Battalion The Parachute Regiment.
Rugby	9th Battalion The Parachute Regiment.
Association Football	7th Battalion The Parachute Regiment.
Swimming	8th Battalion The Parachute Regiment (Command Championship winners).
Water Polo	8th Battalion The Parachute Regiment.
Tug of War	3rd Battalion The Parachute Regiment.

1948

Boxing	8th/9th Battalion The Parachute Regiment (Command Championship winners).
Cross-Country Running	2nd/3rd Battalion The Parachute Regiment.
Hockey	2nd/3rd Battalion The Parachute Regiment.
Rugby	2nd/3rd Battalion The Parachute Regiment.
Association Football	6th Airborne Divisional Royal Engineers.

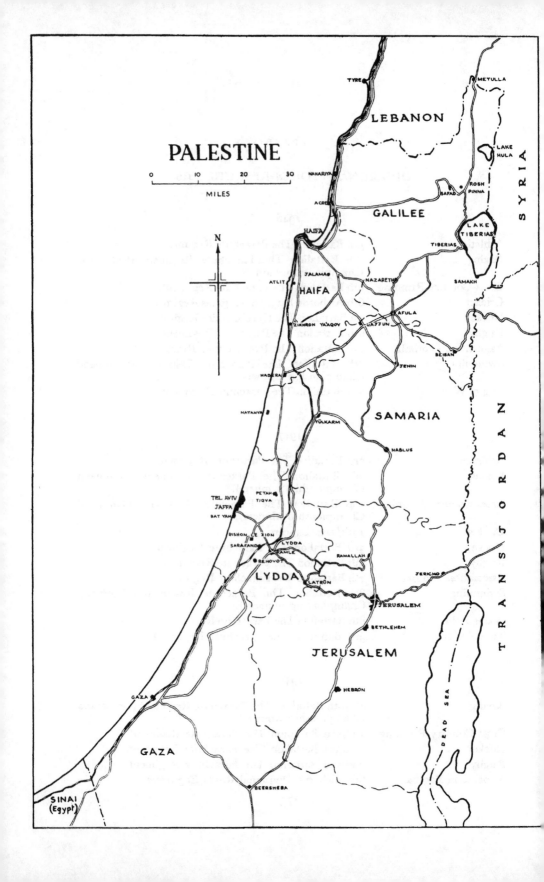